"LIGHTNING."

String Figures

and How to Make Them

A Study of Cat's-Cradle in Many Lands

by
Caroline Furness Jayne

With an Ethnological Introduction by
Alfred C. Haddon

Illustrated

Dover Publications, Inc.
New York

Published in Canada by General Publishing Company, Ltd., 30 Lesmill Road, Don Mills, Toronto, Ontario.

Published in the United Kingdom by Constable and Company, Ltd., 10 Orange Street, London WC 2.

This new Dover edition, first published in 1962, is an unabridged republication of the work first published by Charles Scribner's Sons in 1906 under the former title: *String Figures*.

Standard Book Number: 486-20152-X
Library of Congress Catalog Card Number: 62-51880

Manufactured in the United States of America
Dover Publications, Inc.
180 Varick Street
New York, N. Y. 10014

PREFACE

THIS book may be regarded as an introduction to the study of String Figures—games which are widespread among primitive peoples, and played by weaving on the hands a single loop of string in order to produce intricate patterns supposed to represent certain familiar objects. I have gathered together the facts already known concerning these games, and, adding my own studies and the unpublished records of other observers, I have here described and illustrated the methods whereby about one hundred string figures are made. My purpose has been twofold: to interest other students in the subject, in order that additional figures and their methods may be collected among various tribes and races; and to reach a still larger public, that more people may share in the fascinations of the games themselves. The games are certainly fascinating, appealing as they do to young and to old, and to those debarred from all pastimes demanding physical exertion. Moreover, they are not unduly difficult; and, capable as they are of infinite variations, their charm ought to be inexhaustible.

It gives me great pleasure to express my thanks to Dr. Alfred C. Haddon, of Cambridge, England, who first interested me in the subject by teaching me the games he had collected, for the permission to use his photographs and unpublished notes; to my brother, Dr. William Henry Furness, 3rd, for the string figures from the Caroline Islands, for the finished patterns from the Marshall Islands, for photographs, and for aid in collecting new figures; to Mr. S. Chapman Simms, of the Field Columbian Museum, Chicago, for assistance in studying the games of the North American Indians and the African Pygmies at the St. Louis Exposition, and for photographs of natives under his charge; to Dr. William P. Wilson, Director of the Philadelphia Commercial Museum, for the opportunity of collecting games on the Philippine Reservation at St. Louis; to Dr. George B. Gordon, Curator in the Philadelphia Free Museum of Science and Art, for the Eskimo and Indian games which he secured for me during his recent trip to Alaska; to Mr. John Lyman Cox, of Philadelphia, for figures collected at the Indian School at Hampton, Virginia; and to Mrs. Morris Cotgrave Betts, for her skill and accuracy in the drawings.

Without constant aid and encouragement from my husband, Dr. Horace Jayne, I should never have written this book.

CAROLINE FURNESS JAYNE.

PHILADELPHIA, October, 1905.

CONTENTS

CHAPTER VI

CHAPTER VII

CHAPTER VIII

CHAPTER IX

CHAPTER X

ILLUSTRATIONS

INTRODUCTION

I N Ethnology, as in other sciences, nothing is too insignificant to receive attention. Indeed it is a matter of common experience among scientific men that
apparently trivial objects or operations have an interest and importance that
are by no means commensurate with the estimation in which they are ordinarily
held.

To the casual observer few amusements offer, at first sight, a less promising
field for research than does the simple cat's-cradle of our childhood; and, indeed,
it is only when the comparative method is applied to it that we begin to discover
that it, too, has a place in the culture history of man.

As a child I had played cat's-cradle and had seen various string tricks, but it
was not until the year 1888 that I saw in Torres Straits some of those elaborate
string figures of savage peoples that put our humble efforts to shame. I found that
a couple of natives do not play together as we do, "taking off" from each other, but
that each plays separately, though in exceptional cases two players may be required
to construct a particular figure. They can make much more intricate devices than
ours and the manipulation is correspondingly complicated, toes and teeth being at
times pressed into service; on the other hand, although many figures pass through
elaborate phases in the making, the final result may be simple.

Travellers in various parts of the world have had a similar experience. We are
informed that these figures are much more complicated than are ours, and they
represent various natural and artificial objects in a state of rest or motion.

Occasionally a list has been published of some of the figures made by a particular people, and in rare instances with illustrations of the completed figure. So
far as my information goes, Dr. Franz Boas (1, p. 229)* was the first to publish a
descriptive account of the method employed by a primitive people in making any of
these figures; unfortunately he gives descriptions of but two of the five Eskimo

* For the full title of a work referred to in parentheses after an author's name consult the bibliography at the end of this volume. Other references are to pages of this book.

figures he illustrates. Mr. Harlan I. Smith (p. 282, Fig. 270) has published sketches illustrating the various stages in the making of two string figures of the Salish Indians of Thompson River, British Columbia.

It became evident to me that no progress could be made in the comparative study of string figures and tricks until a definite nomenclature had been devised which would indicate with precision all the stages involved in making a figure. A second visit to Torres Straits afforded me the requisite opportunity, and Dr. W. H. R. Rivers and I (p. 146) managed to devise a method of recording string figures and tricks which enabled us to write down some thirty Papuan examples. Since then the nomenclature has been adopted for the recording of the string figures of other peoples, and now my friend Mrs. Jayne has simplified our procedure and has produced this elaborate volume, which will enable any one to indulge in this fascinating amusement. Not only has she added a new joy to life, but this book will undoubtedly be the means of considerably increasing our knowledge of the forms of the game and their distribution, and therefrom we may hope for more light upon the various problems that await solution.

On making a general survey of string figures, or, to adopt the English colloquial term, "cat's-cradles," it seems that they fall into two main groups; but as our knowledge increases we may find that this generalization will have to be somewhat modified. In the European and Asiatic type two strings pass around the back of each hand, and the crossing loops are taken up by the middle fingers. In the Oceanic and American type there are no strings at the back of the hand, and the crossing loops are taken up by the indices. The former invariably requires two players, while one person suffices for the usual figures of the latter type. I propose to designate these two types as the Asiatic and the Oceanic respectively.

ASIATIC TYPE

In **Korea,** according to Culin (**2,** p. 30), "cat's-cradle is usually played by girls. The figures, which are the same as in our own children's play, are named as follows: 1, Cover for hearse; 2, chess-board; 3, chop-sticks; 4, cow's eyeball; 5, rice-mill pestle." The game is called "woof-taking."

My friend Dr. H. H. Weir informs me that "the Koreans play cat's-cradle almost as in England, but there are two actions with which I am not familiar. The first six figures are as in England, but 6 (cat's-eye) is made into a new figure which reverts to 3 (candles)."

"In **Japan**," according to Culin (**2**, p. 30), "cat's-cradle is called *aya ito tori*, 'woof pattern string-taking.' The figures are identical with those in Korea, but receive different names: 1, Unknown; 2, a mountain cat into which a domestic cat is supposed to transform itself; 3, a musical instrument, or the two pieces of wood under the sole of clogs; 4, horse-eye; 5, a musical instrument."

Culin (**2**, p. 30) states that in southern **China** cat's-cradle is called "well-rope." It is spoken of as an amusement of girls, but is known to most Cantonese laborers; they make the same figures as those of Korea and Japan. Miss Fielde (p. 87) says that the children of Swatow play cat's-cradle precisely as do the children in America and Europe; but the Chinese call it "sawing wood," in allusion to the final act in the performance.

This last statement evidently refers to a figure which is made thus: make the "manger," or "inverted cradle"; the other player picks up one of the straight strings in the middle, passes it under the other, and holding the latter in the middle, draws these two strings as far apart as possible; the first player releases all the strings except those on the little fingers; the two players make sawing movements with the strings. I have an impression that this figure is played in England.

"Sawing Wood" was taught to me by Zia Uddin Ahmad of Trinity College, Cambridge, who said it was known in Delhi and Lucknow under the name of *Qainchi*, "scissors." It is made thus: Opening A (cf. p. 11), the other player passing his left hand over all the strings, pulls the straight little-finger string toward the original player, and with his right hand, under the remaining strings, pulls the straight thumb string toward himself; the first player releases all but the index loops; the sawing movement can then be made. This figure and the trick described on p. 345, and one very similar to "The Lizard" (p. 337), which Dr. S. Levinstein taught me, are all the string games that I have yet heard of from India. A Scottish method of making this figure is described by Maclagan (p. 190), the two operators chant alternately:

> "See saw, Johnnie Maw,
> See san, Johnnie man."

East Indian Archipelago. A. R. Wallace (p. 183) tells us: "One wet day in a Dyak house [Borneo], when a number of boys and young men were about me, I thought to amuse them with something new, and showed them how to make 'cat's-cradle' with a piece of string. Greatly to my surprise, they knew all about it, and more than I did; for, after I and Charles had gone through all the changes we could make, one of the boys took it off my hand and made several new figures, which quite puzzled me. They then showed me a number of other tricks with pieces of string, which seemed a favorite amusement with them." De Crespigny (p. 344) writes of the Dusuns of Borneo: "Near me were two children playing at cat's-cradle exactly as I remember to have played it in my childhood." This precisely coincides with my own experience in the same island.

When I visited the Philippine Reservation at the St. Louis Exposition, in 1904, I played cat's-cradle with some of the natives, and I found they played in the same manner as we do. My time was too limited to learn the names of the figures or to see what others they knew. Mrs. Jayne was more diligent, and she learned a few new figures from some of the natives. It will be noticed that the Bagobo Diamonds (pp. 43, 46) begin with Opening A. Schmeltz (p. 230) says girls are skilled at this game in Soerabaja in Java, and he states that Matthes records it as a very favorite child's game among the Macassarese and Bugis of South Celebes. It is called *toêkâ-toêkâ*, "the ladder game," derived from *toêkâ*, "steps." We have no indication whether this is the Asiatic or the Oceanic type.

Europe. So far as I am aware no description of the British form of cat's-cradle has been published sufficiently explicit to enable one to play the game thoroughly. Mrs. Gomme in her excellent monograph (p. 61) gives illustrations of the figures, and states they are produced seriatim as follows: 1, Cradle; 2, soldier's bed; 3, candles; 4, cradle inversed or manger; 5, soldier's bed again or diamonds; 6, diamonds or cat's-eye; 7, fish in dish; cradle as at first. Other English names are barn-doors, bowling-green, hour-glass, pound, net, fish-pond, the lady's bed, fiddle; but it is not clear to what figures all these names refer. Three or four figures are described and figured by E. Nister (p. 73), but he does not describe the whole series, neither does he give names to any of the figures.

I have heard of cat's-cradle from Denmark, Germany, Austria, Switzerland, France and Netherlands, but details are lacking.

My friend, Miss B. Freire-Marreco, informs me that a Dane of her acquaintance does exactly the same as in the English cat's-cradle though giving different names to the various figures; they are as follows, the English name preceding the Danish: 1, Cradle, cradle; 2, church-window, unknown; 3, pound of candles, mirror; 4, cradle, cradle; 5, soldier's bed, hour-glass; 6 [7, ?], fish in dish, whale.

De Cock and Teirlinck record *Afpakken: Dradenspel* ('Taking off : String-game') from Molenbeek-Brüssel; they give three figures illustrating the method of making the cradle and three figures from Mrs. Gomme. They add the following information : " In Germany it is also known under the name of *Abheben* (' Taking off '), *Faden-abheben* (' Taking-off strings '), and *Fadenspiel* (' String-game '). The figures are variously named; in Brabant they are known as *Wasser* (' Water '), *die Schere* (' Scissors '), *die Geige* (' Fiddle '), *die Wiege* (' Cradle '), (cf. Georgens, Sp. für Knaben, bl. 263). Andree (*Braunschw. Volkskunde*) calls it *Hexenspiel* (' Witch's game '), and *Auf- und abnehmen* (' picking-up and taking-off '). In the neighborhood of the town of Nantes it is known as *la scie* (' Saw '); the best known figures are called: *le berceau* (' Cradle '), *les chandelles* (' Candles '), *les carreaux* (' Squares '), *les ciseaux* (' Scissors '), etc. (R. des Trad. pop. XIII, 15.) "

OCEANIC TYPE

There is no need to give all the references by travellers of the occurrence of cat's-cradle over this vast area, but the following will suffice to indicate its universal occurrence:

Australia. Eyre (p. 227) refers to the " varied and singular figures " made by the Australians and remarks that " our juvenile attempts in this way are very meagre and uninteresting compared to them." Bunce (p. 75) says: " Some were playing with a puzzle made of string, '*Cudgi Cudgick.*' This puzzle was played between two individuals and required two pairs of hands, in the same manner as the juvenile game of ' cat's-cradle ' common to our own country." It is not clear from this description whether they played as we do or whether, as elsewhere in Australia, two people are required to make some figures.

Roth (p. 10) has paid more attention to this subject than any one else in Australia. He states: " With any fair length of twine, adult women and young children, of both sexes, will often amuse themselves for hours at a time. It is thus used in the form of an endless string to play the game known to us Europeans as ' cratch-cradle.' Thus played with, it is met with everywhere throughout North Queensland. In some districts it is even indulged in by adult men; it is the women and children, however, who are most partial to it. Some of the figures are extremely complicated, passing through at least eight or nine stages before completion. During the process of manufacture such a one requires not only the hands, but even the mouth, knees, etc., to make the different loops, twists, and turns. In addition to variations in complexity, certain of the figures may be made with two endless strings, while to complete others again it may be necessary to have one or even two assistants. Strange to say, similar figures may be met with at distances extremely remote, with and without similar interpretations. Occasionally the endless string may be arranged on the flat, or on the ear." Dr. Roth has given careful drawings of seventy-four North Queensland cat's-cradles and to most he has added a small figure to illustrate the original object which is copied, but unfortunately he does not give any indication of how they are made. My friend, Mr. W. Innes Pocock, has, however, been able to discover ways in which many of these figures can be constructed; these I hope will be published by the Anthropological Institute of London in *Man*. One (pl. V, Fig. 6), which is called a "Duck in Flight," is the same as the Torres Straits "Casting the Fish-spear" (p. 131).

New Guinea. Turner (p. 483) was the first to record cat's-cradle from New Guinea, where he found it played by the Motu children of Port Moresby. Later, Finsch (1891, p. 33) found it as a child's game in Bentley Bay, and I have seen it played by children at Hula, Port Moresby, Delena, and on Kiwai Island. Thilenius (p. 20) hazards the suggestion that the figures made in this game may even have had an influence upon the decorative art and wood carving of the Papuans. I have more than once (**1**, p. 361; **2**, p. 224; **3**, pp. 38, 175, 201) alluded to its occurrence among the Papuans of Torres Straits. The general name for the game among the Western Islanders is *Womer*, and by the Eastern Islanders it is called *Kamut*. In 1888 I transferred on to cardboard a few figures that were made for me by a native of the Western Islands ; three of these have been published by Edge-Partington & Heape (pl. 341, 1-3), they are *Gud*, mouth, *Umai*, dog, and *Ger*, sea-snake (cf. p. 34). Several examples from this region have been published by Dr. Rivers and myself, a few more will be found in this book, and some additional ones will be published in Vol. IV of our Reports. The thirty-four figures we wrote down fall into Mrs. Jayne's three groups (cf. p. 4). Of the patterns, 16 were figures at rest and 11 figures in motion; there were 6 tricks and 1 catch, and we know of the occurrence of many others; altogether the figures in motion appear to be as numerous as those at rest. More than one-third represent animals. Two of the fish, besides being well known as fish, are the subjects of a very popular folk-tale of the Murray Islands. One figure which represents boys playing is subsequently converted into two rings, which represent two of the sacred grounds of Mer (Murray Island), in which the very important initiation ceremonies into the Malu fraternity were held; and another is supposed to represent the passing of the stone-headed clubs from hand to hand during one of the Malu dances, as is described in Vol. VI of the Reports. With these exceptions there does not appear to be anything of a religious nature in the game as played in Torres Straits, and I think that these figures have no such significance. Words are said or sentences muttered while most of the figures are being made, but it is difficult to make sense of some of these, and it is quite impossible to understand others. In Murray Island these are called *Kamut wed*, "Kamut songs."

Nageg upi seker dike, abele lar upige seker dike.
Nageg tail comb* it is here, that fish on the tail comb it is there.

Le sik, le sik, sik erapei, le sikge, le sikge, uteidi
Man bed, man bed, bed breaks, man on a bed, man on a bed, asleep lies,

uteidi. sik erapei.
lies asleep, bed breaks.

Mònan patibili Peibri-em enau aroem.
Monan rolls to Peibri enau fruit† for eating.

Tup igoli umi Waierge, Waier kesge, Waierge Waier kesge.
Tup swim round to Waier, Waier in the channel, to Waier Waier channel.

Pageia mai nagedim upi etauerida kai amarem pekem.
Sea-snake you to where tail strikes I to side.

The natives of Torres Straits do not know how to play the Asiatic form of cat's-cradle.

Melanesia. "It was interesting to me," writes Finsch (1888, p. 143), "that the taking off of a thread stretched between the fingers is also found in New Ireland; fairly large lads occupied themselves with it. They were able to make very beautiful figures and in so doing sang a not unpleasant melody." Codrington (p. 341) records that "cat's-cradle, in Lepers' Island *Lelegaro*, in Florida *Honggo*, with many figures, is common throughout the islands." He also says (p. 30) that the people of Florida are grouped into six exogamous divisions, or *Kema*. The names of two of these are *Honggo-kama* and *Honggo-kiki*, respectively the "Great" and the "Little Cat's-cradle." Buchner (p. 269) records the game from Fiji, and he makes the improbable suggestion that the natives had been taught it by the missionaries.

---

* This has reference to the series of small spines at the base of the tail of the *Nageg* fish, i. e. "trigger fish" or "leather jacket" (*Monocanthus*); in the folk-tale *Nageg* is the mother of *Geigi*.
† The Wangai "plum" (*Mimusops Kaukii*).

Polynesia. The knowledge of this pastime was certainly common to the members of the Polynesian stock before they separated off into different groups, as we find it played from the Hawaiian Islands in the north to New Zealand in the south, and as far east as the Hervey group.

Culin (**1,** p. 222) figures sixteen examples from Hawaii and refers elsewhere (**3,** p. 106) to three more, but says, "many others are said to be known." They are known as *Hei,* "net." Elmer E. Brown (p. 163) refers to the unpublished investigations of Mr. J. S. Emerson into the folk-lore of the Hawaiian Islands. "With reference to the Hawaiian cat's-cradle," says Mr. Emerson, "I have collected most carefully a considerable amount of valuable information, which I propose to publish as soon as I can get at it. The last bit of information with regard to the subject I came upon almost unexpectedly this morning at South Cape (Ka Lae). It was the last resting-place (in stone) of the famous rat that saved the human family from starvation when the god Makalii hung up the food in a net to a cloud in the heavens. Thus, little by little, scrap by scrap, all over the islands, I gather the detached materials of a most strangely interesting structure that requires all my patience and ingenuity to dovetail together. There is no native now living who knows enough to give a full and connected story of this remarkable Hei, Koko or Makalii. Part of it comes from Iole, the home of the rat in Kohala. Part must be looked for in Waioli, Kanai, where the net was hung up to the cloud. And at last I have stumbled unawares upon the stars (Pleiades), the home of Makalii, his net, and the rat, all in the rock at South Cape." Mr. Brown goes on to say: "I think Mr. Emerson has fully established its connection with superstitious rites and beliefs in the Hawaiian Islands."

Two early travellers give us the following account of the game as played in New Zealand. Dieffenbach (p. 32) writes: "In the game of *Maui* they are great proficients. This is a game like that called cat's-cradle in Europe, and consists of very complicated and perplexing puzzles with a cord tied together at the ends. It seems to be intimately connected with their ancient traditions, and in the different figures which the cord is made to assume, whilst held on both hands, the outlines of their different varieties of houses, canoes, or figures of men and women are imagined to be represented. Maui, the Adam of New Zealand, left this amusement to them as an inheritance." Taylor (p. 172) says: "*He whai,* or *maui,* the 'cat's-cradle,' is a game very similar to our own, but the cord is made to assume many more forms, and these are said to be different scenes in their mythology, such as Hine-nui-te-po, Mother Night bringing forth her progeny, Maru and the gods, and

Maui fishing up the land. Men, canoes, houses, etc., are also represented. Some
state that Maui invented this game." Tregear (1, p. 115; 2, p. 58) calls the game
Whai, huhi or *maui,* and says sometimes a whole drama was played by means of
the changing shapes. Two of the favorites were the ascent of Tawhaki, the Lightning God, to heaven and the fishing up of the land by the hero Maui. There were
proper songs chanted as accompaniments to the movements of the players' hands.
Gill (p. 65) informs us that in the Hervey group "cat's-cradle (*Ai*) was a great
delight of old and young. Teeth were called into play to help the fingers. One
complication, in which the cord in the centre is twisted into a long slender stem,
and therefore called 'the coco-nut tree,' I have never known a European to
unravel."

America. Several authors have recorded the occurrence of cat's-cradle among
the Eskimo (Hall, 1, p. 316; 2, p. 129). Klutschak (pp. 136–139) found even old
men of King William Land playing it with reindeer sinews. They showed him 139
named figures; of these he gives 3 illustrations, *Tuktuk* (Reindeer), *Amau* (Wolf), and
Kakbik (Pig). Andree very truly points out that there is no pig in this region,
but his suggestion that the natives learned the game from Europeans ("Nordmen")
is untenable. Tenicheff (p. 153) copies the first two of the figures, but does not
say what they are meant to represent nor where he obtained them. As previously
mentioned, Boas (1, p. 229) has published a few figures, and elsewhere (4, pp. 151,
161) he gives the observations of Capt. G. Comer that in Iglulik, "While the sun is
going south in the fall, the game of cat's-cradle is played, to catch the sun in the
meshes of the string, and to prevent his disappearance" (p. 151). Also on the west
coast of Hudson Bay, "boys must not play cat's-cradle, because in later life their
fingers might become entangled in the harpoon-line. They are allowed to play this
game when they become adults. Two cases were told of hunters who lost their
fingers, in which the cause was believed to be their having played cat's-cradle when
young. Such youths are thought to be particularly liable to lose their fingers in
hunting ground-seal " (p. 161).

According to Murdoch (p. 383), "the [Point Barrow] women are very fond
of playing cat's-cradle whenever they have leisure. One favorite figure is a very
clever representation of a reindeer, which is made, by moving the fingers, to run
down-hill from one hand to the other." Nelson (p. 332) was amused for an hour
or more by an old man at Cape Darby, near Behring Strait, who "made a constant
succession of patterns with his sinew cord, forming outlines of various birds and
other animals of the region."

In a criticism of Andree's statement (**2**, p. 214, subsequently repeated, **3**, p. 96) with regard to the distribution of cat's-cradle, that its occurrence among the Eskimo is quite isolated and probably due to European influence, Boas (**2**, p. 85) affirms that the game is known to all the eastern Eskimo peoples and the figures made by them are very numerous, although it appears each has only a limited range. Thus the Cumberland Sound Eskimo did not know the figures given by Klutschak. The game is known on the Mackenzie, and it is probably played all along the whole coast of arctic America. Boas also states that it is known along the north-west coast of America and, as among the Eskimo, is played only by one person at a time. The Tlingit, Tsimshian, and Kwakiutl all play it; the most southerly point at which Boas saw it played was at Comox, on Vancouver Island. He goes on to say : "The way in which the game is played is very interesting. While the figure is being made, the player sings the song belonging to it, which describes what the figure illustrates. Many of these figures illustrate actions. The Eskimo have a figure which illustrates two reindeer fighting, the Tsimshians have dancing shamans, the Comox (Catloltq) a mink which runs along the sea-shore. The game is also known to the Salish tribes of upper Frazer River and Thompson River."

Cat's-cradle has been recorded from various North-west tribes as well as among the Cherokee, Omaha, Pawnee, Navaho (Haddon, **5**), and Pueblo Indians; indeed, it seems to be spread over the whole of North America.

So far as I am aware records are lacking of its occurrence in Central America. It does occur in South America, for Ehrenreich (p. 30) states that the game of cat's-cradle representing animal figures is played by the Karaya of the Rio Araguaya (Goyaz), and quite recently I have heard of string games amongst the Chaco Indians of Paraguay, but details are not forthcoming.

As in so many other subjects, E. B. Tylor (p. 26) was the first to draw the attention of students to this game and to treat it from a comparative point of view. He states quite correctly that it is evident the Dayaks and Polynesians did not learn these string games from Europeans "and," he continues, "though cat's-cradle is now known over all Western Europe, I find no record of it at all ancient in our part of the world. It is known in South-east Asia, and the most plausible explanation seems to be that this is its centre of origin, whence it migrated westward into Europe, and eastward and southward through Polynesia and into Australia."

I, too, can find no early mention of this game in Europe, and as our method is precisely similar to that of Eastern Asia I can only conclude that, like the kite, it was introduced directly into Europe from that part of the world. At present it is impossible to say more exactly where it arose, whether in Korea, China, or Indo-China; presumably it passed from the main-land to the Asiatic Islands.

We should expect to find the overlap of the Asiatic and Oceanic types of the game in the East Indian Archipelago, and therefore we need not feel surprised that Mrs. Jayne has discovered the latter form (p. 43) among the Filipinos. My friend, Miss A. Hingston, has worked out a method by means of which the ordinary Asiatic opening can be converted to the Oceanic Opening A, but I do not know that it is actually practised. Her method is as follows: Cat's-cradle opening. With little fingers take up the ulnar (far) middle-finger strings below the point where they cross. Pass the straight string from the radial (near) side of the indices to the ulnar (far) side of the little fingers. Press thumbs against the indices to hold the radial (near) index string firm. Bring the straight ulnar (far) string that passes over the back of the hand over the tips of all fingers and thumbs. Transfer middle-finger loops to indices. Result, Oceanic Opening A.

So far as I am aware the only figure in Europe which begins with the Oceanic Opening A is that known as "The Leashing of Lochiel's Dogs" (p. 116). I am unable to explain the significance of this anomaly.

It is a highly significant fact that the American cat's-cradles belong to the Oceanic type, and that nowhere in this whole region, so far as is yet known, does the Asiatic type occur. This type must be extremely ancient, otherwise it would not occur among such widely different races as the Australians, Melanesians, Polynesians, Eskimo, and North American Indians.

It is surprising what an enormous number of figures can be made from an endless loop of string, and there are very numerous varieties in every place where the Oceanic type of the game is played. No surprise, therefore, need be felt if similar figures occur in various places; at all events if they are of simple construction, a complex figure or one with difficult manipulation is not so likely to be often invented independently.

So far as our knowledge goes the figure known as "The Leashing of Lochiel's Dogs," "Crow's Feet," etc. (p. 116), is the most widely spread of all, as versions of it occur in North Queensland (Roth), East Africa, North America, and the British Islands. Mr. W. Innes Pocock has discovered that it can be made by a dozen different methods.

The "Fish-spear," which is a simple figure, has also a wide distribution. It is found in Torres Straits ("Fish-spear"). H. I. Smith described it from the Salish of Thompson River, B. C. ("Pitching a tent"). I found it played by the Clayoquaht Indians, Nootka tribe, Vancouver Island, at the St. Louis Exposition ("Sea-egg [Echinus] spear"), and there is a Zuñi, N. M., example in the Philadelphia Museum.

No cat's-cradles or string tricks have hitherto been recorded from Africa. I have for some time been aware of the sparse occurrence of one or two string tricks from that continent, but very recently my friend, Dr. C. W. Cunnington, has collected fifteen patterns and three tricks from various tribes in East Africa, mainly in the neighborhood of Lake Tanganyika ; these will, I hope, be published by the Anthropological Institute of London. Three of these begin with Opening A, the rest have varied beginnings. In four cases the final patterns are similar, but the construction differs in each case. Three figures possess movement. The pattern known as *Umuzwa*, " a wooden spoon " made by the Ulungu, of the south end of Tanganyika, is " practically the same in result as the Cherokee figure, ' Crow's Feet.' " One string trick from Wajiji " is precisely the same as *Kebe mokeis*, ' the mouse,' from Murray Island, Torres Straits, a trick also known to the Omaha Indians." Several patterns are known to widely separated tribes, but under different names. Mrs. Jayne's discovery of a Batwa Pygmy pattern is of great interest, and it will be noticed that, like the majority of those since known from Africa, it has an original opening.

It may seem a superfluous question to some to ask, Why is this game played? But the Ethnologist is bound to do so, for he knows from experience that practically everything man does has a meaning, and it is his business to endeavor to find out whether there is any reason for the performance of any action, and if so to discover its significance.

The Asiatic type, so far as our present knowledge goes, does not appear to possess much interest; but two facts seem to be significant with regard to the Oceanic type. These are: (1) The widely spread accompaniment of words or chants, and (2) The frequent representation of persons, incidents, or objects connected with religion or mythology. These facts are interesting and suggest that we have here to do with some symbolism that has in course of time become obscured. On the other hand, it may merely be a pastime, and the figures and designs may be nothing more than casual illustrations of mythology, as they are of innumerable natural objects.

The Eskimo evidence proves that cat's-cradle may, in part, have a magical significance and suggests a line for future inquiry, for we know that all over the world strings, cords, and knots enter largely into magical practices. The information at present available is too scanty for us to discuss these questions with profit.

ALFRED C. HADDON.

CAMBRIDGE, ENGLAND, July, 1905.

CHAPTER I

IN our childhood we have all doubtless enjoyed the fascination of the game of Cat's-Cradle, and experienced a sense of being hopelessly baffled, when, after completing the series of familiar movements, we were at the end of our knowledge, and all our attempts to go on further ended in a complete tangle of the string. We did not know that the game, as we then played it, is one of a host of similar games played with a loop of string by savage or primitive people all over the world, and that, while our childish game is also known in many and widely separated lands, it is possibly only a survival of others now lost, and crude enough compared with the intricate and beautiful patterns devised by savage races.

For many years travellers have been calling attention to the fact that a game resembling our Cat's-Cradle is played in various parts of the world; hence we now have some idea of its geographical distribution.

We know that certain simple patterns are common in Great Britain, Europe, and the United States (in addition to the Indian games), and have been reported from India, Japan and Korea (Culin, 2, p. 30 and Weir) and China (Culin, 2, p. 30; Fielde, p. 87). Ehrenreich (p. 30) tells us that string games are played in South America, and I have found a few figures among the Batwa pygmies from Africa. Reports of their occurrence come chiefly, however, from explorers of the various islands of the Pacific Ocean, and from observers of the North American Indians. Thus we learn of string figures in Java from Schmeltz (p. 230); in Borneo from Wallace (p. 183), Haddon, and Furness; in Celebes from Matthes (p. 129); in the Philippines from my own studies at the St. Louis Exposition; in Australia from Bunce (p. 75), Smyth (Vol. I, p. 178), Eyre (II, p. 227), and Roth (p. 10); in New Guinea from Finsch (1891, p. 33), Rivers and Haddon (p. 151), and Turner (p. 483); in Torres Straits from Rivers and Haddon (p. 146); in New Ireland from Finsch (1888, p. 143); in the Solomon Islands and the New Hebrides from Codrington

(p. 341); in the Loyalty Islands from Rivers and Haddon (p. 148); in the Fijis from Buchner (p. 269); in New Zealand from Dieffenbach (Vol. II, p. 32), Taylor (p. 172), and Tregear (**1**, p. 115; **2**, p. 58); in the Hervey group from Gill (p. 65); in the Hawaiian Islands from Culin (**1**, p. 223) and Brown (p. 163); in the Caroline Islands from Furness; and in the Marshall Islands from Stephen. In America we learn of their prevalence among the Eskimos from Boas (**1**, p. 229; **2**, p. 85; **3**, p. 569; **4**, pp. 151, 161), Hall (**1**, p. 316; **2**, p. 129), Klutschak (p. 138), Murdoch (p. 383), Nelson (p. 332), and Tenicheff (p. 153); among the Salish from Smith (p. 281); the Tlingits, Tsimshians, and Kwakiutls, from Boas (**2**, p. 85); the Clayo-quahts from Haddon; the Tewas and Zuñis from Culin; the Pawnees, Omahas, and Cherokees from Haddon (**5**, p. 217); and among the Navahos from Haddon (**5**, p. 219) and Culin. Mr. John L. Cox has gathered games for me from the Kla-maths, Tewas, Omahas, and Onondagas, and I collected string figures from the Navahos, Osages, Chippewas and Apaches at the St. Louis Exposition.

Of the name "cat's-cradle," which is confined, of course, to the English game, no satisfactory derivation has ever been given (see Murray, *N.E.D.*). Comparatively few of the native names have been recorded. The Eskimos of Cumberland Sound call it *ajararpoq;* the Navahos, *na-ash-klo*, "continuous weaving"; the Japanese, *aya-ito-tori*, "woof-pattern string-taking"; the Caroline Islanders, *gagai* (the word also employed for the pointed stick used to open coco-nuts); the Hawaiians, *hei*, or "net"; the New Zealanders, *he-whai, huhi*, or *maui;* the natives of Lepers' Island in the New Hebrides, *lelagaro*, and of Florida in the Solomon Islands, *honggo*. In the eastern islands of Torres Straits it is known as *kamut*, in the western islands as *wormer*. The Bugis and Makassars of the Celebes call it *toêkâ-toêkâ*, from *toêkâ*, "a ladder." In some places in Australia it is named *cudgi-cudgick*. In North Queensland the various tribes of blacks have different names for it. The Koko-yimidir of Cape Bedford call it *kápan* (used also for "words, letters, writing," etc.); the Ngaikungo and Ngatchan of Atherton, etc., *morkuru;* the Nggerkudi of the Pennefather and Batavia rivers, *ane-inga;* the Kungganji of Cape Grafton, *man-jing;* the Koko-lama-lama of the Hinterland and coast of Princess Charlotte Bay, *yirma;* the Koko-rarmul of the same, *mianman;* the Koko-wara of the same, *andai-ibi;* the Mallanpara of the lower Tully River, *kumai* or *kamai*.

Although the existence of the game has been known for years, no one had described how the figures are made until Dr. Boas, in 1888, recorded the methods employed in two Eskimo games. In 1900 Mr. Harlan I. Smith figured certain stages of two games played by the Salish Indians of British Columbia. To Dr. W. H. R. Rivers and Dr. Alfred C. Haddon, however, must be attributed the real impetus given to the study of string games: their paper, published in 1902, gives us the first plan whereby all these intricate and difficult figures may be described so that anyone can repeat them; their simple and accurate nomenclature now makes it possible to record all future discoveries. A second paper, in 1903, by Dr. Haddon (**5**) on the string games of the American Indians, and a paper, in 1903, by the Rev. John Gray on several Scotch cat's-cradles, include, probably, all the descriptive records on the subject.

My brother, Dr. William Henry Furness, 3rd, in his recent trip among the Caroline Islands, by following Drs. Rivers and Haddon's directions and nomenclature, was able to record fifteen new and extremely interesting string figures; and at Dr. Haddon's suggestion I visited the St. Louis Exposition several times in 1904, and was fortunate enough to secure thirty-one additional games from natives of the various races and tribes there congregated. Of the ninety-seven figures set forth on the following pages seventy-one are now described for the first time. To this list have been added drawings of a number of finished patterns obtained by other observers who did not record, however, the methods by which they were made.

Just what value the study of the string games of different races will have to the ethnologist, it is difficult to say at this time. That evidences of racial or tribal relationship, or of migration, may be found in them, is not unlikely; that they bring us in closer touch with the folk-lore of savage people is already clear. While games in general of native races, and their connection with folk-lore, have by no means been neglected, string figures have appeared so difficult and require relatively so much time and such intimate relations for their collection, that, as yet, few careful observations have been made. Gradually, however, we are learning more about them; we know that many are closely connected with racial history and mythology, with traditional tales and fortune-telling; some are accompanied by muttered chants or songs; in others a consecutive story follows from movement to movement, or perhaps a touch or a word is associated with a certain turn or twist of the string.

Concerning the relations, which the finished patterns produced in the string games of different countries, bear to one another, we know that a few simple figures are practically universal, that several others are formed by widely separated races, but that the great majority are peculiar to definite localities. We cannot suppose that the natives set to work deliberately to form figures of familiar objects, but rather that of the many patterns—formed by chance, in sheer idleness or from an inventive turn, whether under tropical suns or in ice huts during long arctic winters—only those were kept up and named which bore resemblances, however slight, to something connected with their daily life or prominent in their thought. How far tradition has preserved the figures unchanged, or time and constant repetition have altered their original form, of course it is impossible to tell. In the finished patterns we find, among all races, representations of men and women, parts of the body, articles of dress, of commerce, and of warfare; and of stars, and natural phenomena—such as storms, darkness, and lightning. Animals and plants are frequently reproduced, the names of course being conditioned by the fauna and flora of the locality, as, for example, the *coral* of the Pacific Islands, the *cariboo* of the Eskimos, and the *owl, snake,* and *coyote* of the American Indians.

The methods employed by different races in making the figures and a comparison of these methods, are more interesting, and of more importance, than the study of the relations between the finished patterns. At present we can venture to express only the belief that, while many of the *methods* must be the same the world over, some of them will exhibit, in every region sufficiently isolated, marked peculiarities which, if enough *figures* are available, will enable us with certainty to recognize their locality. Thus the methods of Caroline Islands figures cannot be mistaken for those of the Navaho Indians, or the New Guinea methods for those of the other two.

These string games may be roughly classified into those figures whereof the purpose is to form final *patterns*, supposed to represent definite objects; those which are *tricks*, wherein, after much complex manipulation of the strings, the entire loop is suddenly drawn from the hand by some simple movement; and those which are *catches*, wherein, when certain strings are pulled, the hand or some of the fingers may be unexpectedly caught in a running noose. Of course, there is no hard and fast rule of classification; several very pretty patterns may be converted into catches.

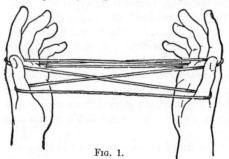

FIG. 1.

String figures are made with a piece of string about six feet long, the ends of which must be tied together to form a single loop about three feet long. In some races a thong of skin is used; in the islands of the Pacific a cord made of cocoa nut fibre, or of human hair finely plaited, serves as a string. A woven cord which does not kink as easily as a twisted cord will prove most satisfactory; unfortunately it cannot be spliced, the ends therefore must be knotted in a small square knot or laid together and bound round with thread.

All string games begin with an *opening*, the object of which is to get the original loop so arranged on the hands that a number of secondary loops shall cross from the fingers of one hand to the fingers of the other, when the hands are held in what is called their *usual position*, namely, with the palms facing each other, and the fingers directed upward (Fig. 1).

The ninety-seven figures described on the following pages show many different openings, but fifty-seven of them begin with the same opening.

In arranging the figures, those with a common opening, and otherwise closely related, are gathered in one series, instead of being distributed into race groups; and in each series, as far as possible, simple figures are placed first.

Every finger loop has, of course, two strings, and as a rule both these strings pass between the hands to form the strings of finger loops on the opposite hand; but sometimes one or both strings of a finger loop, before crossing to the other hand, pass across the palm of the hand or around other fingers and is a string, or strings, common to two finger loops of the same hand (Fig. 2). When you have arranged loops on the fingers, and the hands are held in the usual position, the loops are

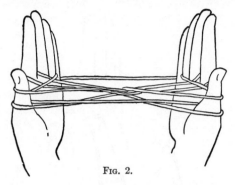

FIG. 2.

named from the fingers on which they are placed; thus, *right index loop, left little finger loop*, and so on; whenever a loop or string is changed to another finger, of course its name is changed to that of the new finger on which it is placed.

The strings of the finger loops which leave the finger from the side nearest you are called *near strings*, and the strings which leave the finger from the side of the finger furthest away from you are called *far strings;* hence we have a *right near middle finger string* or a *left far thumb string*, etc. A finger may have two loops on it, in which case they are called *upper* and *lower loops;* and we have *upper* and *lower near strings* and *upper* and *lower far strings*. A string crossing the palm is a *palmar string* (Fig. 2).

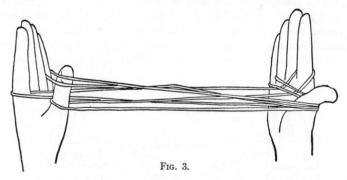

FIG. 3.

The movements which are necessary to form a final pattern are many, and in some cases most complex. They consist of a series of manipulations of the loops and strings which have been put on the fingers by the opening movement. Loops and strings are drawn over other loops and strings (Fig. 3), or under them; or are dropped and new ones formed by drawing out a straight string on one hand by a finger of the other hand (Fig. 4); loops are threaded through other loops (Fig. 5), or twisted, or the loop on the finger of one hand is exchanged for a loop from a

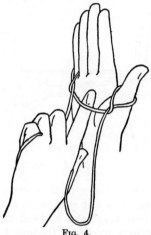

Fig. 4.

finger of the other hand (Fig. 6); and strings crossing between the hands, or in the centre of the growing pattern, are picked up by the fingers of one or of both hands (Fig. 7).

It should be remembered that the object is to form the pattern on the hands, and, as far as possible, that the loops on the fingers of one hand shall be arranged by the fingers of that hand; the hands working together simultaneously. Of course, at times it is necessary for the fingers of one hand (usually the index and thumb) to arrange loops on the other hand (Fig. 8). A loop or a string on the hand is arranged by a finger of the same hand as follows: pass each index

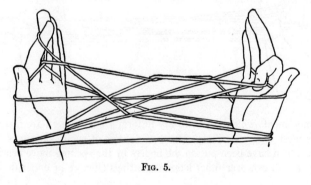

Fig. 5.

toward you, over the upper far thumb string, and pick up from below on the back of the index the lower far thumb string, and draw it up and away from you by returning the index to its usual position (Fig. 9). When you pass a finger down and under a string to pick it up, as in this example, you must naturally pick

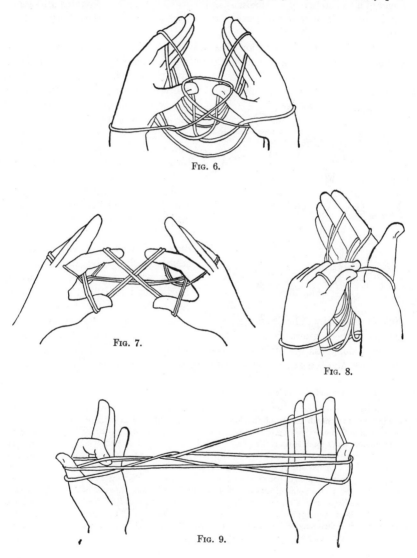

FIG. 6.

FIG. 7.

FIG. 8.

FIG. 9.

it up on the back of the finger; but if you pass a finger over a string to pick it up, you must pick it up on the ball of the finger, or in the bend of its first joint (Fig. 5).

In some figures the hands alone are not sufficient to carry out the necessary steps, and certain strings or loops must be held by the teeth (Fig. 10), or on the finger of a second person. Almost all of the string figures here recorded are solitary games, only a few need two persons and only one two persons and two loops of string.*

I have divided the description of each figure into a number of *movements*, every one of which represents a step toward the completed pattern; in this way it is easy

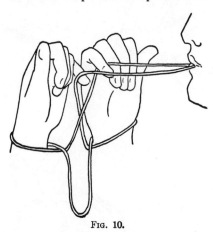

FIG. 10.

to remember the order of the steps, and it enables reference to be made to one or more steps in a figure without the necessity of further description, for some figures are mere variations of others, and a few are made by combining movements of several figures with one or two new ones. The descriptions have been prepared with the utmost care, and have been tested on people who knew nothing of the game. There is, therefore, a reason for every direction which is given; some may seem superfluous, but these mark the points where experience has shown that a pupil is liable to make a mistake. None of the figures is very difficult, the really difficult ones are yet to be recorded, as we can see by examining the finished patterns from the Marshall Islands given at the end of the book

No trouble has been found in teaching string games to children of the kindergarten age, and the games can be made as interesting to all children as to adults,

* Drs. Rivers and Haddon's nomenclature is as follows:

"A string passed over a digit is termed a loop. A loop consists of two strings. Anatomically, anything on the thumb aspect of the hand is termed 'radial' and anything on the little-finger side is called 'ulnar'; thus every loop is composed of a radial string and an ulnar string. By employing the terms thumb, index, middle-finger, ring-finger, little finger, and right and left, it is possible to designate any one of the twenty strings that may extend between the two hands. A string lying across the front of the hand is a palmar string, and one lying across the back of the hand a dorsal string. Sometimes there are two loops on a digit, one of which is nearer the finger tip than the other. Anatomically, that which is nearer to the point of attachment is 'proximal,' that which is nearer the free end is 'distal.' Thus, of two loops on a digit, the one which is nearer the hand is the proximal loop, that which is nearer the tip of the digit is the distal loop; similarly, we can speak of a proximal string and a distal string. * * * A digit may be inserted into a loop from the proximal or distal side, and in passing to a given loop the digit may pass to the distal or proximal side of other loops."

and at the same time aid materially in cultivating manual dexterity and a nice coordination of brain and hand.

Moreover, two persons can play string games together, the right hand of one and the left hand of the other forming one figure while the other hands are forming an entirely different figure; in the same way many persons can play together.

It should be remembered that the following descriptions follow exactly the methods used by the natives; doubtless other ways of forming the same figures exist, or can be devised, but I have not deemed it right, on the ethnological grounds given above, to change the methods shown to me at first hand or recorded by others.

The invention of new figures is a fascinating diversion, and is of value because thereby a student becomes more expert and therefore better trained to observe and record native games. One pretty figure I invented, as I flattered myself, only to find out later that it is common among the natives of the Caroline Islands. A few of these invented games have been added at the end of the book merely as examples of what may be done.

In the illustrations which accompany the descriptions we have the first serious attempt to show the successive steps in string games by pictures of the fingers picking up and arranging the strings and of the result produced by each movement. Heretofore, as a rule, only finished patterns have been drawn, or stretched out on cards for exhibition in a museum. Moreover, the illustrations represent the various steps *as they are seen by the person making the figure.* We have observed great care to have the strings and the loops, and their manner of crossing one another, accurately drawn. In a few figures only, where the strings run into small twists or knots in the centre between the hands, it has not been possible to trace individual strings throughout their entire course, but wherever this has been possible, even in the most complex figures, I think the artist has been unusually successful and has rendered faithfully the effects of strain and of deflection produced by crosses, knots, and twists. In illustrating a step which requires that each hand shall perform, independently, the same movement at the same time, in order to reduce the number of drawings without sacrificing any important stages in the process, one drawing, as a rule, serves to show two stages: one hand, usually the left, being represented as beginning the movement, the other hand as completing it (see Fig. 9).

CHAPTER II

FIRST POSITION

THE following movements put the loop on the hands in what for convenience may be called the First Position. Very many string games begin in this way; and the movements should be learned now, as we shall not repeat the description with every figure.

First : Put the little fingers into the loop of string, and separate the hands.

You now have a single loop on each little finger passing directly and uncrossed to the opposite little finger.

Second : Turning the hands with the palms away from you, put each thumb into the little finger loop from below, and pick up on the back of the thumb the near little finger string; then, allowing the far little finger string to remain on the

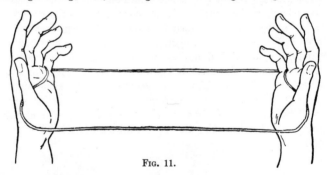

FIG. 11.

little finger, turn the hands with the palms facing each other, return the thumbs to their extended position, and draw the strings tight (Fig. 11).

In the First Position, therefore, there is, on each hand, a string which crosses the palm, and passing behind the thumb runs to the other hand to form the near thumb string of the figure, and passing behind the little finger runs to the other hand to form the far little finger string.

It is not essential that the loop shall be put on the hands by the movements just described; any method will answer, so long as the proper position of the string is secured. This method, however, has been found to be as easy as any other. The First Position is, of course, absurdly simple, yet it not infrequently puzzles the beginner, largely because it is the reverse of the first steps in the ordinary English Cat's-Cradle known to every child.

OPENING A

More than half of the string figures described in this book open in the same way; to avoid constant repetition therefore, we may follow Drs. Rivers and Haddon (p.

Fig. 12.

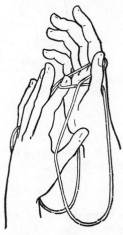

Fig. 13.

148), and call this very general method of beginning Opening A. It should be learned now, because in the descriptions of the figures in which it occurs, the first movement will be simply noted as Opening A. It is formed by three movements.

First : Put the loop on the hands in the First Position.

Second : Bring the hands together, and put the right index up under the string which crosses the left palm (Fig. 12), and draw the loop out on the back of the finger by separating the hands.

Third : Bring the hands together again, and put the left index up under that part of the string crossing the palm of the right hand which is between the strings on the right index (Fig. 13), and draw the loop out on the back of the left index by separating the hands.

You now have a loop on each thumb, index, and little finger (Fig. 14). There is a near thumb string and a far little finger string passing directly from one hand to the other, and two crosses formed between them by the near little finger string of one hand becoming the far index string of the other hand, and the far thumb string of one hand becoming the near index string of the other hand.

In forming many of the figures beginning with Opening A it is absolutely necessary to follow the order just given, and take up, first, the left palmar string with the right index, and then the right palmar string with the left index; it will save trouble, therefore, if this order be always followed, even if it make no difference in

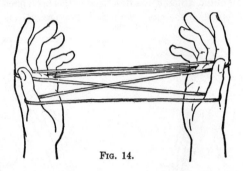

Fig. 14.

the result. If the reverse of this order is ever required, of course it will be noted in the description.

AN APACHE DOOR

This figure was taught to me by an Apache girl, Lena Smith, from Jicarilla, New Mexico, at the St. Louis Exposition in September, 1904. Lena spoke very little English and touched a door to signify the name of the figure. I could not get from her the Apache name. She was much amused at my blunders. A Navaho girl told me that all Indians know this figure. In the Philadelphia Free Museum of Science and Art, there are four examples of the finished figure collected by Mr. Stewart Culin and preserved on cards: (1) *Li-sis* = a Poncho, 22722, Navaho, from St. Michael's Mission, Arizona; (2) *Pi-cho-wai-nai*, 22604, Zuñi, New Mexico; (3) *Pi-cho-wai, a-tslo-no-no-nai* = a Sling, 22610, Zuñi, New Mexico, and (4), 22729, from Isleta, New Mexico.

First: Opening A.

Second: With the right thumb and index pick up the left near index string close to the left index, and lift the loop entirely off the left index; then put the loop over the left hand and let it drop down on the left wrist. With the left thumb and index pick up the right near index string close to the right index, and lift the loop entirely off the right index; then put the loop over the right hand and let it drop down

LENA SMITH, A JICARILLA APACHE.
(Courtesy of Mr. S. C. Simms.)

PASI, A MAMOOSE, OR CHIEF, OF DAUAR, TORRES STRAITS.
See Haddon's *Head Hunters: Black, White and Brown*.
(Courtesy of Dr. A. C. Haddon.)

on the right wrist. Separate the hands and draw the strings tight. You now have a loop on each thumb, a loop on each little finger, and a loop on each wrist (Fig. 15).

Third: With the right thumb and index pick up the left near little finger string (not the whole loop) close to the left little finger, and, drawing it toward you,

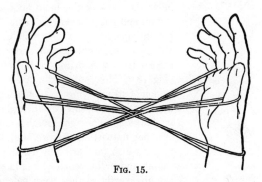

FIG. 15.

pass it between the left index and thumb, and release it. With the right thumb and index pick up the left far thumb string close to the left thumb, and, drawing it away from you, pass it between the left ring and little fingers, and release it.

With the left thumb and index pick up the right near little finger string close to the right little finger, and, drawing it toward you, pass it between the right index and thumb, and release it. With the left thumb and index pick up the right far

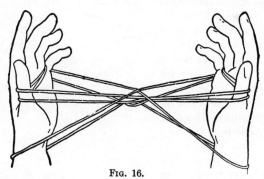

FIG. 16.

thumb string close to the right thumb, and, drawing it away from you, pass it between the right ring and little fingers, and release it.

You now have a loop on each wrist, and two strings crossing each palm in the First Position (Fig. 16).

Fourth : Keeping all the loops in position on both hands, with the left hand grasp tightly all the strings where they cross in the centre of the figure, and pass this collection of strings from left to right between the right thumb and index, that is, from the palmar side to the back of the hand, and let them lie on the back of the hand midway between the thumb and index finger (Fig. 17). Then with the left thumb and index take hold of the two loops already on the right thumb, and, without pulling them out, draw them over the tip of the right thumb (Fig. 18). Now, still holding the loops, let the collection of strings lying low down between the right index and thumb, slip over the right thumb to the palmar side. The right thumb is now entirely free. Without untwisting the two original right thumb loops, which you are still holding with the left thumb and index, replace these loops on the right thumb exactly as they were before the collected strings were placed between the right index and thumb (Fig. 19). Separate the hands, and draw the strings tight. Now repeat exactly the same movement on the left hand as follows:

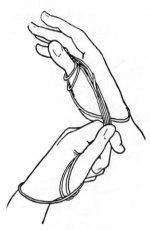

Fig. 17.

Keeping all the loops in position on both hands, with the right hand grasp tightly all the strings where they cross in the centre of the figure, and pass this collection of strings from right to left between the left index and thumb, that is, from the palmar side to the back of the hand, and let them lie on the back of the hand midway between the index and thumb; then with the right thumb and index take hold of the two loops already on the left thumb and, without pulling them out, draw them over the tip of the left thumb. Now, still holding these loops, let the collection of strings lying low down between the left index and thumb, slip over the left thumb to the palmar side. The left thumb is now entirely free.

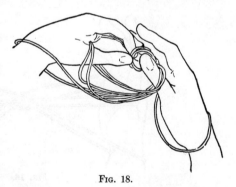

Fig. 18.

Without untwisting the two original left thumb loops, which you are still holding with the right thumb and index, replace these loops on the left thumb exactly as they were before the collected strings were placed between the left index and thumb. Separate the hands, and draw the strings tight.

You now have a loop on each wrist, two twisted loops on each thumb, and two twisted loops on each little finger (Fig. 20).

Fifth : With the right thumb and index lift the left wrist loop from the back of the left wrist up over the tips of all the left fingers, and let it fall on the palmar side. With the left thumb and index lift the right wrist loop from the back of the right wrist up over the tips of all the right fingers, and let it fall on the palmar side.

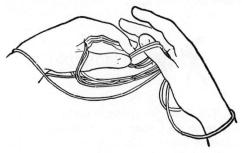

Fig. 19.

Sixth : Retaining the loops on the thumbs and little fingers, rub the palms of the hands together; then separate the hands, and draw the figure tight (Fig. 21).

This is a beautiful figure, and not at all difficult. Moreover it retains its shape no matter how tight you may pull it. It contains several interesting movements:

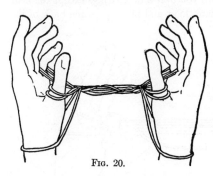

Fig. 20.

In the *Second*, the method of transferring the index loops to the wrists is unusual; as we shall see further on, a more complicated method is almost always employed. In the *Third* movement the changing of a string from one finger to another by means of the thumb and index of the other hand is a process not often observed. Indeed one may easily believe that the methods given in these two movements are short cuts peculiar to the individual who taught me the figure, and that, some day, other Indians will be seen doing these movements in the usual elaborate style, whereby the strings on either hand are shifted and arranged by the fingers of that hand only. As far as I know, the *Fourth* movement has not been observed in any other string figure. The rubbing of the hands together in the

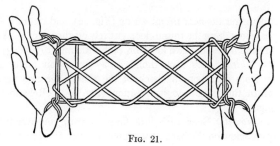

Fig. 21.

Sixth movement is, of course, only for effect; it has no bearing on the success of the figure. The manner of showing the finished pattern, what we call its "extension," is of the most simple type; indeed the figure practically extends itself when the hands are drawn apart.

 FIGHTING HEAD–HUNTERS

This figure was taught to me by Dr. Haddon in August, 1904. He obtained it when on the Cambridge Anthropological Expedition to Torres Straits; it is described by Rivers and Haddon (p. 150). In Mer (Murray Island), Torres Straits, it is called *Ares* = Murray and Dauar men fighting. One twisted loop of the finished figure represents the Murray man, who always carries off the Dauar man's head.

First : Opening A.

Second : Bend each little finger toward you over all the strings except the near thumb string, and then down into the thumb loop, and pick up on the back of the

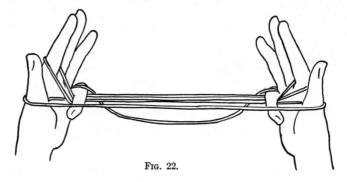

Fig. 22.

little finger the near thumb string (Fig. 22), and return the little finger to its original position, taking the thumb loop entirely off the thumb. You now have a single loop on each index and two loops on each little finger (Fig. 23).

Third : Pass each thumb away from you under the index loop, and take up from below on the back of the thumb the two near little finger strings, and return the thumb to its position (Fig. 24). Release the loops from the little fingers.

Fourth : Bend each little finger toward you over the index loop, and take up from below on the back of the finger the two far thumb strings (Fig. 25, Left hand),

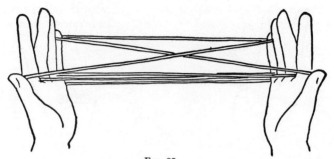

Fig. 23.

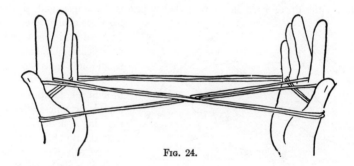

Fig. 24.

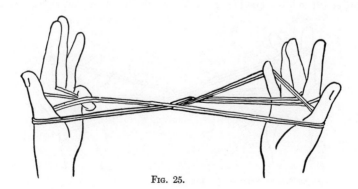

Fig. 25.

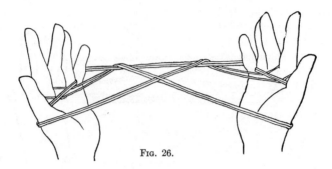

FIG. 26.

and return the little finger to its position, retaining the loops on the thumb (Fig. 25, Right hand).

Fifth : In the centre of the figure there is now a distinct triangle formed of double strings (Fig. 26).

Insert the tip of each index from below into this triangle, and, pulling out

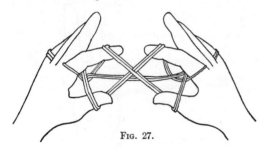

FIG. 27.

the sides of the triangle on the backs of the index fingers (Fig. 27), separate the hands. You should now have two loops on each thumb, two loops on each little finger, and three loops on each index, one at the base of the finger and two together near the tip (Fig. 28).

Sixth : Keeping all the strings securely on the right hand, with the right thumb and index lift the lower left single index loop over the two upper left index loops (Fig. 29), and over the tip of the left index, and let it

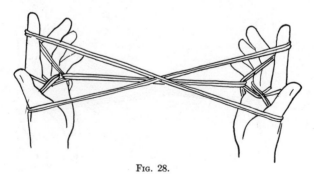

FIG. 28.

fall on the palmar side. In doing this movement be careful not to let the loops slip off the right fingers. In like manner with the left thumb and index remove the lower right index loop from the right index. Release the loops from the thumbs.

The two loops which are now on each index and little finger are bound together not far from the palm (Fig. 30).

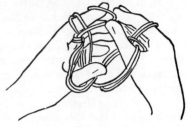

Seventh : Twist tightly the two loops on each index finger about three times, by rotating the index away from you (or by dropping the loops from the index and twisting them with the thumb and index).

Eighth : The loops should now be dropped from the index (if this has not

Fig. 29.

been already done to twist them with the thumb and index) and the figure turned so that these twisted index loops shall hang down. With the left little finger pull

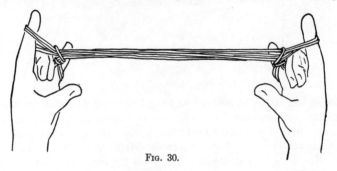

Fig. 30.

gently on the left near little finger strings, which will cause the right twisted hanging loops (one head-hunter) to move toward the other hanging loops (the other head-hunter) (Fig. 31); then they meet, and by jerking the left hand strings slightly

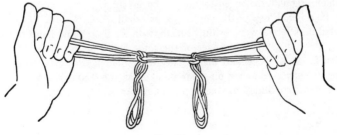

Fig. 31.

"they fight and they fight and they fight." The result of the contest is always uncertain; either "they kill each other" and fall apart, or "one may kill the other and travel home," toward the right hand, "with his enemy's head" (Fig. 32).

If, in forming Opening A, the right palmar string be taken up first, and if, when the figure is completed, the *right* near strings be pulled upon, then the victorious head-hunter will travel home toward the left hand.

There are not many figures like this one which have definite stories attached to them. Doubtless the stories exist, but have not been told and recorded; in some instances the stories have been forgotten by the natives themselves, or have degenerated into formulæ the meanings of which are no longer known.

The Fighting Head-Hunters is a good example of that simple type of figure in which most of the movements consist in passing the fingers away from you and

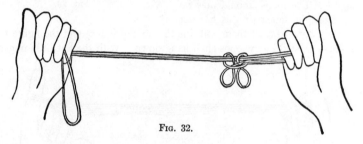

FIG. 32.

toward you, and taking up strings and loops from other fingers of the same hand. The picking up of the strings forming the sides of the central triangle is not a common movement. In the *Second* movement a loop is transferred from one finger to another and turned over during the transfer. In the *Sixth* movement we have the first example of an almost universal procedure: When two loops are on a finger the lower loop is lifted over the upper loop and off the finger to form, toward the centre of the figure, a running noose or ring upon the upper loop. If there be three loops on a finger the lower one may be lifted over the upper two, or the lower two over the upper one, but in all cases the principle is the same, namely, to thread the upper loop, which originally belonged to another finger, through the lower loop, which is usually the original loop of the finger. As we shall see further on, this movement is executed in different ways: with the teeth, with the thumb and index of the other hand, by the aid of another finger of the same hand, or merely by twisting the finger itself. It is so general in the Navaho Indian figures that, following Dr. Haddon, in conversation we often speak of it as the "Navaho movement," or, coining a new verb, direct that the loops on a finger shall be "Navahoed."

A SUNSET

The "Sunset" is closely related to the preceding "Fighting Head-Hunters."
It was obtained by Dr. Haddon in Torres Straits (see Rivers and Haddon, p. 150,

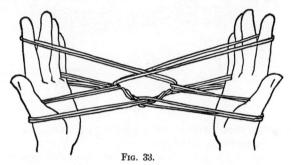

FIG. 33.

Fig. 4). In Murray Island it is known as *Lem baraigida* = a Setting Sun; in
Mabuiag as *Dògai* = a Star.

First, Second, Third, Fourth: Similar to the first four movements of the
Fighting Head-Hunters.

Fifth: Exchange the loops on the index fingers by bringing the hands together
and putting the right index loop on the left index and then putting the left index
loop on the right index; in this way the right index loop is passed through the left

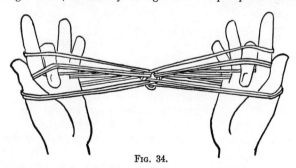

FIG. 34.

index loop. You now have a single loop on each index, two loops on each thumb,
and two loops on each little finger (Fig. 33).

Sixth: Bend each middle finger down, and put it from above through the index
loop; pick up from below on the back of the finger the two far thumb strings (Fig. 34),

and return the middle finger back through the index loop to its original position (Fig. 35).

Release the loops from the thumbs and index fingers, and transfer the two

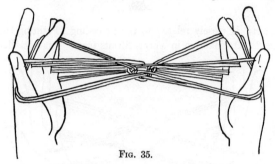

Fig. 35.

loops on each middle finger to the thumb, by putting the thumb from below into the loops and withdrawing the middle finger.

Seventh : In the centre of the figure is a small triangle the base of which is on the far side and is formed by the two strings passing from one little finger to the other; each side of the triangle is formed of the two near thumb strings after they have crossed the corresponding strings from the other thumb (Fig. 36). Pick

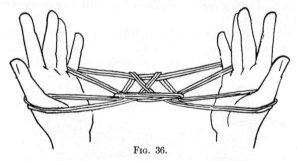

Fig. 36.

up from below on the back of each index the strings forming the corresponding side of the triangle (Fig. 37), and return the index to its position.

You now have two loops on each thumb, two loops on each index, and two loops on each little finger.

Eighth : Put each middle finger from above through the two index loops, and (as in the *Sixth* movement) pick up from below on the back of the middle finger the two far thumb strings (Fig. 38), and return the middle finger, through the two index loops (Fig. 39), to its former position.

Ninth : Release the loops from the thumbs and index fingers, and, keeping the loops on the little fingers, extend the figure by putting each index finger into the middle finger loop to make it wider (Fig. 40).

The far little finger strings drawn straight represent the horizon, the central semicircle is the sun, and the three other double strings on each side are the sun's rays. These latter may be made more apparent by transferring, on each hand,

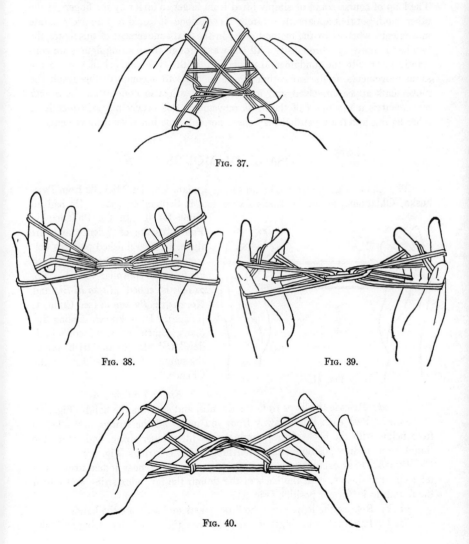

FIG. 37.

FIG. 38.   FIG. 39.

FIG. 40.

one of the middle finger loops to the index. The sun is made to set by releasing the loops held by the index and middle fingers, and drawing the hands apart.

In this figure we have as a new movement the exchange of loops between opposite fingers. We also see the method of transferring a loop from one finger to another finger of the same hand, without turning the loop over in the transfer. The loop of course could be simply lifted from finger to finger by the fingers of the other hand, but that apparently is rarely, if ever, done; it would require two separate movements, whereas by the method given in the *Sixth* movement of this figure, the two hands move synchronously. All the way through these string figures we constantly meet with the fundamental principle that the two hands shall execute the same movements at the same time; in some cases to accomplish this result the movements appear involved and indirect. You will also notice that the *Eighth* movement is a repetition of the *Sixth* movement; this occurs not infrequently in other figures and the repetition may cover not only one but several movements.

OSAGE DIAMONDS

This figure was shown me by an Osage Indian, Charles Michelle from Pawhuska, Oklahoma, at the St. Louis Exposition, in September, 1904. He had no

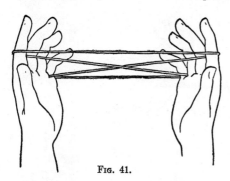

name for it. In the Philadelphia Free Museum of Science and Art there are two finished patterns collected by Mr. Stewart Culin; both are from the Hawaiian Islands. No. 21447 is called *Ma-ka-lii-lii*, and No. 21514, *Pu-kau-la* (see Culin, **1**, p. 222). It is known among Indians, sometimes as "Jacob's Ladder," and also to the Irish, under the names of the "Ladder" or the "Fence."

FIG. 41.

First: Opening A.

Second: Release the loops from the thumbs, and separate the hands (Fig. 41).

Third: Pass each thumb away from you under all the strings, and take up from below with the back of the thumb the far little finger string, and return the thumb to its former position without touching the other strings (Fig. 42).

Fourth: Pass each thumb away from you over the near index string, and take up, from below, with the back of the thumb the far index string and return the thumb to its former position (Fig. 43).

Fifth: Release the loops from the little fingers and separate the hands.

Sixth: Pass each little finger toward you over the near index string and take

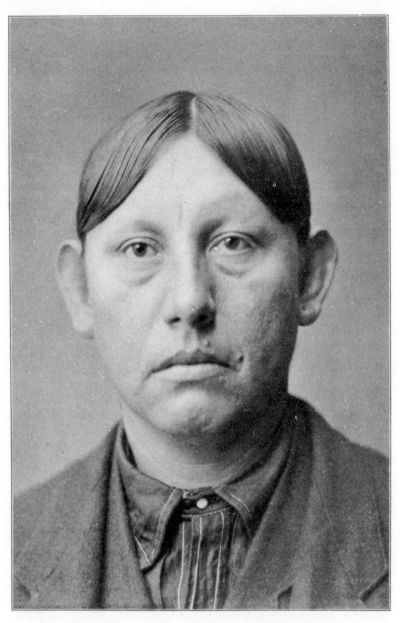

CHARLES MICHELLE, AN OSAGE INDIAN OF PAWHUSKA, OKLAHOMA.
(Courtesy of Mr. S. C. Simms.)

WARIA, A MAMOOSE, OR CHIEF, OF MABUIAG, TORRES STRAITS.

An intelligent and literary Papuan. See Haddon's *Head Hunters: Black, White and Brown.*

(Courtesy of Dr. A. C. Haddon.)

up from below on the back of the little finger the far thumb string (Fig. 44, **Left** hand), and return the little finger to its former position (Fig. 44, **Right** hand).

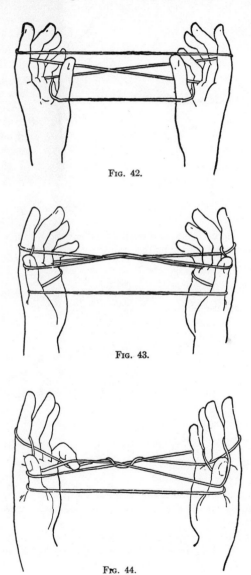

Fig. 42.

Fig. 43.

Fig. 44.

Seventh: Release the loops from the thumbs (Fig. 45).

Eighth: Pass each thumb away from you over the index loop, and take up, from below, with the back of the thumb the near little finger string and return the thumb to its position (Fig. 46).

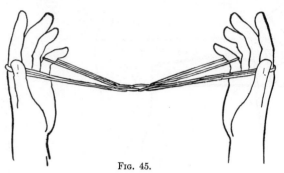

Ninth: With the right thumb and index pick up the left near index string (close to the left index and above the left palmar string) and put it over the left thumb (Fig. 47). With the left thumb and index pick up the right near index string (close

Fig. 45.

to the right index and above the right palmar string) and put it over the right thumb. Separate the hands (Fig. 48).

Tenth: Bending each thumb toward the other hand and then up toward you, slip the lower near thumb string off the thumb, without disturbing the upper thumb loop (Fig. 49, Left hand).

Eleventh: Insert each index from above into the small triangle formed by the palmar string twisting around the thumb loop (Fig. 49, Right hand), and, turning the palms down, release the loop from the little fingers; then separate the hands, turn the palms away from you, and the finished figure will appear (Fig. 50).

This figure is extremely simple; the majority of the movements are most direct. The *Ninth* movement appears to be rather a clumsy way of taking an additional loop on the thumb, but if you try the usual Indian way of putting each t h u m b

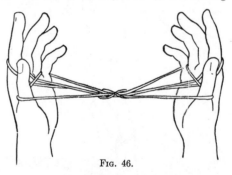

Fig. 46.

simultaneously up into the index loop between the palmar string and the index, and then separating the thumbs from the index fingers, you will find it rather difficult.

In the *Tenth* movement we see a new way of slipping the lower thumb loop over the upper loop and off the thumb. The turning of the palms away from you to form the finished figure is a movement we shall meet with repeatedly; in this figure

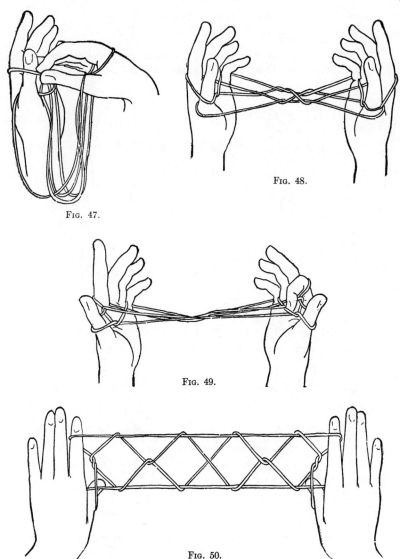

Fig. 47.

Fig. 48.

Fig. 49.

Fig. 50.

it is not essential to the success of the pattern, but in many other figures the final pattern will not appear unless the far strings are drawn tight by turning the palms away from you.

OSAGE TWO DIAMONDS

The Osage Indian who taught me the preceding game gave me this one also; he had no name for it. There is a Hawaiian example done with a single string

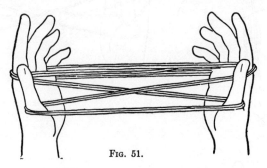

FIG. 51.

loop preserved in the Philadelphia Free Museum of Science and Art. It was collected by Mr. Stewart Culin, is numbered 21448 and called *Pa-pi-o-ma-ka-nu-i-nu-i* (see Culin, **I,** pl. xiv, *a*).

First: Opening A, with the string doubled and used throughout as if it were a single string (Fig. 51).

Second: Release the loops from the thumbs.

Third: Pass each thumb away from you over the index loops and the near

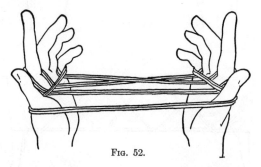

FIG. 52.

little finger strings, and take up, from below, on the back of the thumb the far little finger strings and return the thumb to its former position (Fig. 52).

Fourth: Insert each thumb from below into the index loops, close to the index, between the finger and the strings which cross the palm and return the thumb to its position (Fig. 53).

Fifth: Turn each thumb down toward the other thumb (Fig. 54, Left hand),

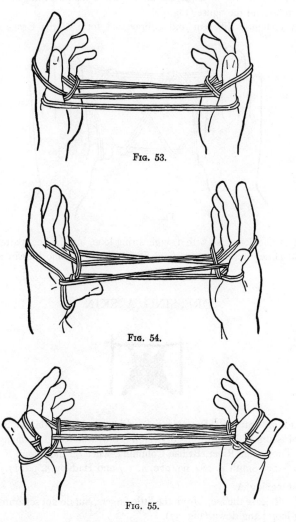

FIG. 53.

FIG. 54.

FIG. 55.

and, letting the lower loops slip off the thumb, turn the thumb up toward you (Fig. 54, Right hand).

Sixth: Insert each index from above into the triangle formed between the thumb and index by the palmar strings looping around the strings of the thumb loops (Fig. 55), then, while turning the palms downward and then away from you, release the loops from the little fingers, and separate the index fingers widely from the thumbs to extend the figure (Fig. 56).

This is a slightly different and abbreviated form of the Osage Diamonds.

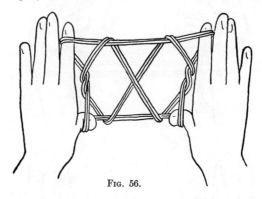

FIG. 56.

Of course it can be done also with a single string loop, but the final pattern is not so effective and closely resembles the final figure of the Navaho "Twin Stars."

DRESSING A SKIN

Dr. Haddon learned "Dressing a Skin" from Mr. Harlan I. Smith of the American Museum of Natural History, New York, who found it among the Salish Indians of Thompson River, British Columbia, when on the Jessup North Pacific Expedition.   (See Smith p. 282, fig. 270, *a*, 1-7 and Haddon 5, p. 217.)

First : Opening A.

Second : Release the loops from the little fingers, but do not separate the hands; let the long loop hang down (Fig. 57).

Third : Toss this long loop toward you over all the other strings and let it hang down on the near side (Fig. 58).

Fourth : Bend each thumb down into its own loop, over that part of the string of the hanging loop which crosses over the thumb loop (Fig. 59 Left hand), and let the original thumb loop slip over the knuckle and off the thumb (Fig. 59, Right hand).

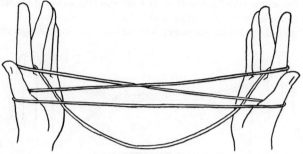

FIG. 57.

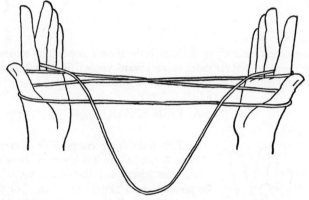

FIG. 58.

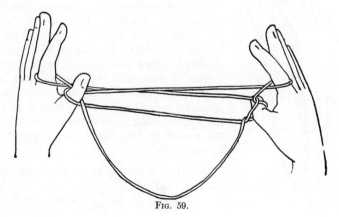

FIG. 59.

Then turn the hands with the palms away from you and, drawing the strings tight, extend the figure between the thumbs and index fingers (Fig. 60).

The object of the *Third* movement is to get each far index finger string into a

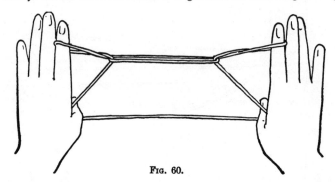

FIG. 60.

convenient position for drawing it through the thumb loop. This movement may be done by drawing each far index string toward you on the thumb and then releasing the little finger loops and the original thumb loops.

A FISH-SPEAR

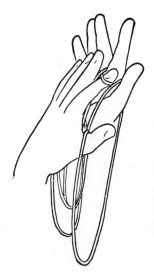

FIG. 61.

This little figure comes from Murray Island, Torres Straits, where it is known as *Baur* = a Fish-spear (see Rivers and Haddon, p. 149, Fig. 1). It is identical with "Pitching a Tent," of the Salish Indians, British Columbia, obtained by Mr. Harlan I. Smith, when he secured "Dressing a Skin." Several stages of "Pitching a Tent" are illustrated by Mr. Smith (p. 282, Fig. 270, *b*, 1-4) and the game itself is described by Dr. Haddon (**5**, p. 217). Dr. Haddon has since found it played by the Clayoquaht Indians, Nootka tribe, Vancouver Island, at the St. Louis Exposition under the name "Sea-Egg (Echinus) Spear." There is a finished pattern in the Philadelphia Free Museum of Science and Art, No. 22608 from Zuñi, New Mexico, collected by Mr. Stewart Culin.

First: Put the loop of string on both hands in the First Position.

Second: Insert the right index, from above, behind the string crossing the left palm, and draw out the loop to the right, twisting it several times by rotating the right index.

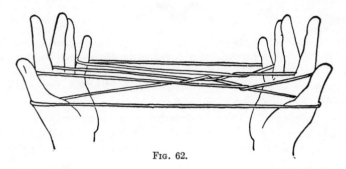

FIG. 62.

Third : With the left index pick up from below the string crossing the right palm, being sure to pick it up between the strings of the right index loop and near

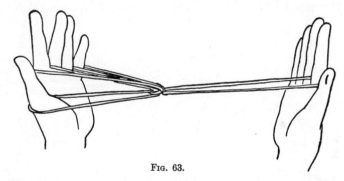

FIG. 63.

the right index where the loop is not twisted (Fig. 61).   Separate the hands and draw the strings tight (Fig. 62).

Fourth : Release the loops from the right thumb and little finger, and separate the hands.   The points of the spear will be on the thumb, index, and little finger of the left hand. and the handle will be held by the index of the right hand (Fig. 63).

A SEA-SNAKE

The "Sea-snake" is played by the natives of Murray Island, Torres Straits, they call it *Pagi* = a Sea-snake. It is described by Rivers and Haddon (p. 152, Fig. 9). Partington (pl. 341, 3) gives a drawing of a finished pattern from Torres Straits, preserved in the British Museum (A. C. Haddon Collection) and labelled "cat's-cradle in the form of a water snake (*garê*)."

First : Opening A. (The *left* palmar string *must* be taken up first.)

Second : Keeping all the loops securely on the fingers, turn the hands with the palms down and the fingers pointing toward one another. Move the right hand

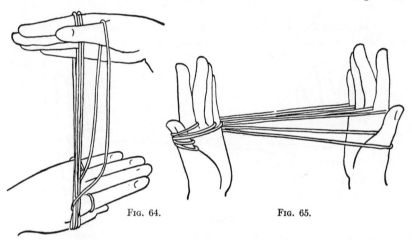

FIG. 64.   FIG. 65.

toward you, then to the left, and carry it up and away from you over and past the left hand (Fig. 64); turn the hands with the fingers pointing upward and draw the strings tight (Fig. 65). This movement brings all the strings from the palm of the left hand around the base of the left thumb over the back of the left hand and then to the right hand from the far side of the left hand.

Third : Put the entire left hand, from above, into the loop on the right index (Fig. 66), and move it away from you over the right little finger loop, and release the loop from the right index as it slips down on the left wrist (Fig. 67). Now carry the right hand around the left hand, by moving it away from you, to the left, and toward you over the left hand (Fig. 68), thus unwinding the strings. Separate the hands and draw the strings tight (Fig. 69).

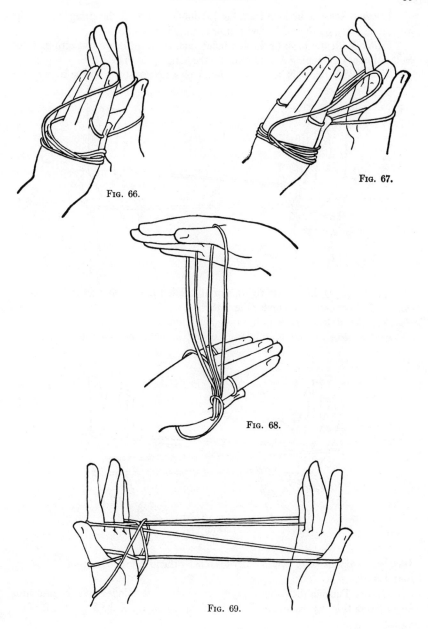

Fig. 66.

Fig. 67.

Fig. 68.

Fig. 69.

Fourth : Release the loop from the left index and draw the strings tight (Fig. 70). The string on the right hand is now in the First Position.

Fifth : With the back of the left index take up, from below, the string on the right palm, as in Opening A, and separate the hands (Fig 71).

Sixth : With the right thumb and index pick up the string on the back of the

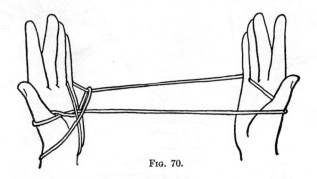

FIG. 70.

left wrist (Fig. 72), lift it over the tips of all the left fingers, and let it drop on the palmar side; separate the hands (Fig. 73).

Seventh : Release the loop from the left thumb.

Eighth : Put the left thumb, from below, into the left index loop and with-

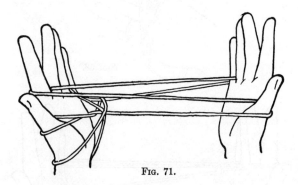

FIG. 71.

draw the left index (Fig. 74), in order to transfer the loop to the left thumb (Fig. 75, Left hand).

Ninth : Turning the palms away from you, bend each index over the near little finger string (Fig. 75, Right hand), and pick up on the tip of the finger the far little

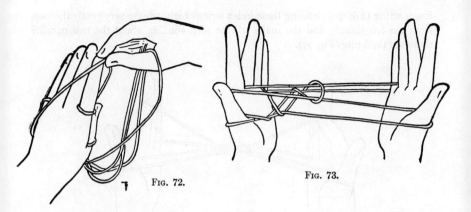

FIG. 72.

FIG. 73.

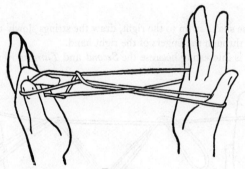

FIG. 74.

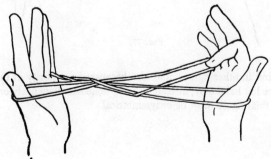

FIG. 75.

finger string (Fig. 76); holding these index strings high, release very gently the loop from the left thumb, and the snake will be seen winding about the two parallel strings of the figure (Fig. 77).

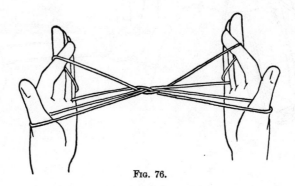

FIG. 76.

To make the snake swim to the right, draw the strings slowly to the left, allowing them to slip through the fingers of the right hand.

This figure is interesting because the *Second* and *Third* movements are unlike

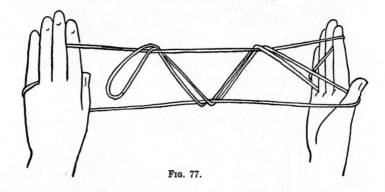

FIG. 77.

anything we find in other figures, and also because the majority of the movements are done on the left hand only, instead of being done simultaneously on both hands. Of course the final figure must be unsymmetrical.

A KING FISH (Also a Catch)

This is another of the games obtained by Dr. Haddon in Torres Straits. In Murray Island it is known as *Geigi* = King Fish, and in Mabuiag as *Dangal* = the Dugong, or Sea-cow (Rivers and Haddon, p. 151, Fig. 7).

First : Opening A. (The *left* palmar string *must* be taken up first.)

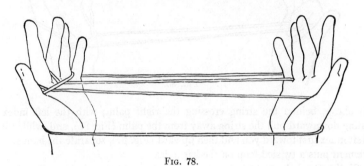

FIG. 78.

Second : Release the loop from the right index. Separate the hands and draw the strings tight (Fig. 78).

Third : Bend the left index down between the two index strings and hold firmly in the bend of the finger, the string which passes across the left palm and over the

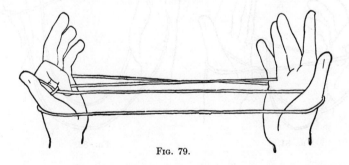

FIG. 79.

index strings (Fig. 79). Turn the left hand with the palm down and the fingers pointing to the right, and let all the strings slip off the left hand except the loop held in the bend of the left index by which the strings can now be pulled tight (Fig. 80).

Fourth : Arrange the loop held by the left index on the left hand in the First Position across the palm and behind the thumb and little finger.

Fifth : Bring the palms together, point the left index downward, and put it,

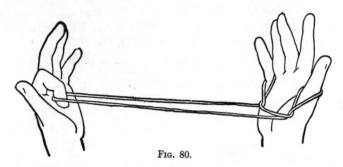

FIG. 80.

from above, behind the string crossing the right palm; with the left index still pointing downward pull the string away from the palm (Fig. 81), and, while turning the left index first toward you and then upward (Fig. 82), separate the hands. This movement puts a twisted loop on the left index.

Sixth : Bend the right index down into the right thumb loop (Fig. 83), and

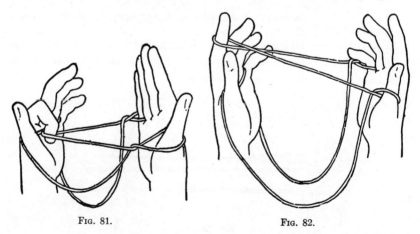

FIG. 81.   FIG. 82.

then, turning the palm away from you, put the right index, carrying the right far thumb string, down into the little finger loop (Fig. 84) and pick up with its tip the right near little finger string (Fig. 85). As you return the index to its original position, of course, the string which was the right far thumb string slips off the index finger. This movement, which appears so complicated, is nothing more than the index finger pulling the near little finger string through the thumb loop.

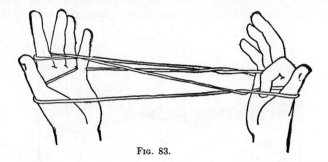

Fig. 83.

You now have on the left hand a string across the palm and a twisted loop on the index; and on the right hand a near thumb string and a far little finger string;

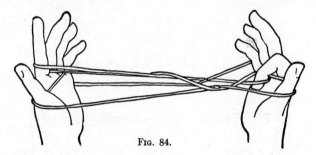

Fig. 84.

the near little finger string is looped around the tip of the index after passing under the far thumb string and pulling it over to the centre of the palm.

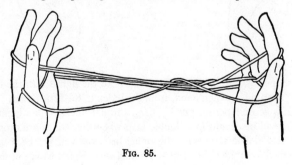

Fig. 85.

Seventh : Bend the left little finger down into the left index loop (Fig. 86, Left hand) close to the index, and pull down and hold securely the left far index string.

Eighth : Bend down the right little finger over the right far thumb string (Fig. 86, Right hand) where it forms the lower string of a triangle, whereof the other

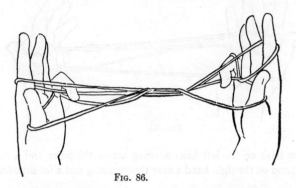

FIG. 86.

two sides are formed by the original near little finger string held up by the tip of the right index. Pull down this far thumb string in the bend of the right little finger.

Ninth : Let the loops slip off the thumbs and extend the figure between the index and little finger of each hand (Fig. 87). The strings on the index fingers must be kept well up toward the tips; if the figure does not come properly it can be

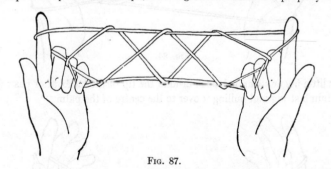

FIG. 87.

worked into shape, by pushing toward the centre of the figure with the thumb the straight string running, on each hand, from the index to the little finger.

Tenth : If a second person put his hand through the middle diamond of the figure his wrist will be caught in a double loop when the strings are dropped from the left hand and pulled tight with the right; his wrist will not be caught if the strings be dropped from the right hand and pulled with the left hand toward the left.

This is an interesting example of a figure which starts unsymmetrically, and then, after a series of very different movements by each hand comes out almost perfectly symmetrical at the end. You will notice that there is a twist at the right end

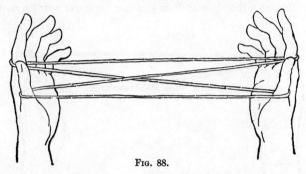

FIG. 88.

of the right lozenge and a simple loop at the left end of the left lozenge. If the right palmar string be taken up first in the formation of Opening A, and then the movements of the hands reversed, the wrist will be caught in a double loop when the right-hand strings are dropped. By forming the figure first one way and then the other you can add to the perplexity of the observer.

BAGOBO DIAMONDS

I was taught this figure by a young man of the Bagobo Tribe in the Philippine Reservation at the St. Louis Exposition in August, 1904. He had no name for it. I found that it was also known to the Philippine Linao Moros.

First: Opening A. (The *left* palmar string *must* be taken up first.)

Second: Release the loops from the little fingers. There is now a loop on each thumb and a loop on each index (Fig. 88).

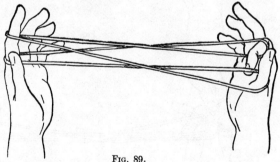

FIG. 89.

Third: Transfer the thumb loops to the index fingers by taking up from below with the back of each index the far thumb string (Fig. 89, Right hand). You now have on each index, two loops, an upper and a lower (Fig. 89, Left hand).

Fourth : Pass each thumb away from you over the lower near index string, and with the back of the thumb pick up, from below, the lower far index string, and return the thumb to the original position (Fig. 90).

Fifth : Pass each thumb away from you over the upper near index string, and

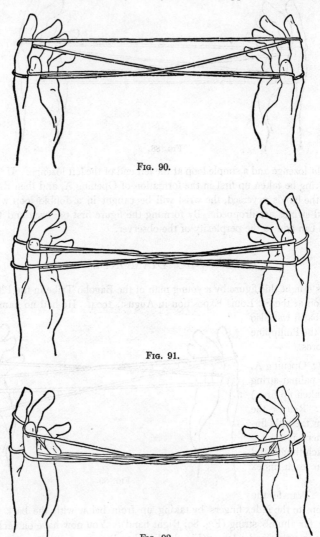

Fig. 90.

Fig. 91.

Fig. 92.

with the back of the thumb pick up, from below, the upper far index string, and return the thumb to the original position.

By these movements the far strings of the t w o i n d e x l o o p s a r e crossed o v e r their corresponding near strings,

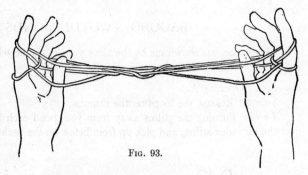

FIG. 93.

and pass around the backs of the thumbs to become lower and upper near thumb strings (Fig. 91).

Sixth : Pass each ring finger over the upper near index string and pick up, from below, on the back of the ring finger the lower near index string (Fig. 92), and return the ring fingers to their positions (Fig. 93).

Seventh : Pick up with the teeth, close to the back of the thumb, the right lower near thumb string, and lift it over the tip of the thumb, and drop it on the palmar side, being careful not to disturb the upper near thumb string. Repeat this movement on the left hand by picking up with the teeth the left lower near thumb string, lift it over the tip of the thumb, and drop it on the palmar side.

Eighth : Keeping the strings drawn tight, swing the left hand down, and turn it palm up with the fingers pointing away from you; turn the right-hand palm down with the fingers pointing toward you and the completed figure appears (Fig. 94).

In this figure the *Fourth* and *Fifth* movements are unlike anything observed in the preceding figures. The interesting point, however, lies in the fact that while both hands do the same movements throughout the figure, the finished pattern will not appear unless one hand is revolved through half a circle. Moreover, when the pattern does appear, it is not perfectly symmetrical.

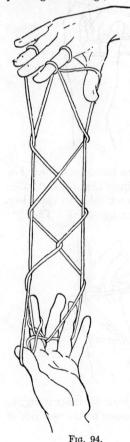

FIG. 94.

BAGOBO TWO DIAMONDS

This figure was shown me by the same young Bagobo who taught me the preceding Diamonds. He had no name for it.

First : Opening A.

Second : Release the loops on the thumbs.

Third : Turning the palms away from you, bend each index away from you over the far index string, and pick up from below on the back of the finger the near

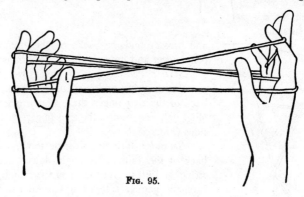

Fig. 95.

little finger string; straighten the index and turn the palms facing each other (Fig. 95, Right hand); then release the loop from each little finger (Fig. 95, Left hand) and draw the strings tight. You now have two loops on each index, an upper loop with a straight far string and a lower loop with a near straight string. The right

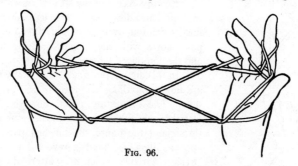

Fig. 96.

lower far index string crosses on the near side of the left lower far index string; in the Bagobo Diamonds, the left lower near index string crosses on the near side of the right lower near index string.

Fourth, Fifth, Sixth and *Seventh :* The same as the corresponding movements of the Bagobo Diamonds.

The finished pattern appears on the completion of the *Seventh* movement (Fig. 96).

This figure closely resembles the preceding figure, but in the *Second* and *Third* movements it is the little finger loops which are transferred to the index fingers. The final figure is symmetrical, and does not require any rotation of the hand .to produce it.

CHAPTER III

 ## MANY STARS

D R. HADDON showed me this figure in August, 1904. He obtained it in Chicago in 1901 from two old Navaho men, and has published a description of it (**5**, p. 222, pl. xv, Fig. 3). I also saw it done by the two Navaho girls who taught me other Navaho figures. It is called *Son-tlani* by the Navahos. Mr. Stewart Culin has preserved two examples of this pattern in the Philadelphia Free Museum of Science and Art, one (22731) from Isleta, New Mexico; the other (22714) from St. Michael's Mission, Arizona.

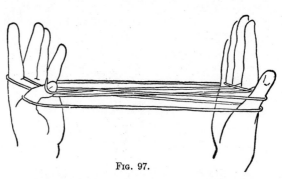

FIG. 97.

First: Opening A.

Second: Pass each thumb away from you over the far thumb string and both index strings, and pick up from below, on the back of the thumb, the near little finger string (Fig. 97, Left hand), and return the thumb to its original position (Fig. 97, Right hand).

Third: Bend each middle finger down toward you over the index strings, and take up from below, on the back of the finger, the far thumb string (Fig. 98, Left hand) and return the middle finger to its original position (Fig. 98, Right hand). Release the loops from the thumbs (Fig. 99). You now have a loop on each index, a loop on each middle finger, and a loop on each little finger.

Fourth: Turning the palms slightly away from you, pass each thumb away from you over the near index string, but under the far index string, both strings on

48

the middle finger and also under both strings on the little finger; then drawing the thumb toward you, take up on the back of the thumb the far little finger string

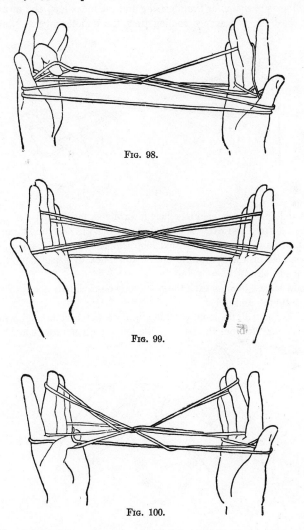

Fig. 98.

Fig. 99.

Fig. 100.

(Fig. 100, Left hand) and return the thumb to its position, bringing back with it through the index loop only the far little finger string (Fig. 100, Right hand). Release the loops from the little fingers.

Fifth : Put the tips of the right thumb and index together, and put the tips of the left thumb and index together, then turning each hand slightly away from you pass these fingers over the far thumb string and the index loop and away from you under and past the two strings coming from the middle finger. Now, drawing

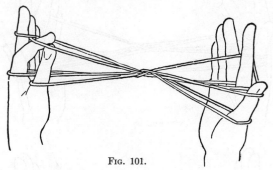

FIG. 101.

the thumb and index (still held together) toward you, take up on their tips the far middle finger string, and draw it toward you under the near middle finger string (Fig. 101, Left hand). Let the twisted loop slip off the middle finger, and widen out the loop held on the tips of the thumb and index by separating these fingers (Fig. 101, Right hand).

You now have a loop on each thumb, a loop on each index, and a loop passing around both thumb and index.

Sixth : Keeping all the loops carefully in place on the right hand, with the right thumb and index lift from the back of the left thumb the lower loop on the left

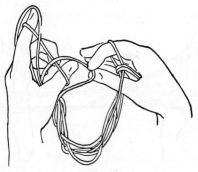

FIG. 102.

thumb up over the upper loop (which passes around both thumb and index), then entirely off the left thumb, being careful *not* to take off also the upper loop, and let it drop on the palmar side of the thumb (Fig. 102). With the right thumb and index in the same way lift the lower left index loop over the upper left index loop and off the left index.

Keeping all the loops carefully in place on the left hand, with the left thumb and index lift the lower loop on the right thumb up over the upper loop, off the right thumb, and let it drop on the palmar side. With the left thumb and index, in the

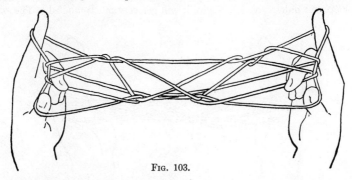

Fig. 103.

same way, lift the lower right index loop over the upper right index loop, then off the right index, and let it drop on the palmar side.

You now have on each hand a single loop passing around both thumb and index. Two other loops are held by that part of the loop passing from the back of the thumb to the back of the index (Fig. 102, Right hand).

Seventh : Put each middle finger from below up on the far side of the lower near string of the four passing around the string running from the back of the thumb

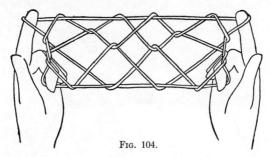

Fig. 104.

to the back of the index; bend the middle finger toward you (Fig. 103), and pull this lower near string down, of course on the near side of the other three strings, and letting the loop slip off each thumb, extend the figure between the index fingers and the middle fingers, bent on the palms (Fig. 104).

Seventh A: According to Dr. Haddon (**5,** p. 222) the Navahos have another way of doing this movement.

Bend each thumb away from you, and pull down the lower near string of the four strings forming the two loops held out by the loop passing around the thumb and index (Fig. 105, Right hand), and extend the figure between the index fingers and thumbs, holding the palms of the hands away from you (Fig. 106).

On the completion of this figure, you will want to have the string again as a single loop, but unless you are careful it will get very much tangled.   The way to

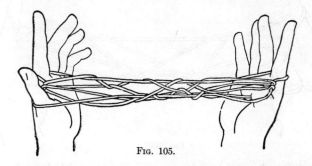

FIG. 105.

prevent this is as follows: Place the completed figure on your lap, and draw apart the straight strings which form the top and bottom of the figure; then the string will pull out into a single loop.   This is true for practically all string figures.

I have put "Many Stars" as the first of a series of ten Navaho figures, which are all done in much the same way, but come out in characteristic patterns in the

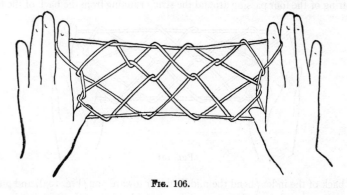

FIG. 106.

end.   They all start with Opening A, or a modification of it; after that, however, some go on as "Many Stars," but end differently; others have a few new movements and then end with some from "Many Stars," while others begin and end as "Many Stars," but have different intermediate movements.

"Many Stars" exhibits several movements which are unlike any we have hitherto studied. The *Fifth*, which appears to be a movement peculiar to these Navaho figures, is a clever way of putting the middle finger loop around the thumb and index and turning it over in the transfer.

The result of the *Sixth* movement is interesting, because when the lower loop on each thumb and on each index is slipped over the upper loop and off the finger, it cannot run down the upper loop toward the centre of the figure in the form of a noose or ring, for the upper loop is a loop common to both thumb and index, hence the two loops are merely strung on the string of this thumb-index loop which passes from the back of the thumb to the back of the index. The *Seventh* movement is very characteristic of the Navaho figures; it may occur in the middle of the figure, or more than once in the same figure.

FIG. 107.

AN OWL

This first "Owl" was obtained by Dr. Haddon from the two old Navaho men who showed him "Many Stars." (See Haddon **5**, p. 222, pl. xv, Fig. 4.) It is called *Nas-ja* = an Owl. There is an example of the finished pattern in the Culin collection in the Philadelphia Free Museum of Science and Art (22716), from St. Michael's Mission, Arizona.

First: First position.
Second: Put the right index from above down behind the string on the left palm (Fig. 107), draw it out and twist it by twice rotating the index toward you and then up. Separate the hands (Fig. 108).

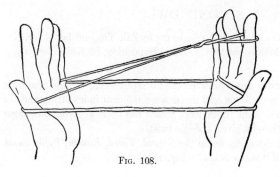

FIG. 108.

FIG. 109.

Third: Take up from below with the left index the string on the right palm, not through the right index loop as is usual, but between the near index string and the thumb (Fig. 109). Separate the hands.

Fourth: Proceed now as in "Many Stars," from the *Second* movement to the very end, concluding with the *Seventh* or the *Seventh A* movement. The "Owl" will then be formed (Fig. 110).

The movements of the "Owl" are all the same as those of "Many Stars" except the *Second* and *Third.* The *Second* movement is about the only way you can put a twist and a half in the index loop, by the index itself, and restore the index to its usual position; if you rotate the index after the usual formation of Opening A you put one twist in the index loop. The *Third* movement is peculiar to this figure.

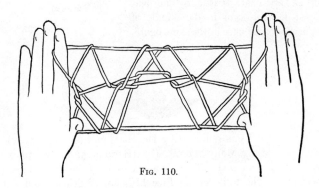

FIG. 110.

A SECOND OWL

The two following "Owls" were taught to me by Zah Tso and her sister, Navahos from Gallup, New Mexico, at the St. Louis Exposition, in November, 1904.

First: Opening A.

Second: Bend each index down between the far index string and the near little finger string, and bring it toward you and up between the near index string and the far thumb string (Fig. 111). The index loop, which has been kept on the finger during this movement, is thereby given a single twist.

Third: Complete the figure by doing the *Second, Third, Fourth, Fifth, Sixth* and *Seventh* movements of "Many Stars" (Fig. 112).

ZAH TSO, AN ARIZONA NAVAHO OF GALLUP, NEW MEXICO.
(Courtesy of Mr. S. C. Simms.)

TWO NATIVES OF MURRAY ISLAND. THE YOUNGER IS JAMES.
(Courtesy of Dr. A. C. Haddon.)

The movements of this figure are similar to those of "Many Stars," except for the additional *Second* movement which puts a twist in the index loops.

A THIRD OWL

An active imagination is required to find this Owl.

First, Second and *Third:* Similar to the *First, Second* and *Third* movements of "Many Stars."

Fourth: Put each thumb from below into the index loop, then bend it away from you over the far index string and under all the other strings; now, drawing

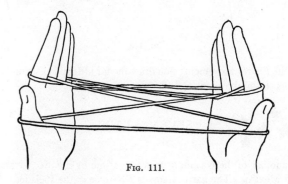

FIG. 111.

the thumb toward you, catch on its back the far little finger string, and return the thumb to its position, thus drawing the far little finger string through the index loop. Release the loops from the little fingers.

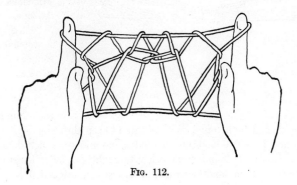

FIG. 112.

Fifth: Complete the figure by doing the *Fifth, Sixth* and *Seventh* movements of "Many Stars" (Fig. 113).

The figure will be extended more perfectly if you give the upper index string one more turn around the tip of each index finger.

The only difference between the movements of this figure and those of "Many

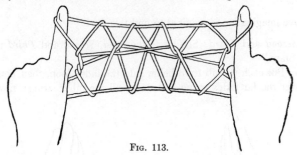

Fig. 113.

Stars" is in the *Fourth* movement; you draw the far little finger string back through the thumb loop from above, instead of from below.

            SEVEN STARS

This is another of the Navaho games taught me by the two Navaho girls from Gallup, New Mexico. The native name is *Dil-ye-he* = the Pleiades. The Philadelphia Free Museum of Science and Art has an example of the finished pattern,

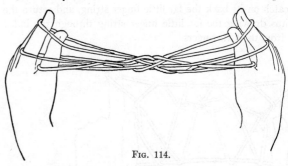

Fig. 114.

No. 22717, collected by Mr. Culin from the Navahos at St. Michael's Mission, Arizona.

The first five movements are the same as the first five movements of "Many Stars."

Sixth: Withdraw each thumb from the loop, passing around both thumb and index, and keep this loop high up on the index. You now have two loops on each index and a loop on each thumb.

Seventh: Pass each thumb from below through both index loops (Fig. 114); then with the right thumb and index lift the lowest (the original) left thumb loop over the upper two thumb loops (which pass around both thumb and index) and entirely off the left thumb (Fig. 115); let it drop on the palmar side. In the same way with the left thumb and index lift the lowest right loop over the upper two thumb loops and entirely off the right thumb.

Eighth: Put each middle finger from below into the thumb loop and then up on the far side of the upper straight string crossing this loop, bend the figure toward you (Fig. 116), and pull this straight string down. Release the loops from the thumbs, and extend the fig-

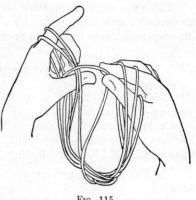

FIG. 115.

ure between the index fingers and the middle fingers closed on the palm (Fig. 117). An extra turn around the index fingers displays the pattern better.

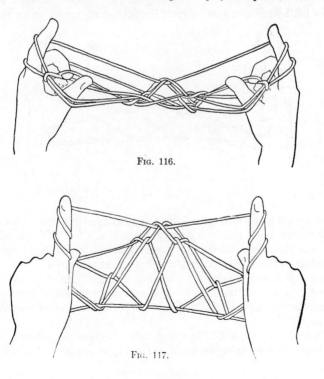

FIG. 116.

FIG. 117.

This figure differs from "Many Stars" only in the *Sixth* and *Seventh* movements; each thumb loop is slipped over the two index loops, instead of both the thumb and index loops being slipped over the loop common to the thumb and index.

TWO-HORNED STAR

This pattern is known to the Navahos as *Son-bi-tere*. I learned it from the same source as the preceding figures. In the Culin collection in the Philadelphia Free Museum of Science and Art a finished pattern, 22716, from St. Michael's Mission, Arizona, is labelled *So-bide-hulonni* = Horned Star. At Grand Canyon, Arizona, a Navaho called it "Cow's Head."

The first five movements are the same as the first five movements of "Many Stars."

Sixth: Withdraw each thumb from the loop passing around both thumb and index, and keep this loop high up on the index (Fig. 118). You now have two loops on each index and a single loop on each thumb.

Seventh: With the right thumb and index pick up from the back of the left index the left lower index loop (whereof the near string passes under the thumb

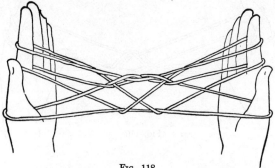

FIG. 118.

loop and nearest to the thumb), and lift it up, over the left upper index loop, entirely off the left index, and let it drop on the palmar side. With the left thumb and index in like manner lift the right lower index loop over the right upper index loop, entirely off the right index, and let it drop on the palmar side.

Eighth: Put each thumb from below into the index loop (Fig. 119) and, with the thumb and index of the other hand, in turn, draw the lower thumb loop over the upper thumb loop entirely off the thumb, and let it drop on the palmar side (Fig. 120).

Ninth: Put each middle finger from below between the strings forming the thumb loop, and then up on the far side of the upper straight string which passes

from one side to the other and forms a loop around the string running from the
back of the thumb to the back of the index. Bending the middle finger toward

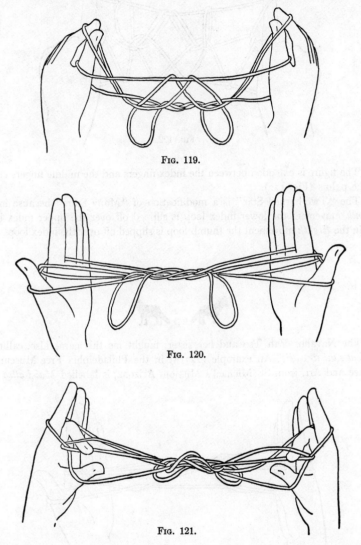

Fig. 119.

Fig. 120.

Fig. 121.

you over this straight string (Fig. 121), pull it down; release the loops from the
thumbs, and draw the strings tight.

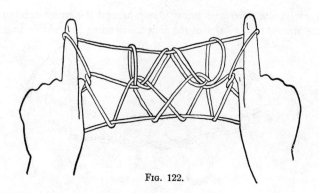

Fig. 122.

The figure is extended between the index fingers and the middle fingers closed on the palms (Fig. 122).

The "Two-horned Star" is a modification of "Many Stars" because in the *Seventh* movement the lower index loop is slipped off over the upper index loop, and in the *Eighth* movement the thumb loop is slipped off over the index loop.

TWO COYOTES

The Navahos, Zah Tso and her sister, taught me this game also, calling it *Ma-i-at-sani-il-watli*. An example (22718) in the Philadelphia Free Museum of Science and Art, from St. Michael's Mission, Arizona, is labelled *Mai-i-atlsa-yill-*

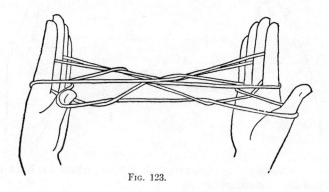

Fig. 123.

aghueli = Two Coyotes Running Apart.

First, Second a n d *Third* movements are the same as the *First, Second* and *Third* movements of "Many Stars."

Fourth : Pass each thumb from below into the index loop, and bend it over the far index string; turning the palm

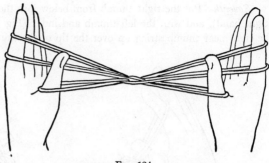

Fig. 124.

away from you, pass the thumb away from you under all the strings, and catch the far little finger string on the far side with the back of the thumb (Fig. 123, Left hand), and return the thumb to its position (Fig. 123, Right hand). Release the loops from the little fingers.

Fifth : Put the tips of the right thumb and index together and put the tips of the left thumb and index together; now, turning the palms slightly away from you, pass these fingers over the thumb and index loops and away from you under and past the two strings of the middle finger loop. Then drawing the thumb and index (still held together)

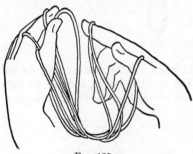

Fig. 125.

toward you, take up on their tips the far middle finger string and draw it toward you under the near middle finger string. Let the twisted loop slip off each middle finger and withdraw the thumb, leaving the loop well ·up toward the tip of the index (Fig. 124).

Sixth : Keeping all the loops carefully on the left hand, with the left thumb and index lift the right lower index loop over the right upper index loop, and entirely off the finger (Fig. 125), and let it drop on the palmar side, being careful not to take

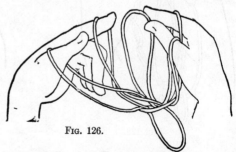

Fig. 126.

off also the upper loop. In the same manner with the right thumb and index lift the left lower index loop over the left upper index loop, and entirely off the index (Fig. 126). Do not pull the strings tight after this movement.

Seventh : Put the right thumb from below into the right index loop (Fig. 127, Right hand), and with the left thumb and index (Fig. 128) or with the teeth, lift the right near thumb string up over the tip of the thumb, without disturbing the

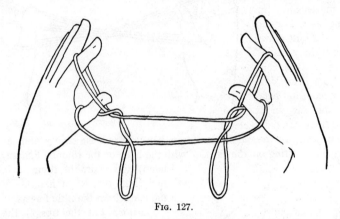

FIG. 127.

string which passes around both thumb and index. In like manner put the left thumb from below into the left index loop (Fig. 127, Left hand), and with the right thumb and index (Fig. 129), or with the teeth, lift the left near thumb string over

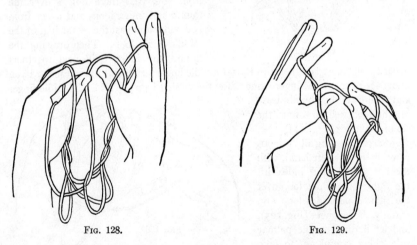

FIG. 128. FIG. 129.

the tip of the left thumb. Do not pull the strings tight after this movement. There are now two straight strings which cross the thumb loop and form a loop around the string passing from the back of the thumb to the back of the index.

Eighth : Put each middle finger from below between these straight strings, so that the lower string is on the far side of it and the upper string on the near side of it (Fig. 130); then bend the middle finger down toward you over the upper string and,

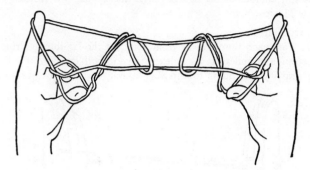

Fig. 130.

holding it in the bend of the finger, draw it down and away from you through the thumb loop, and release the loops from the thumbs. Closing each middle finger down on the palm, hold the index strings high on the finger tips and separate the

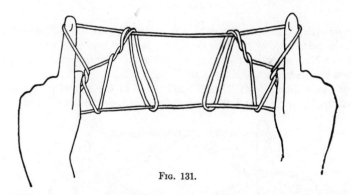

Fig. 131.

hands (Fig. 131). If the strings be permitted to slip around the index fingers the "coyotes" will run away from each other.

When we analyze this figure we see that it has the first four movements of the "Third Owl," the *Fifth* of "Many Stars," and the *Sixth, Seventh* and *Eighth* of the " Two-horned Star."

BIG STAR

This is still another of the figures taught me by the two Navaho girls from Gallup, New Mexico.

First: Opening A.

Second: Pass each thumb away from you over the far thumb string and the near index string and under the far index string and both strings of the little finger loop; then, drawing the thumb toward you, take up on the back of its tip the far

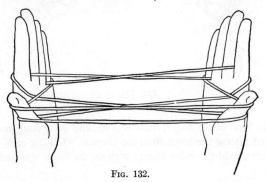

FIG. 132.

little finger string and bring it toward you, under the near little finger string and through the index loop, by restoring the thumb to its position (Fig. 132).

Third: Now complete the figure by doing the *Third, Fourth, Fifth, Sixth* and *Seventh* movements of "Many Stars" (Fig. 133).

This figure differs from "Many Stars" only in the second movement. In "Many Stars" it is the near little finger string that is drawn toward you over the

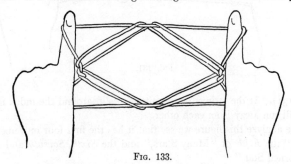

FIG. 133.

index loop. In this figure it is the far little finger string which is drawn toward you through the index loop—in other words, the *Second* movement is like the *Fourth*.

NORTH STAR

I obtained this figure in the same way as the preceding figure. The Philadelphia Free Museum of Science and Art has an example of the finished pattern,

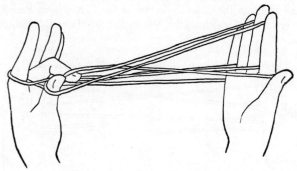

Fig. 134.

No. 22713, collected by Mr. Stewart Culin at St. Michael's Mission, Arizona, and called *Tsun-tsi* = Big Star.

First: Opening A.

Second: Transfer the thumb loops to the middle fingers, by bending each middle finger toward you over the index loop, and taking up from below on the back of the finger the far thumb string (Fig. 134, Left hand); withdraw each

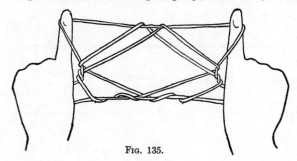

Fig. 135.

thumb from its loop, and return the middle finger to its position (Fig. 134, Right hand).

Third: Then complete the figure by doing the *Fourth, Fifth, Sixth* and *Seventh* movements of "Many Stars" (Fig. 135).

The "North Star" differs from "Many Stars" only by the omission of the *Second* movement.

CARRYING WOOD

Dr. Haddon taught me this figure in August, 1904. He learned it in Chicago in 1901, from the two old Navaho men who showed him " Many Stars " (5, p. 221, pl. xv, Fig. 2). It is called by the Navahos, *Chiz-jŏ-yĕt-lĭ*. There are two examples of the finished figure in the Culin Collection of the Philadelphia Free Museum of Science and Art, one (22724) from the Navahos at St. Michael's Mission, Arizona,

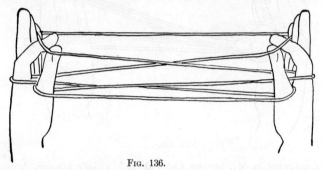

FIG. 136.

is labelled *Chizh-joyeli* = Hacking the Wood, the other (22605) from Zuñi, New Mexico, is called *Pish-kap-po-a, pi-cho-wai-nai*.

First: Opening A.

Second: Put the tips of the thumb and index of each hand together, and bind these fingers away from you over the far index string, and pick up from below the

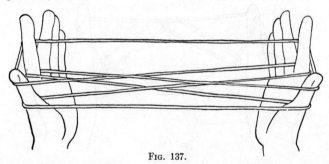

FIG. 137.

near little finger string, and return the thumb and index to their usual positions (Fig. 136); then separate their tips and release the loop from the little finger. This movement transfers the little finger loop to both thumb and index (Fig. 137).

Third: Keeping all the loops carefully in place on the right hand, with the right thumb and index lift the lower loop on the left thumb up over the upper loop (the one passing around both thumb and index), then entirely off the left thumb (Fig. 138), and let it drop on the palmar side, being careful not to take off also the upper loop. Then with the right thumb and index lift the left lower index loop over the

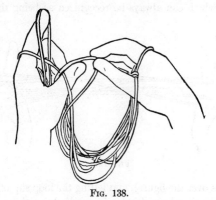

Fig. 138.

upper index loop (the one which passes around both thumb and index) and off the index, and let it drop on the palmar side.

In the same manner, keeping the loops in place on the left hand, with the left thumb and index lift the right lower thumb loop up over the right upper thumb loop (the one passing around both thumb and index), entirely off the thumb, and let it drop on the palmar side. Then with the left thumb and index lift the right lower index loop up over the right upper index loop (the one passing around both thumb and index), entirely off the right index, and let it drop on the palmar side.

You now have on each hand a single loop passing around both thumb and index, and on that part of this loop which passes from the back of the thumb to the

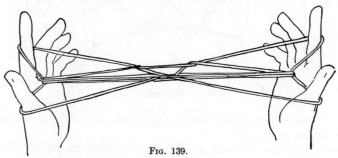

Fig. 139.

back of the index are two more loops (Fig. 139). Of the four strings forming these two loops, two are upper strings and two are lower strings when the figure is held horizontally. Of the upper strings, the far one runs obliquely away from you and passes over the far index string, but the near one passes straight across to the other side.

Fourth : Now bend each thumb away from you, and pull down this near upper string (Fig. 140), (which can always be recognized as being the only free straight

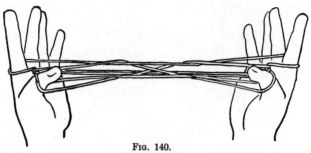

Fig. 140.

string passing across over the figure), and letting the loop slip off the thumb, extend the figure between the thumbs and index fingers, holding the palms away from you (Fig. 141).

"The two central strings that lie side by side represent the carrying band of the Navaho; the other strings represent the wood that is being carried." (Haddon.)

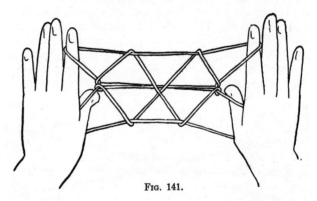

Fig. 141.

The Navahos have another, more characteristic, way of doing the *Fourth* or final movement, as follows:

Fourth A: Put each middle finger from below up on the far side of the near upper straight string, and bending the middle finger, pull this string down, of course on the near side of the other three strings; then letting the loop slip off each thumb, extend the figure between the index and middle fingers, and at the same time turn the palms away from you.

"Carrying Wood" is made up of some of the simple movements of "Many Stars" and a new one, the *Second*.

OWL'S NET

This figure was obtained for me by Mr. John L. Cox, at Hampton, Virginia, from a Klamath Indian, Emma Jackson, from Oregon.

First: Opening A.

Second: Pass each thumb away from you over the far thumb string and the

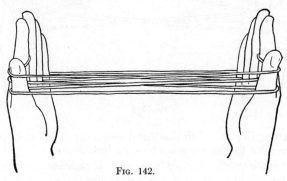

FIG. 142.

near index string, and pick up from below on the back of the thumb the far index string, and return the thumb to its position (Fig. 142).

Third: Bend the index and middle finger of each hand down into the upper thumb loop, and then pass the index to the near side of the lower near thumb

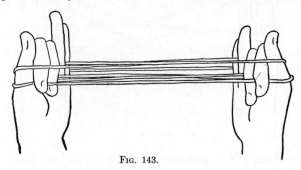

FIG. 143.

string, and pass the middle finger through the lower thumb loop (Fig. 143). Holding the lower near thumb string tightly between the index and middle fingers, draw these fingers away from you, straighten them, and by turning the palms away from you, put the lower near thumb string around the tip of each index (Fig. 144). Release the loops from the thumbs and draw the hands apart.

Fourth : Pass each thumb away from you over the near index string and under all the other strings, and, drawing the thumb toward you, catch on its back the far

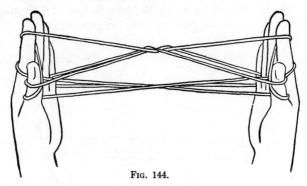

FIG. 144.

little finger string (Fig. 145, Left hand) and return the thumb to its position (Fig. 145, Right hand). Release the loops from the little fingers.

Fifth : Put the middle, ring and little fingers of each hand from below (toward you) into the thumb loop (Fig. 146), and pull this loop down by closing these fingers on the palm; withdraw the thumbs. Transfer each upper index loop to the thumb

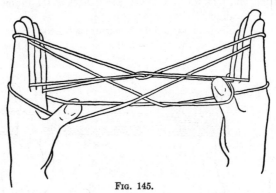

FIG. 145.

by putting the thumb into it from below, withdrawing the index and returning the thumb to its position.

Sixth : Keeping each middle finger still in the loop it is helping to hold to the palm, pass it toward you over the far thumb string (Fig. 147), and draw this string through the loop held to the palm (Fig. 148). Now take the ring and little fingers

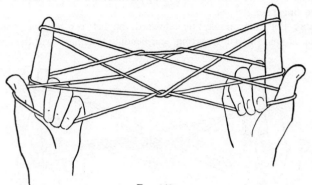

FIG. 146.

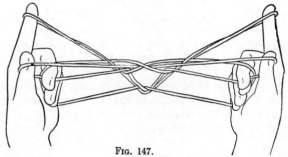

FIG. 147.

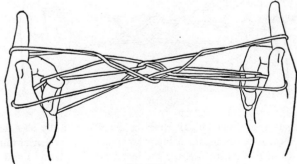

FIG. 148.

from the loop they have been holding and pass them toward you into the loop with the middle finger (Fig. 149).

Seventh : Put each middle finger toward you between the two strings which form a loop around the palmar string, and bending the finger over the lower string

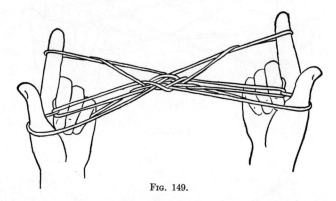

FIG. 149.

(Fig. 150, Left hand), draw it away from you, releasing the loop held down by the ring and little fingers (Fig. 150, Right hand). Put the ring and little fingers into the loop held down by the middle finger and withdraw the middle finger (Fig. 151).

Eighth : Pass each middle finger from below through the index loop (Fig. 152, Left hand), then bend it toward you under the near thumb string, then bend the index toward you down on the near thumb string, which is thus held securely between the first joints of the index and middle finger (Fig. 152, Right hand). Now draw

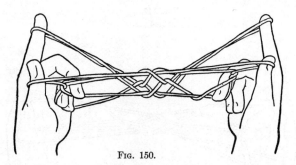

FIG. 150.

these two fingers away from you, allowing the index loop to slip over their tips to the palmar side, and by turning the palms away from you, put the near thumb string around the tip of the index. Release the loops from the thumbs and draw the hands apart (Fig. 153).

The finished pattern is practically the same as the pattern of "Many Stars," the end diamonds of the middle row, however, are not looped to the diamonds of

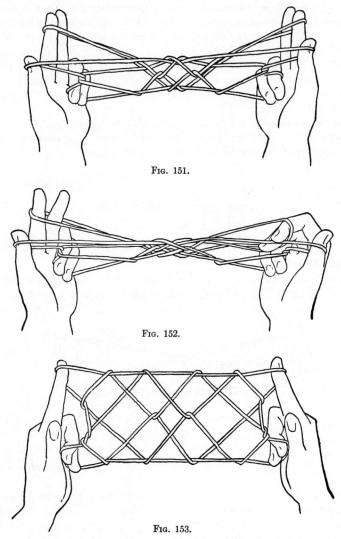

Fig. 151.

Fig. 152.

Fig. 153.

the upper row, as in "Many Stars," but the strings merely cross each other at these points. If, in the *Second* movement, you pick up the near little finger string with the thumb, instead of the far index string, the "Many Stars" pattern will be formed. Apparently the methods of forming the two figures are very different, only the *Fourth* movement being the same in both; yet, if you examine them closely, you will notice that the *Third* movement of the "Owl's Net" accomplishes the turning over of the middle finger loop (originally the thumb loop) observed in the *Fifth* movement of "Many Stars"; the *Fifth* movement of the "Owl's Net" merely shifts the loops to other fingers; the *Sixth* and *Eighth* movements of the "Owl's Net" together produce the same results as the *Sixth* movement of "Many Stars"; and the *Seventh* movement in both figures, although done differently, twists the side strings in precisely the same manner.

The methods used in the "Owl's Net" exhibit the highest type of native skill. Every movement is carried on by both hands simultaneously, and there is no arranging of loops on the one hand by the fingers of the other hand.

TWO ELKS

This is a Klamath Indian figure from the same source as the "Owl's Net."

First: Opening A.

Second: Pass each thumb away from you over the far thumb string, both strings of the index loop, and under both strings of the little finger loop. Now

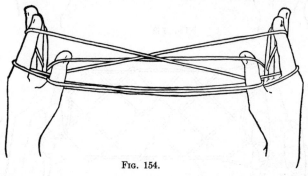

FIG. 154.

lift up the near little finger strings temporarily on the tips of the index fingers (Fig. 154), and draw toward you on the back of the thumb the far little finger string, by returning the thumb to its usual position and dropping the near little finger strings from the tip of each index (Fig. 155).

Third: Bend the index and middle finger of each hand down through the upper thumb loop and pass the index to the near side of the lower near thumb

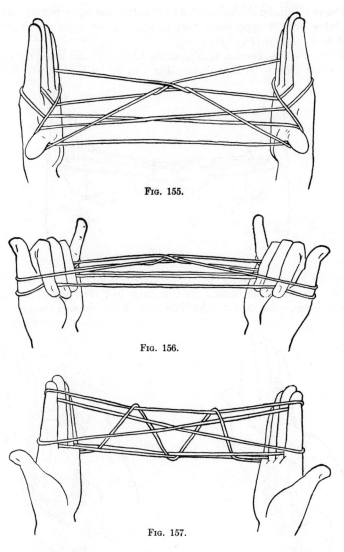

FIG. 155.

FIG. 156.

FIG. 157.

string; then pass the middle finger to the far side of the same string (Fig. 156), draw the string up between the two fingers, and put it on the tip of the index by turning the palm away from you. Release the loops from the thumbs and draw the hands apart (Fig. 157).

Fourth : Transfer the upper index loops to the thumbs, by putting each thumb from below into the upper index loop, withdrawing the index and returning the thumb to its position (Fig. 158).

Fifth : Pick up, between the tips of the left thumb and index, the right near thumb string (close to the right thumb) (Fig. 159), lift the loop entirely off the right

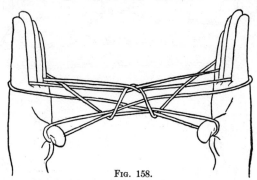

FIG. 158.

thumb, turn it over so that its near string becomes its far string and then place the loop over the two strings of the right little finger loop (Fig. 160). Now with the left thumb and index draw the far little finger string through the original right

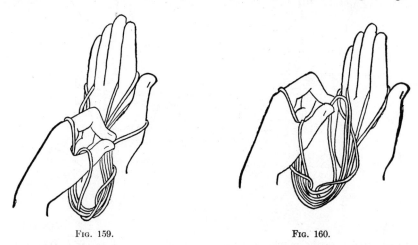

FIG. 159.   FIG. 160.

thumb loop (Fig. 161); put the right thumb under the far little finger string just pulled through the loop, and pick up from below on the back of the right thumb the string of the former thumb loop which you have just been holding with the left thumb and index (Fig. 162) and return the thumb to its position (Fig. 163, Right hand). Repeat the same movement on the left hand as follows: Pick up, between the tips of the right thumb and index, the left near thumb string (close to

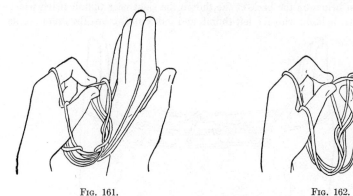

FIG. 161.   FIG. 162.

the left thumb), lift the loop entirely off the left thumb, turn it over so that its near string becomes its far string and then place the loop over the two strings of the left little finger loop; now with the right thumb and index draw the far little finger string through the original left thumb loop; put the left thumb under the far little finger string just pulled through the loop, and pick up from below on the back of

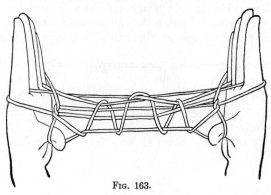

FIG. 163.

the left thumb the string of the former thumb loop which you have been holding with the right thumb and index and return the thumb to its position (Fig. 163).

Sixth : Pick up, between the tips of the left thumb and index, the right near thumb string (close to the right thumb), lift the loop entirely off the right thumb, turn it over so that its near string becomes its far string, and then place the loop over the strings of the right little finger loop. Now, with the left thumb and index, draw the near little finger string through the original right thumb loop; put the right thumb under this near little finger string just pulled through the loop, and pick up from below on the back of the thumb the right near thumb string which you have been holding with the left thumb and index and return the thumb to its

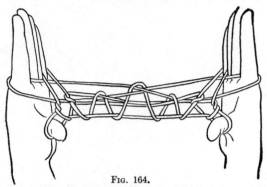

Fig. 164.

position. Repeat the same movement on the left hand, as follows: Pick up, between the tips of the right thumb and index, the left near thumb string (close to the left thumb), lift the loop entirely off the left thumb, turn it over so that its near string becomes its far string and then place the loop over the two strings of the left little finger loop. Now, with the right thumb and index, draw the near little finger string through the original left thumb loop; put the left thumb under the near little finger string just pulled through the loop, and pick up from below on the back of

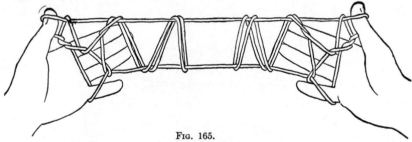

Fig. 165.

the left thumb the near string of the former thumb loop which you have been holding with the right thumb and index and return the left thumb to its position. Separate the hands (Fig. 164).

Seventh: Release the loops from the index fingers and separate the hands, drawing the strings very tight and moving the hands alternately up and down to make the "Elks" appear (Fig. 165).

The *Fifth* and *Sixth* movements of this figure exhibit what appear to be artificial methods, and yet it is difficult to see how the same results could be produced by any quicker or more simple procedure.

A RABBIT

This is another Klamath game obtained in the same way as the "Owl's Net."

First : Opening A.

Second : Bend each middle finger down toward you into the thumb loop, and bend each index down toward you on the near side of the near thumb string (Fig. 166, Left hand), then, holding this string tightly between these two fingers, straighten the fingers and turn the

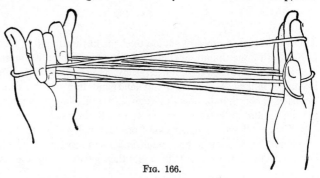

FIG. 166.

palms away from you to put the string around the tip of the index (Fig. 166, Right hand). Release the loops from the thumbs.

Third : Pass each thumb from below into the little finger loop and draw toward you, on the back of the thumb, the near little finger string, the upper far index string and both strings of the lower index loop (Fig. 167).

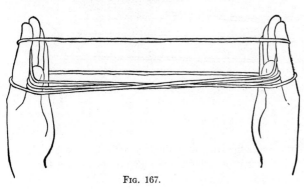

FIG. 167.

Fourth : Pass each thumb up and away from you over the upper near index string, and pull this string down on the ball of the thumb, letting the other strings slip off the thumb (Fig. 168). Turn the palms away from you and, still holding down the string with the thumbs, pass each thumb away from you under the far little finger string

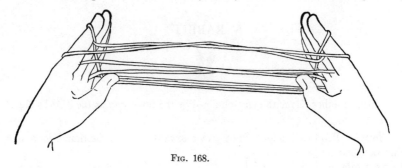

FIG. 168.

and draw this string toward you on the back of the thumb. The string which was held down by the thumb, of course, is released during this movement (Fig. 169).

Fifth : Insert each thumb from below (close to the index) into the small ring-like upper index loop (Fig. 170, Left hand) and draw the upper near index string, on the back of the thumb, down through the thumb loop, this latter loop slipping off the thumb during the movement (Fig. 170, Right hand).

Sixth : Release the upper loop from each index (Fig. 171).

Seventh : Pass the index, middle and ring fingers of each hand toward you and down into the thumb loop (Fig. 172); then gently release the loops from the little

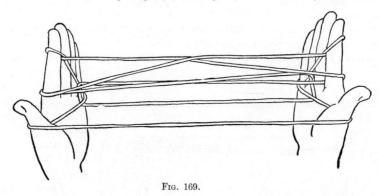

FIG. 169.

fingers, and put each little finger toward you in the loop with the ring, middle and index fingers. Hold all four fingers of each hand down on the palm; turn the hands with the palms facing each other. Lift up the near thumb string on the tip of each

Fig. 170.

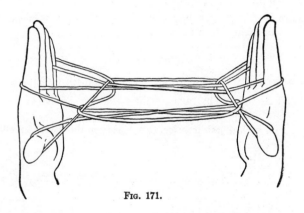

Fig. 171.

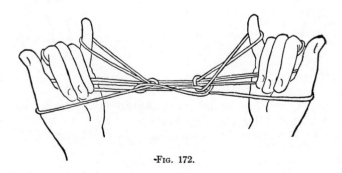

Fig. 172.

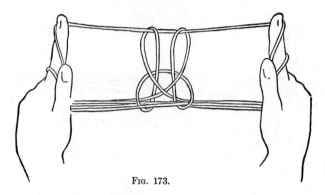

Fig. 173.

index, and withdraw the thumb. Some working of the strings is usually required to make the "Rabbit" appear (Fig. 173).

This is an interesting figure because the majority of the movements are unusual, and are met with again only in the following figure.

THE SUN

Mr. Cox secured "The Sun" also from the Klamath Indian.

First and *Second*: The same as the *First* and *Second* movements of the "Rabbit."

Third: Pass each thumb from below up between the lower index loop and the

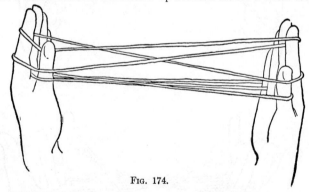

Fig. 174.

little finger loop and draw toward you, on the back of the thumb, both strings of the lower index loop (Fig. 174, Right hand).

Fourth: The same as the *Fourth* movement of the "Rabbit" (Figs. 174, Left hand; 175, 176).

Fifth: Release the loops from the little fingers.

Sixth : Insert the middle, ring and little fingers of each hand toward you (from above) into the thumb loop (Fig. 177) and withdraw the thumb.

Seventh : Pass the thumb from below into the upper index loop in order to make this loop wider. Bend each middle finger down toward you over the upper

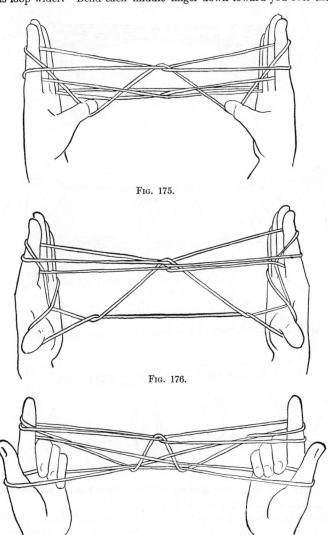

Fig. 175.

Fig. 176.

Fig. 177.

far index string and both strings of the lower index loop (Fig. 178) and draw these strings down to the palm. Withdraw the ring and little fingers of each hand from

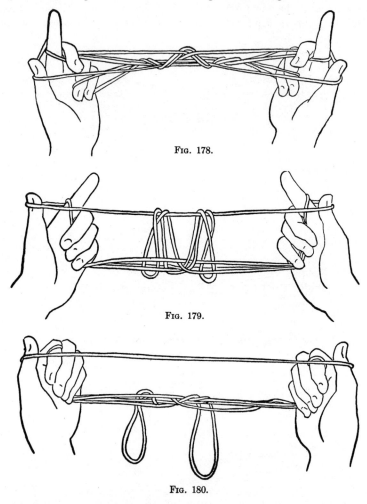

FIG. 178.

FIG. 179.

FIG. 180.

the loop which they have been holding and bend them toward you and down over the strings held down by the middle finger.

Eighth : The "Sun" is made to appear by raising each thumb, thus lifting up the near index string which passes across its back (Fig. 179); if raised too high, the sun "sets" (Fig. 180).

CHAPTER IV

A WELL

I OBTAINED this figure in August, 1904, from Dr. Haddon, who learned it
from a native of Lifu, Loyalty Islands, who happened to be residing in Mabuiag in Torres Straits. (See Rivers and Haddon, p. 149, Fig. 2.) In Lifu
it is known as *Tim*, = a Well. It is precisely similar to the Torres Straits figure
which in Murray Island, is called *Ti Meta*, = the Nest of the *Ti* bird, and in
Mabuiag, *Gul* = a Canoe.

First: Opening A.

Second: Keeping the hands well separated, with the strings quite tight, and
turning the palms slightly away from you, pass each index away from you over the far

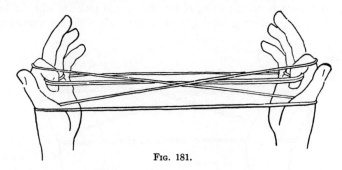

FIG. 181.

index string and the near little finger string and then well down into the little finger
loop. Now, turning the palms gradually toward you, bend each index carrying
these two strings toward you (with the tips pointed toward each palm), and then up
between the near index string and the thumb (which must be kept upright), but
not touching the thumb loop (Fig. 181). This movement brings the far index string
and the near little finger string up toward you while the near index string slips away
from you over the knuckle of the index and entirely off that finger. Now turn each

85

index completely up, and straighten it (Fig. 182), when it will be seen that the original far index string and the near little finger string have both become far index strings. Release the strings passing around each little finger.

You now have two loops on each index, twisted toward the centre of the figure; and a loop on each thumb (Fig. 183).

Third: Turning the palms toward you, with the middle, ring and little fingers

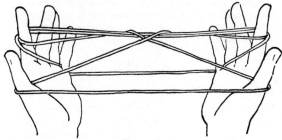

Fig. 182.

of each hand pull straight down, as far as possible, the two far index strings (Fig. 184).

Fourth: Gently withdraw each thumb (Fig. 185, Right hand).

Fifth: Bend each thumb away from you into the former thumb loop (now hanging from the top straight string of the figure), and pick up, with the back of the thumb, the diagonal string passing from the near side of the index down around

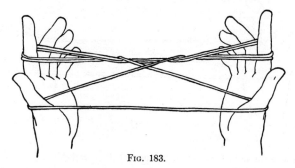

Fig. 183.

the two strings at the bottom of the figure (Fig. 185, Left hand), and pull it toward you through the hanging loop.

Raise the thumbs toward you and the index fingers away from you, and keep the lower strings well down, by bending the middle, ring and little fingers around them, and the finished figure will appear (Fig. 186).

The well is said to be "full of water" when the inverted pyramid of the figure is made high, and to be "dry" when the base and apex of the pyramid are brought

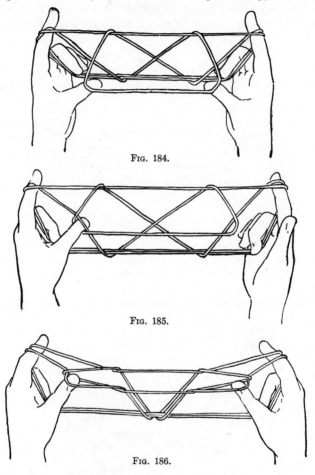

Fig. 184.

Fig. 185.

Fig. 186.

to the same level, by letting the lower strings, held down by the fingers, come up to the same plane as the other strings.

The *Second* movement is a new one; its purpose is to put the little finger loop on the index, above the original index loop, and turn it over in the transfer. The original index loop gets, of course, a twist in the process. The *Fifth* movement is the only practicable method of drawing the index string through the thumb loop from above.

FENCE AROUND A WELL

This game is a continuation of "The Well"; it is called *Sihnag*, = "a Fence Around a Well," in Lifu, Loyalty Islands.   It was taught Drs. Rivers and Haddon by the same native who taught them "The Well" (p. 149, Fig. 3).

First: Form "The Well."

Second: Pass each thumb away from you and put it up under the two near index strings, close to the index (Fig. 187); then, with the thumb and index of the

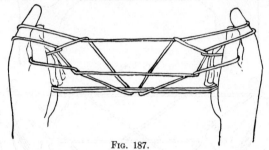

FIG. 187.

right hand, pick up from the back of the left thumb the lower single left thumb loop, and draw it over the upper two loops and off the thumb, and drop it on the palmar side.

With the thumb and index of the left hand, in the same manner, pick up the

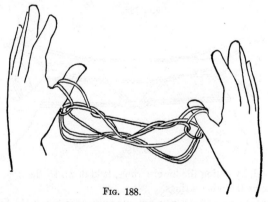

FIG. 188.

lower single right thumb loop, and draw it over the upper two loops, off the thumb, and drop it.

Release the loops from the index fingers.

Third: Take all the fingers of each hand out of the lower loops which they

have been holding, and let the figure hang on the thumbs (Fig. 188). Then put
the four fingers of each hand toward you into the ring-like loops held by the thumb;

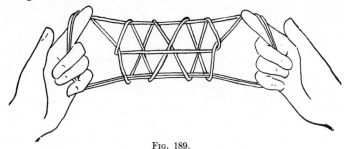

FIG. 189.

remove the thumb; close the middle, ring and little fingers on the palm, and separate the hands (Fig. 189).

There are few string figures in which the final pattern is extended in such a
simple manner as in this one.

A CRAB

Dr. Haddon obtained the "Crab" at Saguane, Kiwai Island, near the mouth
of the Fly River, British New Guinea, where it is known as *Kokowa,* = a Crab.
(See Rivers and Haddon, p. 151, Fig. 8.)

First : Go through the movements necessary to form "The Well."

Second : Turn the palms toward you and slightly upward, and slacken a little
the strings held down by the little fingers; then insert each little finger from below
into the thumb loop, bend it over the near thumb string, and take the loop off the
thumb (Fig. 190, Right hand), and hold it down together with the two lower strings

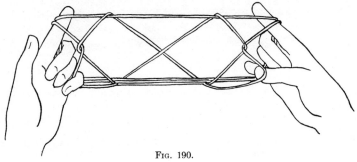

FIG. 190.

of the figure. Separate the hands. The palms now face each other again, and the middle finger and the ring finger of each hand should be slipped out of the

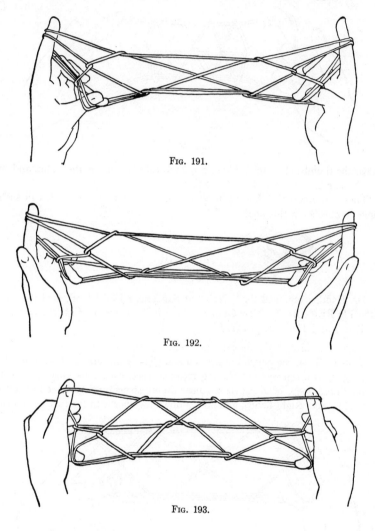

Fig. 191.

Fig. 192.

Fig. 193.

triangle close to the hand, and the three lower strings held down by the little finger alone (Fig. 190, Left hand).

Third : Turn the palms away from you, and insert each thumb away from you into the little finger loop, then, turning the palms toward you, draw toward the palm with the bent thumb the diagonal string which runs upward from the little finger and serves to separate the two triangles near the hand. Now, still

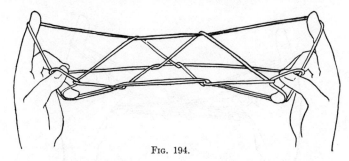

FIG. 194.

holding the string on the thumb, insert the thumb away from you behind the two strings running from the little finger to the far side of the index (Fig. 191, Right hand), and draw these strings toward you with the back of the thumb, withdrawing the little finger (Fig. 191, Left hand).

Fourth : Turn the palms toward you, and insert each little finger toward you into the two thumb loops, and remove the thumb (Fig. 192).

Fifth : Hold the loops well down with each little finger ; pick up from below with the back of each thumb the near index string which runs directly from index to index and draw it toward you; remove each index from its loops (Fig. 193).

Sixth : Insert each index toward you into the loop held by the thumb, and with the back of the index pick up the near thumb string; return the index to its position and remove the thumb.

Seventh : Keep the index loop well up on the tip of the finger; pass each thumb away from you, and pick up on the back of the thumb, and draw toward you (Fig. 194) the horizontal string which holds the side lozenge of the central figure to the vertical string running from the little finger to the near side of the index.

FIG. 195.

Eighth : Bend each middle finger toward you down over all the strings, and hold them down tightly while you exchange the loops on the thumbs, putting the right thumb loop from the right thumb entirely on the left thumb and the left thumb loop from the left thumb entirely on the right thumb (Fig. 195); being careful not to twist the loops or let the loops slip off the index fingers. Straighten the middle fingers and the index fingers, and separate the hands (Fig. 196).

Ninth : Bend each middle finger toward you over the index loop, and bring it into the thumb loop from below; and take the loop off the thumb by lifting up the

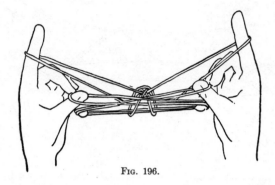

FIG. 196.

far thumb string (Fig. 197), returning the middle finger to its former position, and withdrawing the thumb (Fig. 198).   Turn the palms toward you, and bend down each middle finger, and with the back of the thumb, inserted into the middle finger loop from above, take up the far middle finger string, and thus turning the loop over, restore it to the thumb by putting the thumb again in its usual position (Fig. 199, Right hand) and withdrawing the middle finger (Fig. 199, Left hand).

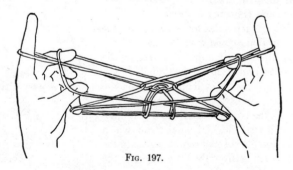

FIG. 197.

Tenth : Insert each thumb from below into the index loop, and with the back of the thumb catch the near index string and draw it down toward you through the thumb loop, and let the thumb loop slip off the thumb (Fig. 200).   Release the loops from the index fingers and separate the hands.

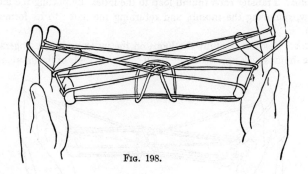

Fig. 198.

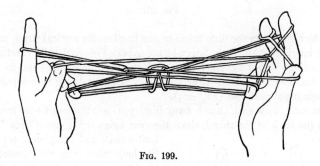

Fig. 199.

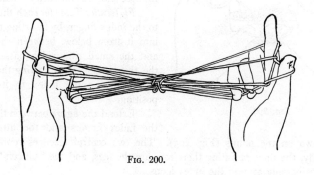

Fig. 200.

Eleventh : Transfer each thumb loop to the index, by putting the index into it from below, removing the thumb, and returning the index to its former position (Fig. 201).

Twelfth : Holding carefully the loops on the index and little fingers, with the back of the thumbs pick up, within the small central triangle of the figure, the crossed

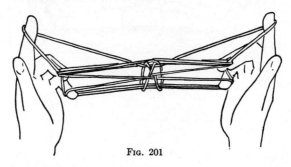

FIG. 201

strings which run from the little finger of one hand to the vertical string passing on the other hand from the little finger to the index (Fig. 202). Be careful to pick up these strings within the small triangle just where they cross, and in doing so keep the backs of the thumbs close together. The hands are then separated and put in their usual positions (Fig. 203).

Thirteenth : Pass each thumb away from you into the index loop from below, and with the back of the thumb draw the near index string toward you (Fig. 204, Left hand), and completely through the two loops already on the thumb; then let these two loops slip entirely off the thumb (Fig. 204, Right hand).

Fourteenth : Release the loops from the index fingers and draw the hands apart.

Fifteenth : Transfer each thumb loop to the index finger, by inserting the index into it from below, between the thumb and the small ring which passes around the thumb loop, withdrawing the thumb, and returning the index to its former position.

Extend the figure between the tips of the index fingers and the little fingers

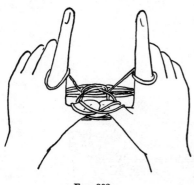

FIG. 202.

closed down on the palms (Fig. 205). The two central lozenges represent the crab's body, the lines radiating therefrom are the legs, and the "pincers" are the small rings passing around the index loops.

The crab is a long figure, but the movements are not difficult; although it is rather hard to remember the order in which they come.   The finished pattern has a

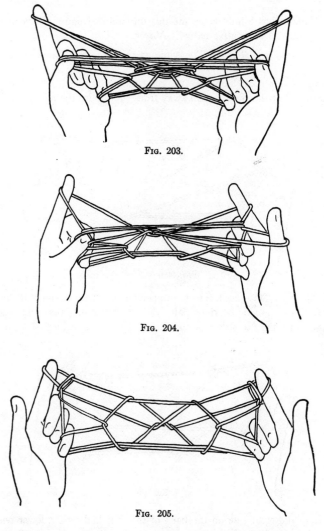

Fig. 203.

Fig. 204.

Fig. 205.

greater likeness to the object it is supposed to represent than some of the string figures.

A TRIGGER FISH

Dr. Haddon has kindly given me this unpublished figure which he collected in Torres Straits. The native name is *Nageg*.

First, Second and *Third :* The same as the first three movements of "The Well."

Fourth : Release the loop from the right thumb and let it hang down in front of the figure. Put the right thumb away from you, under the middle of the upper

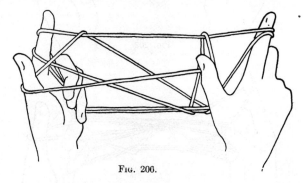

FIG. 206.

string of the figure (Fig. 206), into the upper middle triangle and with the ball of the thumb draw toward the right palm the string forming the right side of the triangle and also the far string of the former right thumb loop (Fig. 207); then

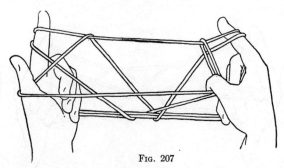

FIG. 207

pick up from the right side on the back of the thumb the right lower near index string (which runs obliquely down to the lower strings of the figure) (Fig. 208) and return the thumb to its position (Fig. 209).

Fifth : Take the right thumb out of the loop and insert it again into the loop, but in the opposite direction away from you. Bend the right thumb down on the right palm and pick up with the back of the thumb the two right far index strings

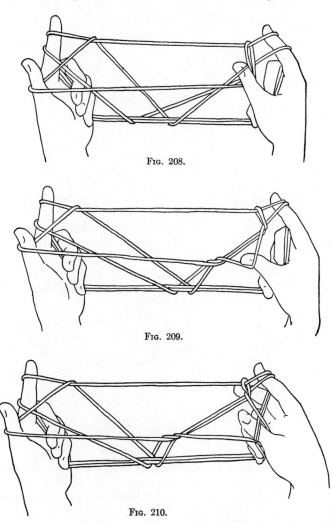

Fig. 208.

Fig. 209.

Fig. 210.

(passing from index to little finger) (Fig. 210) and draw them through the thumb loop which you allow to slip off the thumb as you return the thumb to its original position (Fig. 211). Transfer the loops held by the right thumb to the right little finger by inserting the little finger toward you (from below) into the thumb

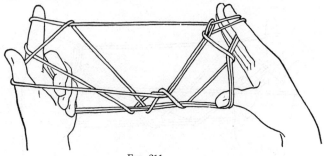

FIG. 211.

loops, and withdrawing the thumb; close the little finger down on the palm (Fig. 212).

Sixth : Pick up from below on the back of the right thumb, close to the right index finger, the upper right near index string (which runs straight across to the

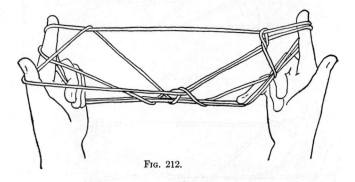

FIG. 212.

left index). Withdraw the right index from *both* its loops and return the right thumb to its position (Fig. 213).

Seventh : Release the loop from the *left* thumb and let it hang loosely. Do not draw its strings tight (Fig. 214).

Eighth : With the left thumb draw down the left lower near index string (which runs obliquely to the lower strings of the figure) (Fig. 215) until it is below these lower strings and let it hang down; then pass the left thumb away from you

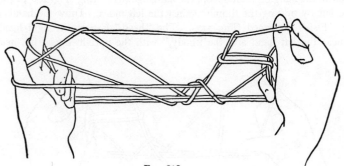

Fig. 213.

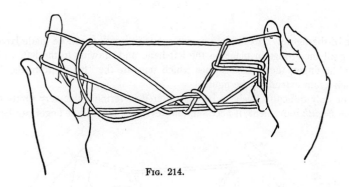

Fig. 214.

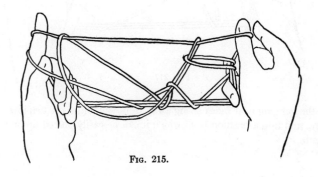

Fig. 215.

over the two lower strings and pick up from below on the ball of the left thumb, to the left of the hanging thumb loop, the hanging index string (Fig. 216), and draw it to the left by putting the thumb against the left index. Draw the hands apart and the "Fish" is formed (Fig. 217). The "head" is near the right hand, the "tail" near the left hand and the "body," with the upright dorsal fin, near the

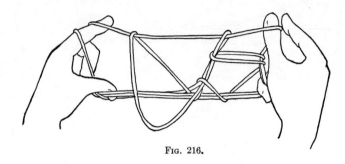

Fig. 216.

middle of the figure. If the body comes out very small, it can be made larger by keeping all the strings in place on the left hand and drawing to the left, with the left middle finger, the crossed strings which separate the "body" from the "tail" and then again extending the figure.

The only difficulty likely to be encountered in forming this very pretty figure is in the *Eighth* movement; if necessary, however, the left middle finger can be used

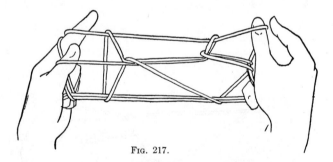

Fig. 217.

to draw the hanging near index string away from you under the two lower strings of the figure, and into a position from which it can be easily picked up on the back of the thumb.

A RATTLESNAKE AND A BOY

This is a Klamath Indian game obtained for me by Mr. John L. Cox, at Hampton, Virginia, from Emma Jackson of Oregon.

First: Opening A.

Second: Transfer the little finger loops to the index fingers, by putting each

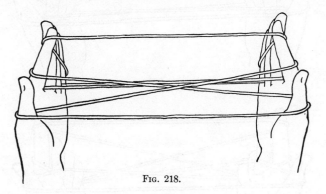

FIG. 218.

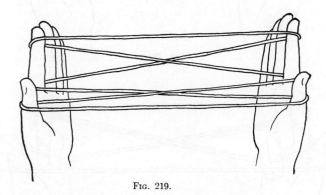

FIG. 219.

index from above down into the little finger loop, and picking up, from below (Fig. 218), the far little finger string, and withdrawing the little finger. You now have two loops on each index and a loop on each thumb (Fig. 219).

Third: Pass the middle, ring and little fingers of each hand toward you over both strings of the lower index loop, and pull them down by closing these fingers on the palm (Fig. 220).

Fourth: Pass each middle finger from below into the thumb loop (Fig. 221); straighten the finger, put it from below into the upper index loop (Fig. 222) and

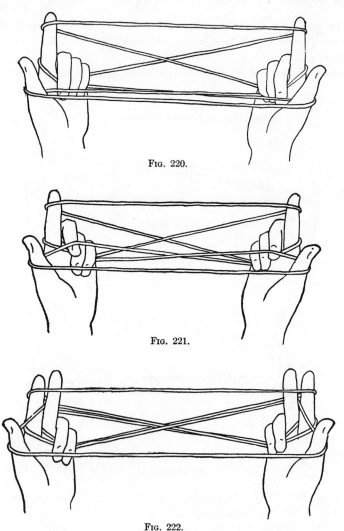

Fig. 220.

Fig. 221.

Fig. 222.

pull down on the ball of the finger the upper near index string, and draw it through the thumb loop (Fig. 223), then away from you past the lower index loop (held to the palm by the ring and little fingers). Release the loops from the ring and little

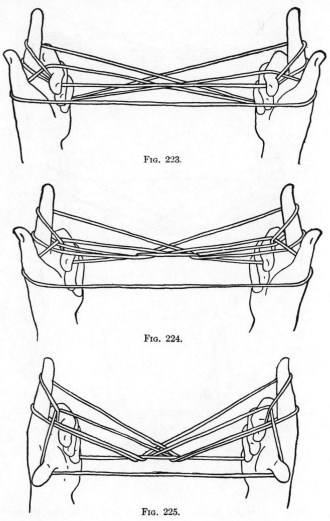

Fig. 223.

Fig. 224.

Fig. 225.

fingers (Fig. 224), and insert these fingers into the middle finger loop beside the middle finger (Fig. 225).

Fifth: Withdraw the middle finger, and pass it toward you through the upper index loop and under the near thumb string; then, keeping the strings tight, bend the index down on the near thumb string (Fig. 226), and draw this string away

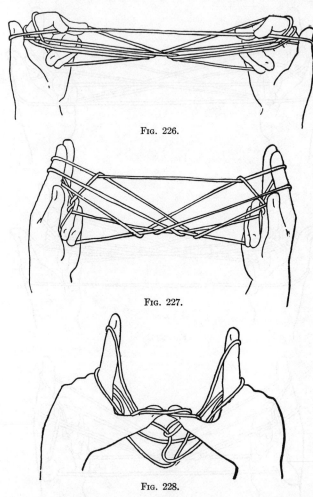

Fig. 226.

Fig. 227.

Fig. 228.

from you (holding it between the index and middle fingers) through the index loop, and put it on the tip of the index by turning the palm away from you. Release the loops from the thumbs (Fig. 227).

Sixth: Pick up with the back of both thumbs (held close together) the two

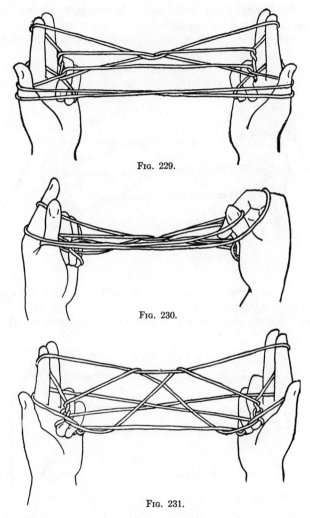

FIG. 229.

FIG. 230.

FIG. 231.

lower index strings just where they cross at the bottom of the figure (Fig. 228) **and** draw these strings out by separating the hands. You now have two straight **near** thumb strings (Fig. 229).

Seventh: Put each thumb against the index, to hold in place the upper **near** index string (Fig. 230), and then throw the two near thumb strings over the **tip of** the index, and let them fall on the far side. Separate the hands (Fig. 231).

Eighth: Transfer the upper index loop to the thumb, by putting the thumb from below into it, and withdrawing the index from *both its loops* (Fig. 232).

Ninth: Put the index toward you, that is from above, into the thumb loop and take the loop off the thumb.

Tenth: Pass each thumb away from you through the corresponding side lozenge below the two straight transverse strings, pick these strings up on the back of the

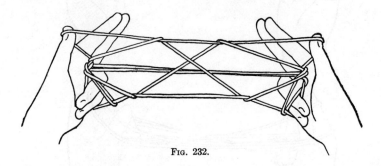

FIG. 232.

thumb (Fig. 233) and return the thumb to its position. Release the loops held down by the ring and little fingers and draw the strings tight (Fig. 234).

Eleventh: Pass the ring and little fingers toward you (from below) into the

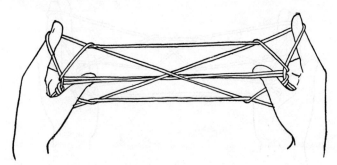

FIG. 233.

two thumb loops and bending the fingers over the two near strings, draw the loops down on the palm and withdraw the thumb (Fig. 235).

Twelfth: Put each thumb away from you into the loops held to the palm by the ring and middle fingers, and, drawing the single upper string of these loops toward the palm (Fig. 236, Left hand) with the back of the thumb pick up from the palmar

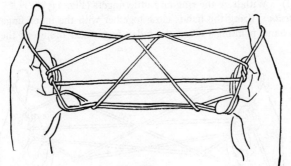

FIG. 234.

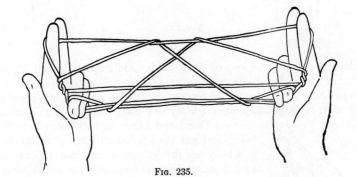

FIG. 235.

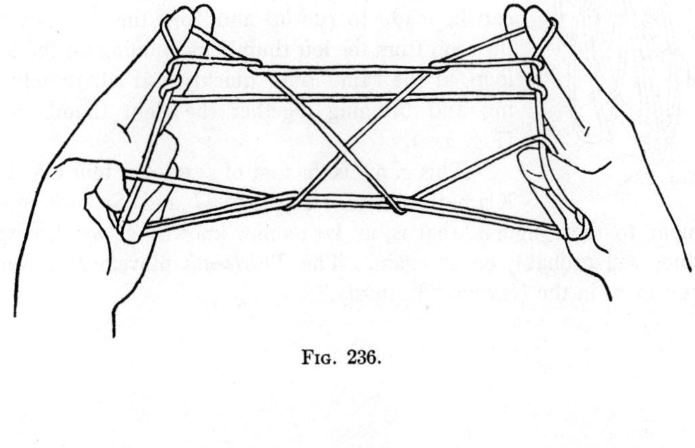

FIG. 236.

side, the string which runs down from the index to the little finger (Fig. 236, Right hand). Withdraw the ring and little fingers (Fig. 237).

Thirteenth : Bring the hands close together with the index finger and thumb of the one hand pointing toward the index finger and thumb of the other hand;

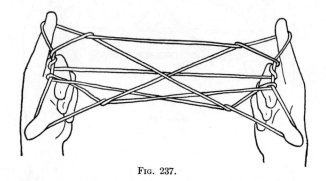

FIG. 237.

then hang the right index loop on the left index and the right thumb loop on the left thumb (Fig. 238). Take up with the right index from the right side the loop which you have just put on the left thumb, and take up with the right thumb, from the left side, the loop which was originally on the left thumb (Fig. 239); then with

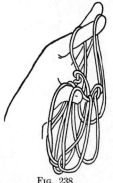

FIG. 238.

the right thumb and index lift both loops from the left index, and put the left index toward you into the loop just hung on the left index, and put the left thumb away from you into the loop originally on the left thumb (Fig. 240). Extend the figure on the thumbs and index fingers (Fig. 241). The "rattlesnake" is at the left side of the figure, the "boy" at the right side. The snake can be made to run up and "bite the boy" by releasing the loop from the left thumb and pulling on the left index loop, at the same time quickly and alternately separating and bringing together the right thumb and index (Fig. 242).

This game is the first of a series of four closely related Klamath games. The *Second* and *Seventh* movements are peculiar to these figures, that is, as far as now known; as we discover more figures they will probably occur again. The *Thirteenth* movement is very much like a movement in the Navaho "Butterfly."

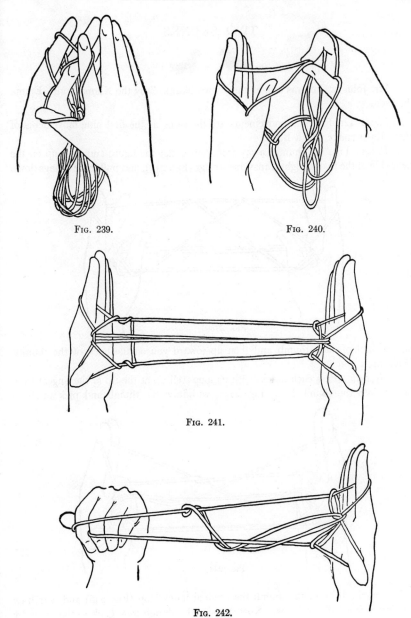

Fig. 239.

Fig. 240.

Fig. 241.

Fig. 242.

TWO SKUNKS

Mr. John L. Cox was taught the " Two Skunks " by the Klamath girl, Emma Jackson.

First : The first nine movements are the same as the first nine movements of the " Rattlesnake and a Boy."

Tenth : Pass the thumbs away from you under the figure and then up on the near side of the two straight transverse strings (Fig. 243), and pull these strings down

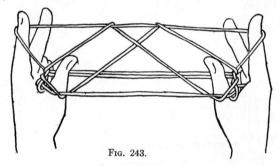

FIG. 243.

on the ball of each thumb and then up toward you on the back of the thumbs (Fig. 244).

Eleventh : Pass each index (with its loop well up at the tip of the finger) from below, into the thumb loop (Fig. 245); withdraw the thumb and pick up from

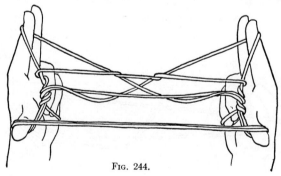

FIG. 244.

below on the back of the thumb the original index loop (Fig. 246) and withdraw the index from all the loops. Now transfer the thumb loop back to the index by putting the index into the loop from below and withdrawing the thumb and straightening the index (Fig. 247).

You now have on each hand a loop on the index and a loop held down by the little and ring fingers. The figure consists of an upper straight string, a lower

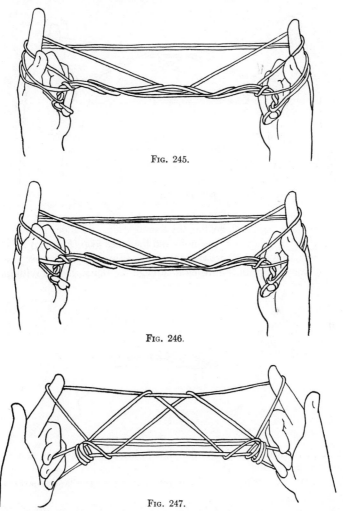

Fig. 245.

Fig. 246.

Fig. 247.

straight string and two middle straight strings, also two diagonal strings on each side, which come from a twist around the little finger loop and pass obliquely to the upper string of the figure. The lower diagonal runs downward and passes under the lower straight string before it runs up to the upper straight string.

Twelfth : Pick up from below on the back of each thumb the lower diagonal close to the twist around the little finger loop and before it passes under the lower

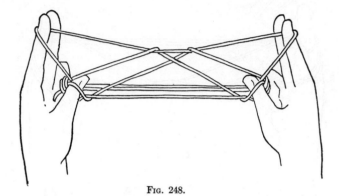

FIG. 248.

straight string (Fig. 248) and, holding the thumb against the index to keep in position the near index string, pass the index and the index loop (Fig. 249) from above into the thumb loop and withdrawing the thumb (Fig. 250) pick up from below on its back the index loop, thus drawing it through the thumb loop. Withdraw the

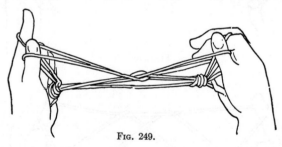

FIG. 249.

index and put it from below into the thumb loop, withdraw the thumb, and straighten the index (Fig. 251).

Thirteenth : Repeat the *Twelfth* movement, and draw the hands apart to extend the figure (Fig. 252).

The last four movements of this figure are all novel methods. In the *Twelfth* and *Thirteenth*, it is necessary to observe care in order to get the proper diagonals and pick them up in the right places.

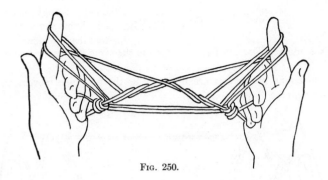

Fig. 250.

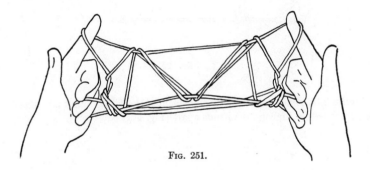

Fig. 251.

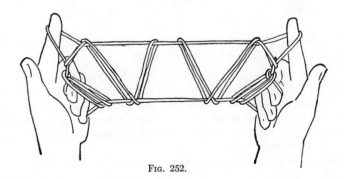

Fig. 252.

TWO FOXES

This is another Klamath figure, secured in the same way as the two preceding games.

The first nine movements are the same as the first nine movements of the "Rattlesnake and a Boy."

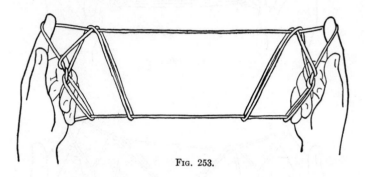

FIG. 253.

Tenth : The same as the *Twelfth* movement of the "Two Skunks." The figure is then extended by drawing the hands apart (Fig. 253).

 TWO SQUIRRELS

This is the last of the "Rattlesnake" series of Klamath figures, obtained by Mr. John L. Cox, from Emma Jackson of Oregon.

First : Hold the string between the tips of the thumb and index of each hand, so that a short piece passes between the hands and a long loop hangs down. Make a small ring, hanging down in the short string, putting the right hand string away from you over the left hand string. Put both thumbs away from you through the small loop and both little fingers away from you through the long hanging loop (Fig. 254), and separate the hands (Fig. 255).

Second : Now go through all the movements of the "Two Foxes" including Opening A, to the very end. Remember that you have two near thumb strings; these must be considered throughout as one string (Fig. 256).

The heads of the "Squirrels" are directed toward the hands; the tails are the loops on the index fingers. The pattern should be held vertically.

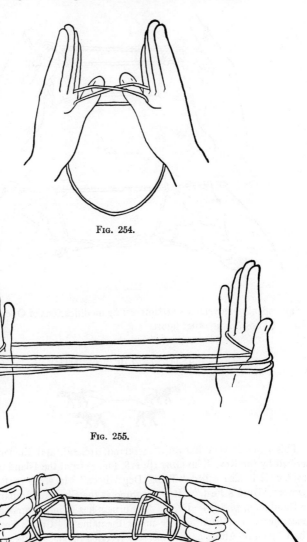

FIG. 254.

FIG. 255.

FIG. 256.

To hang up the "Squirrels," pick up on each thumb the straight string crossing the figure (Fig. 257). Release the index loops and separate the hands (Fig. 258).

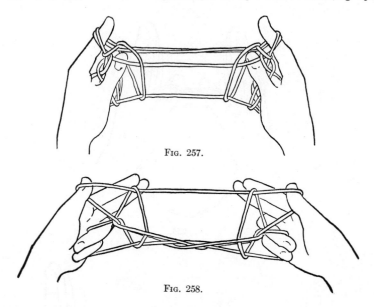

FIG. 257.

FIG. 258.

The opening movements are interesting modifications of Opening A, and occur, so far as I know, in no other figure.

THE LEASHING OF LOCHIEL'S DOGS

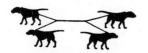

This game is well known in Scotland, Ireland, and England. It has been described by the Rev. John Gray (p. 118, Fig. 4) from the Island of Eriskay, Outer Hebrides; it is also called "Tying Dogs' Feet." In some parts of Ireland, it is known as "Duck's Feet." It is the same as the Cherokee Indian "Crow's Feet." (See Haddon, **5,** p. 217.) Dr. W. H. Furness has found it among the Kabyles of Algeria, introduced from France under the name of "Cock's Feet." It is known to the Ulungu of Africa as *Umuzwa*=a Wooden Spoon. Roth gives a similar pattern from Australia (pl. xii, 1). It closely resembles the "Two Hogans" of the Navaho Indians, just before the completion of that figure.

First: Opening A.

Second: Turn the palms toward you, draw the strings tight and close the four fingers over all the strings except the near thumb string (Fig. 259, Left hand);

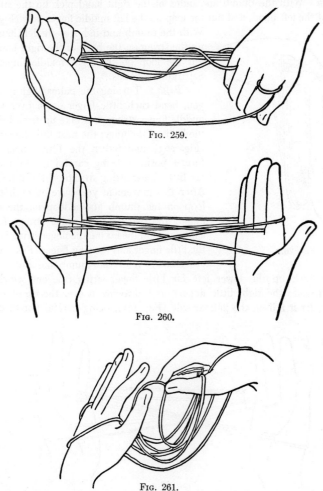

FIG. 259.

FIG. 260.

FIG. 261.

turn each hand down and then up toward you (Fig. 259, Right hand) under the near thumb string, to put this string around the four fingers (Fig. 260).

Third: With the thumb and index of the right hand lift the loop from the left index and place it on the left thumb (Fig. 261). With the thumb and index of the left hand lift the loop from the right index and place it on the right thumb. This movement can also be made by putting each thumb from below into the index loop and withdrawing the index.

Fourth : With the thumb and index of the right hand pick up the string on the back of the left hand, and put the loop on the left middle finger only (Fig. 262).

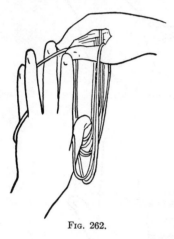

With the thumb and index of the left hand pick up the string on the back of the right hand, and put the loop on the right middle finger only. Separate the hands.

Fifth : Turning the palms slightly toward you, bend each little finger down over the far middle finger string, and take up from below on the back of the finger the near little finger string (Fig. 263), and return the little finger to its former position, being careful not to allow the far little finger string to slip off the little finger. After this movement you have on each hand a loop on the thumb and a loop on the middle finger, and two far little finger strings forming a loop around the far middle finger string between the little finger and the ring finger (Fig. 264).

Fig. 262.

Sixth : With the thumb and index of the right hand pick up the lower left far little finger string (the one which runs straight across to the right little finger), and, drawing it over the tip of the left little finger, let it fall on the palmar side (Fig. 265), being careful not to disturb

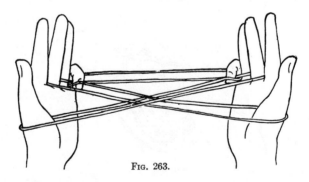

Fig. 263.

the upper far little finger string (the one that crosses over to the far side of the right thumb). With the thumb and index of the left hand, in the same way pick up the lower right far little finger string, lift it over the tip of the right little finger, and drop it on the palmar side. Separate the hands (Fig. 266).

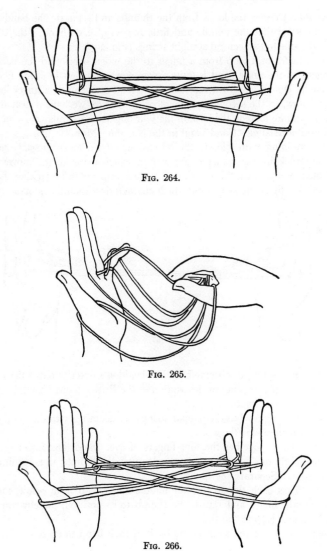

Fig. 264.

Fig. 265.

Fig. 266.

This movement may also be made by bending each little finger down over the upper far little finger string, and picking up from below on the back of the finger the lower far string, which will slip to the palmar side as the little finger is straightened.

Seventh : Release the loops from the thumbs and separate the hands, when it will be observed that the middle and little fingers of each hand, "the dogs," are leashed by loops to two central straight strings (Fig. 267).

The transfer of a loop from a finger to the wrist, or around the backs of the four fingers, of the same hand is quite a common movement in string figures. In the "Apache Door" we saw a very simple method of changing a finger loop to the wrist, and now, in the second movement of this figure, we have a neat method of putting the thumb loop on the back of the four fingers. A similar movement occurs in the Caroline Islands "Coral" and in the Navaho "Man."

On examining more closely the "Leashing of Lochiel's Dogs," one cannot fail to be struck by the rather crude way in which many of the movements are carried out; except in the Fifth movement, there appears to be lacking that expert use of both hands at the same time which characterizes the figures made by savage

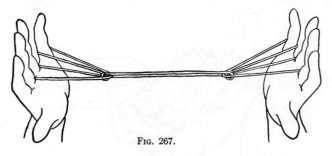

Fɪɢ. 267.

races. It is interesting to observe that Dr. Haddon's description of the Cherokee "Crow's Feet" differs from our description of the British figure; his description, in my own words, is as follows:

First : Opening A; but the palmar strings are taken up with the middle fingers instead of with the index fingers.

Second : Close together the four fingers of each hand, and insert them from above into the thumb loop, then take this loop off the thumb; thus turning it over in the transfer. Separate the hands.

Third : Pass each thumb into the middle finger loop from below, then withdraw the middle finger and return the thumb to its position, thereby transferring the middle finger loop to the thumb.

Fourth : Transfer the loop on the back of each hand to its respective middle finger.

Fifth : Pass each near little finger string from below through the middle finger loop and replace it on the far side of the little finger.

Sixth : Transfer each far little finger string over the little finger to the near side of that finger.

Seventh : Release the loops from the thumbs and draw the strings tight. "Crow's Feet" was taught to Dr. Haddon by a Pullman porter of European, negro and Cherokee parentage, which may account for the absence of what, for lack of a better term, we may call "savage characters."

From the figure shown to Mr. John L. Cox by an Onondaga Indian, Charles Doxon, we know that "Crow's Feet" is done by the Indians in the typical Indian way. This method differs from "The Leashing of Lochiel's Dogs" only in the *Third* and *Fourth* movements:

Third : Insert each thumb from above into the index loop, and pick up from below the far index string; return the thumb to its position, and withdraw the index.

Fourth : Turning the hands toward you and closing the fingers on the palms, let the far wrist string slip toward you along the fist until it comes to the index finger, when the whole wrist loop can be readily transferred to the middle finger.

TWO HOGANS

Hogan is the Navaho name for a tent ; two tents are *Naki-hogan* or *Atl-sa-hogan.* This game was taught to Dr. Haddon, in 1901, by the two old Navahos in Chicago. (Haddon, **5,** p. 221, pl. xv, Fig. 1.) An example of the finished pattern is preserved

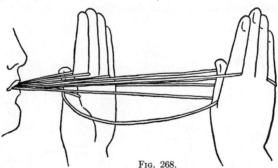

Fig. 268.

in the Philadelphia Free Museum of Science and Arts; No. 22723, collected by Mr. Culin, from the Navahos at St. Michael's Mission, Arizona.

First : Opening A.

Second : With the mouth, take up, from the centre of the figure, the four crossed strings, and draw them toward you and hold them firmly (Fig. 268).

Third : Release the loops from the thumbs and index fingers, and let them hang down; the index loops form two short hanging loops, the thumb loops form one long hanging loop.

Fourth : Put each hand up from below completely through the loops held by the little finger (Fig. 269); bend the hands down away from you, with the palms facing each other and the fingers pointing downward, and pick up from the near side

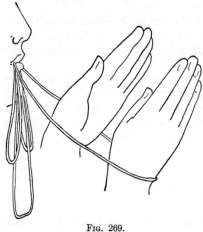

with the backs of both little fingers the long hanging loop, drawing it out away from you under and past the far wrist string. Turn the hands with the fingers pointing upward (Fig. 270).

You now have a lower loop held by the mouth and passing around both wrists to become the lower far string of the figure; and a triangle produced by a string on each side passing from the mouth and running between the ring and little finger to become the upper far string of the figure. The original index loops hang down from the mouth.

Fifth : Still holding the strings in the mouth, and keeping the loops securely on the little fingers, turn the palms slightly toward you, and, bending each little finger down over the near little finger string, pick up from below on the

Fig. 269.

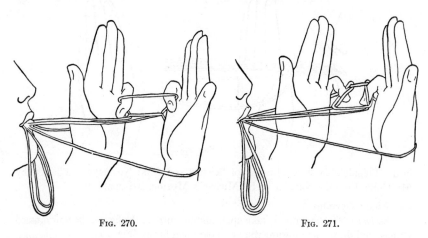

Fig. 270.   Fig. 271.

back of the finger the diagonal string running from the mouth to the little finger, and return the little finger to its usual position, drawing the diagonal string upward and outward through the little finger loop (Fig. 271).

Sixth : Release the strings held by the mouth and separate the hands (Fig. 272).

Seventh : Take up with the mouth the middle of the two strings passing between the knots in the figure, and turn the hands with their palms up and the fingers

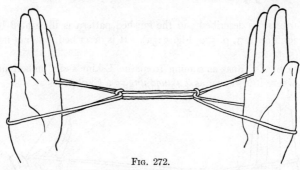

Fig. 272.

directed away from you; in this way a hogan, or tent, is formed on each hand by the wrist and little finger loops (Fig. 273).

"Two Hogans" is interesting because the loops are held by the teeth almost throughout the entire figure. It is not unusual for one or more loops to be taken up by the teeth, but, as a rule, it is done merely through one or two movements, in order

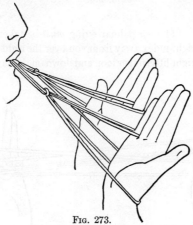

Fig. 273.

to bring the strings into a position from which they can be conveniently taken up by the fingers. The figure produced by the *Sixth* movement is similar to the finished figure of the "Leashing of Lochiel's Dogs"; the loops, however, being held on the wrists and little fingers instead of on the middle fingers and little fingers.

A CARIBOO

The "Cariboo" is described and the finished pattern is illustrated by Dr. F. Boas (**1**, p. 229, Fig. 1, **3,** p. 570, Fig. 525a). It is described, but not figured, by Dr. Haddon (**5,** p. 216).

It is given by Dr. Boas as coming from the Eskimos of Cumberland Sound, Baffin Land, where it is known as *Tuktuqdjung* = a Cariboo.

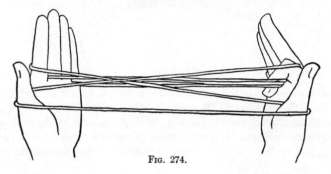

Fig. 274.

First: Opening A. (The *left* palmar string *must* be taken up first.)

Second: Bend the right index away from you over the right far index string and over both strings of the right little finger loop and down on the far side of the right far

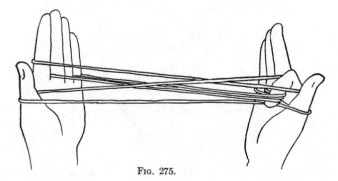

Fig. 275.

little finger string (Fig. 274); then draw toward you on the near side of the right index both right little finger strings and the right far index string, allowing the right near index string to slip over the knuckle of the index and to the far side of the finger. Now put the right index (still bent and holding the strings on its near side) from below into the thumb loop, by pressing the near side of the bent index toward you against the right far thumb string, and putting the tip down toward you over and on the near side of the right near thumb string (Fig. 275).   Pick up, on the far side

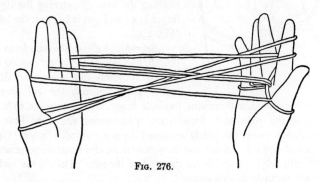

FIG. 276.

of the bent right index, this right near thumb string, and lift it and the former near index string up by turning the index away from you and up to its usual position (Fig. 276).

Third : Release the loop from the right thumb (Fig. 277).

Fourth : Give the loops on the right index a twist by rotating the index

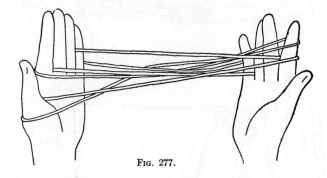

FIG. 277.

away from you, down on the near side of the little finger loop and then up toward you.

Fifth : Put the right thumb from below into the two loops on the right index, and draw the thumb away from the index in order to enlarge the loops.

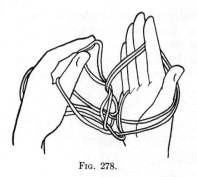

FIG. 278.

Sixth : With the left thumb and index take the loop from the left index, and pass it from above and away from you through the two loops passing around the right thumb and index (Fig. 278), without twisting the loop or touching the right little finger loop, and put it back on the left index (Fig. 279).

Seventh : Release the loop from the left thumb, and release the loops passing around the right thumb and index, and draw the hands apart; putting the left thumb into the left little finger loop, withdrawing the little finger, and putting the right thumb and index into the right little finger loop, withdrawing the right little finger. Extend the figure between the widely separated thumbs and index fingers (Fig. 280).

The finished figure is curious and unsymmetrical, and bears some resemblance to a cariboo with the head and horns directed to the left. The *Second* and *Third* movements are peculiar to this figure.

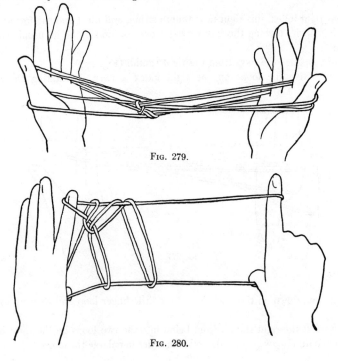

FIG. 279.

FIG. 280.

THE CIRCLE

Dr. Boas has described and illustrated (**1**, p. 230, Fig. 5) a game known to the Eskimos of Cumberland Sound, Baffin Land, as *Ussuqdjung*. I have called it the "Circle."

First : Put the loop on the hands in the First Position.

Second : Pass the right index, middle, ring and little fingers from below, behind the left palmar string, and draw the loop out. Pass the left index, middle, ring and

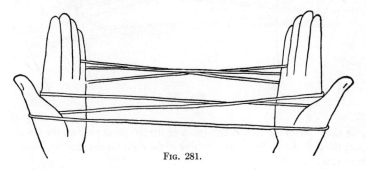

Fig. 281.

little fingers, from below, behind the right palmar strings; draw the loop out and separate the hands. This movement, which is like Opening A, puts each palmar string on the back of the opposite hand (Fig. 281).

Third : Release the loops from the thumbs and separate the hands.

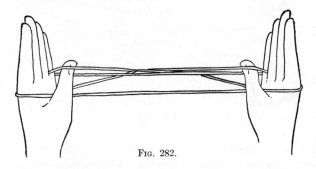

Fig. 282.

Fourth : Bend each thumb over the string which passes between the hands and then between the thumb and index of each hand, and pick up from below, on the back of the thumb, the near little finger string (Fig. 282), and return the thumb to its position.

Fifth : Pick up the palmar strings with the index fingers as in Opening A (Fig. 283).

Sixth : With the thumb and index of the right hand pick up the string on the back of the left hand, lift it over the tips of the left fingers, and let it drop on the

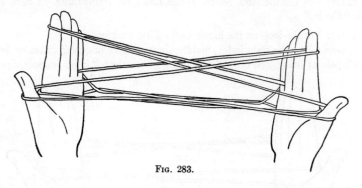

Fig. 283.

palmar side. With the thumb and index of the left hand pick up the string on the back of the right hand, lift it over the tips of the right fingers, and let it drop on the palmar side.

Seventh : Draw the hands apart and the central circle will appear (Fig. 284).

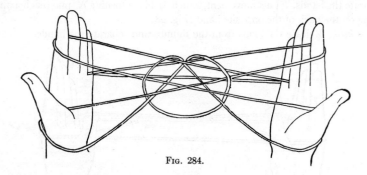

Fig. 284.

This is not an interesting figure, and appears more like a figure in process of development than one worked out to the end. The *Second* movement is the direct way of putting the loop on the backs of the four fingers.

TWO STARS

I learned this figure at the St. Louis Exposition, in November, 1904, from the two Navaho girls, from Gallup, New Mexico, who taught me the other Navaho figures.

First: Opening A.

Second: Transfer the index loops to the thumbs, by putting each thumb from below into the index loop, withdrawing the index, and returning the thumb to its position.

Third: Transfer the little finger loops to the thumbs, by bending each thumb away from you over the far thumb strings, and taking up from below on the back of the thumb the near little finger string; and then withdrawing the little finger, return the thumb to its position.

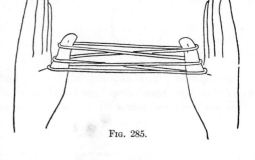

FIG. 285.

You now have three loops on each thumb (Fig. 285). Keep them well separated on the thumb: the original loop down at the base, the loop taken from the index half-way up, and the loop taken from the little finger near the tip.

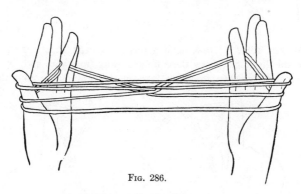

FIG. 286.

Fourth: Put each ring finger from below through the two lower thumb loops, and, pushing the two lower far strings away from you with the back of this finger (Fig. 286), bend the ring finger toward you over the upper far thumb string (the far string which passes directly from thumb to thumb), draw it down, and hold it by closing the ring and little fingers over it on the palm (Fig. 287).

Fifth: Turn the hands so that the thumbs, index fingers and middle fingers point away from you; then bending the index and middle finger pass the middle

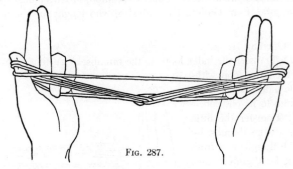

Fig. 287.

finger toward you through the thumb loops, and pass the index toward you into the two upper thumb loops and then between the two upper near thumb strings and the lower near thumb string (the near string which passes directly from thumb

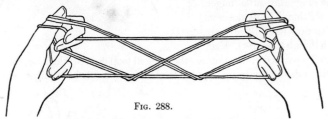

Fig. 288.

to thumb) (Fig. 288).   Now, holding this lower near thumb string between the index and middle finger, draw these fingers away from you, and, by turning the index down and then away from you, take the string up on the tip of the finger.

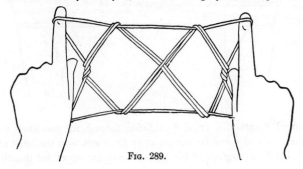

Fig. 289.

Sixth : Release the loops from the thumbs, and, turning the palms away from you, extend the figure between the index fingers and the ring and little fingers closed on the palm (Fig. 289).

So far as I know, this figure is the only one in which, after Opening A, three loops are arranged on both thumbs.

CASTING THE FISH–SPEAR

Dr. Haddon has given me this unpublished Torres Straits figure.

First : Opening A. (The *left* palmar string *must* be taken up first.)

Second : Exchange the index loops so that they will catch, by bringing the hands together (with the fingers pointed toward one another) and putting with the left index the left index loop on the right index over the right index loop, and down to the base of the finger; then lift off with the left index the original right index loop, and separate the hands. In this way the right index loop is drawn through the left index loop (Fig. 290).

Third : Release the loop from the right index. You

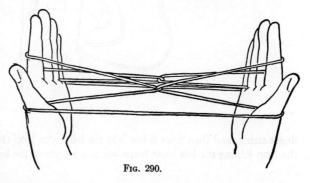

FIG. 290.

now have a loop on each thumb and little finger and a loop on the left index; the loops on the left hand form the fish-spear, which is brought out more plainly by closing all the fingers of the right hand down on the palm, and letting the strings of the little finger loop come out between the index and middle finger (Fig. 291).

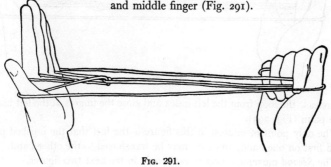

FIG. 291.

Fourth : The spear is "cast" from the left hand to the right hand, by putting the right index down between the right far thumb string and the right near little

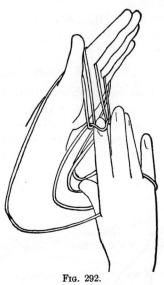

FIG. 292.

finger string, and then from below into the left index loop (Fig. 292), and drawing the loop joining the left hand loops out to the right on the back of the right index.

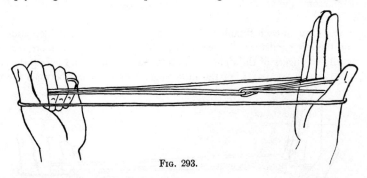

FIG. 293.

Then release the loop from the left index and close the fingers of the left hand down on the palm (Fig. 293).

The only point of interest in this figure is the fact that the finished pattern is formed first on one hand, and then may be transferred to the other hand.

The *Second* movement occurs again only in the next two figures.

AN ARROW

This very pretty figure was shown to me by the two girls from whom I learned the other Navaho figures, at the St. Louis Exposition, in November, 1904. The native name is Ka = an Arrow.

First: Opening A. (The *left* palmar string *must* be taken up first.)

Second: The same as the *Second* movement of "Casting the Fish-Spear."

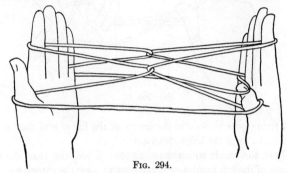

FIG. 294.

Third: Pass the right thumb away from you over the right far thumb string and under all the other strings, and, as you begin to return the thumb, catch on its

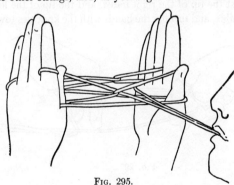

FIG. 295.

back the right far little finger string, and draw it back under the right near little finger string and the strings of the right index loop (Fig. 294, Right hand).

Fourth: With the teeth pick up from the right thumb this right far little finger string, which you have just drawn toward you, remove the right thumb (Fig. 295), and moving the hands away from you, release the loops from the little fingers and draw the strings tight.

You now have a loop on each thumb and a loop on the left index. The loop held by the teeth makes one twist near the mouth, and then the right string passes to the far side of the right index, around that finger and to the centre of the figure,

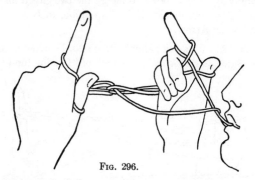

FIG. 296.

while the left string goes at once to the centre of the figure and then to the far side of the left index, to form the left index loop.

Fifth : Turn the hands with the palms toward you and close the middle, ring and little fingers of the left hand down on the palm, over the thumb and index loops; and close the middle, ring and little fingers of the right hand down on the palm, over the near index string and the thumb loop (Fig. 296). Now put the tip of the right thumb against the tip of the right index, and the tip of the left thumb against the tip of the left index, and turning the hands with the knuckles toward one another,

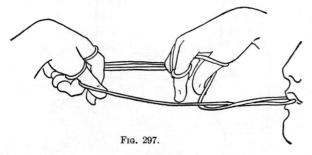

FIG. 297.

and the palms down, put the thumb and index (still held together) of each hand down between the two strings of the loop held by the mouth, below (to the far side of) the twist in the loop (Fig. 297). The middle, ring and little fingers must be kept closed on the palms throughout the following movement.

By lifting the elbows and bending the hands down at the wrists, direct the thumb and index (still held together) of the right hand toward the right, under the right string of the loop held by the teeth; and direct the thumb and index (still held together) of the left hand toward the left, under the left string of the loop held by

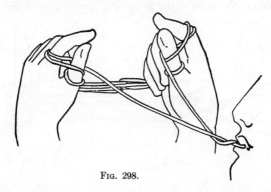

Fig. 298.

the teeth. Now, if both hands be moved up toward the chin and turned at the wrist toward you and upward, while you drop your elbows, each string of the loop can be caught around the thumb and index of the hand of the same side, and when the hands are put in the usual position each string will pass from the teeth to the far side of the index finger, between the index and middle fingers to the back of the hand, and

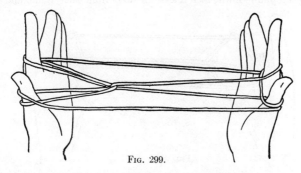

Fig. 299.

then toward you across the backs of the thumb and index, around the thumb to the palm, and again between the index and middle fingers (Fig. 298).

Sixth : Release the loop held by the teeth; separate the hands, and draw the strings tight (Fig. 299).

You now have on each hand: A single lower loop on the thumb, a single lower loop on the index, and an upper loop which passes around both thumb and index.

Seventh : With the thumb and index (or with the teeth) lift the lower loop off the thumb, and lift the lower loop off the index of each hand in turn, passing the loop over the loop which goes around both thumb and index, but permitting that loop to remain around these fingers. The single loops which you have slipped from each thumb and each index are now looped around the string passing from the back of the thumb to the back of the index (Fig. 300). One of the four strings

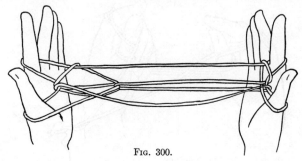

FIG. 300.

of these loops, the upper near one, passes straight across the figure and above the other three strings.

Eighth : Put the middle finger of each hand from below between the strings forming the thumb loop, and then on the far side of this upper straight near string passing directly across the figure, and bending the middle finger toward you over this string (Fig. 301), pull it down; then release the loop from each thumb and draw the

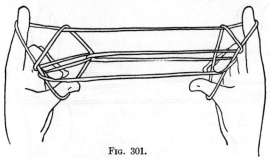

FIG. 301.

strings tight. The figure is extended between the index fingers and the middle fingers closed on the palms (Fig. 302).

The head of the "Arrow" is near the left hand; the feathered end near the right hand. By pushing together with the thumb the loops forming the point of the "Arrow," the head can be rendered very distinct; in the same way the feathered end can be made perfectly symmetrical.

The "Arrow" begins, practically, with an unsymmetrical movement, and although the subsequent movements are done with both hands the figure does not again become entirely symmetrical. The *First* and *Second* movements are similar to the same movements in "Casting the Fish-Spear." The object of the *Third,*

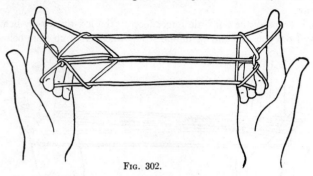

F. 302.

Fourth and *Fifth* movements is to wrap the far index strings (which usually form the little finger loops) around both the index and thumb. The *Seventh* and *Eighth* movements are characteristic Navaho movements.

A PORCUPINE

The "Porcupine" is a Klamath Indian game obtained by Mr. John L. Cox, at Hampton, Virginia, from Emma Jackson, of Oregon.

First: Opening A. (The *left* palmar string *must* be taken up first.)
Second: The same as the *Second* movement of "Casting the Fish-Spear." With the right thumb and index pull in turn the left near thumb string and the left

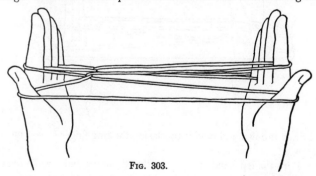

F. 303.

far little finger to the right, in order to bring central crossings of the strings near the left hand (Fig. 303).

Third : Transfer the left index loop to the left thumb, by putting the thumb from below into the index loop, withdrawing the index, and returning the thumb to its position.

Fourth : Transfer the left little finger loop to the left thumb, by bending the thumb away from you over the far thumb strings and taking up from below on the

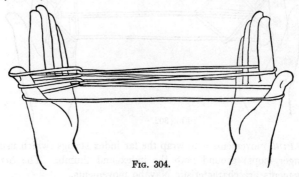

FIG. 304.

back of the thumb the near little finger string; then withdrawing the little finger, return the left thumb to its position. Keep the three loops on the right thumb well separated (Fig. 304).

Fifth : Put the left ring finger from below through the two lower loops on the left thumb, and, pushing the two lower far strings away from you with the back of the finger (Fig. 305), bend the ring finger toward you over the upper far thumb string (the far string which passes directly from the left thumb to the right little

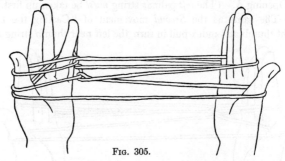

FIG. 305.

finger) and draw it down and hold it by closing the ring finger over it on the palm (Fig. 306).

Sixth : Turn the left hand so that the thumb, index and middle fingers point away from you; then bending the left index and middle fingers, pass the middle finger toward you through all the left thumb loops and pass the left index toward you into the two upper left thumb loops and then between the two upper near thumb strings and the lower near thumb string (the near string which passes directly from thumb to thumb) (Fig. 307). Now, holding this lower near thumb string between

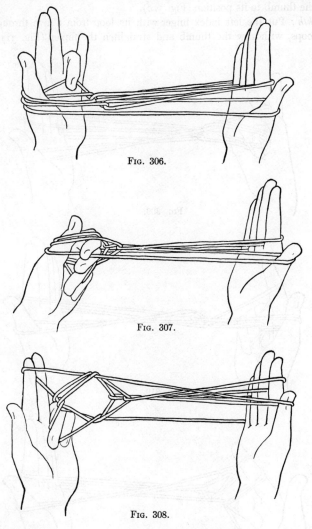

Fig. 306.

Fig. 307.

Fig. 308.

the index and middle finger, draw these fingers away from you, and by turning the index down and then away from you take the string up on the tip of that finger. Release the left thumb (Fig. 308).

Seventh : Put the left thumb under the two right lower strings of the lozenge now formed near the left hand (Fig. 309) and pick them up on the back of the thumb. Return the thumb to its position (Fig. 310).

Eighth : Put the left index finger with its loop from above through the left thumb loops, withdraw the thumb and straighten the finger (Fig. 311); transfer

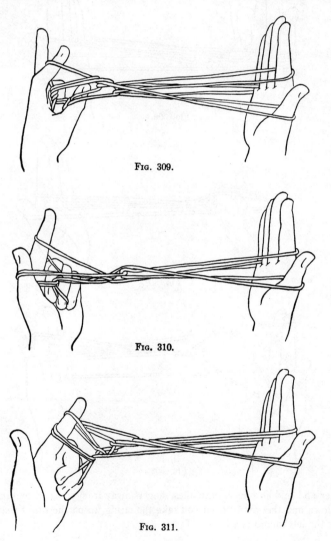

Fig. 309.

Fig. 310.

Fig. 311.

the original left index loop to the thumb by picking up from below the near index string and withdrawing the index from all its loops (Fig. 312). Transfer the left

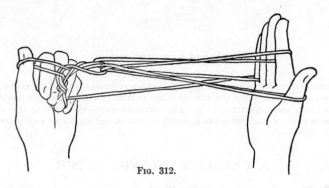

Fig. 312.

thumb loop to the index, by pulling the index into it from below and withdrawing the thumb.

Ninth : Release the loops from the right thumb and little finger and draw the hands apart and the porcupine is formed near the left hand (Fig. 313).

This is a very easy figure because the *Third, Fourth, Fifth* and *Sixth* move-

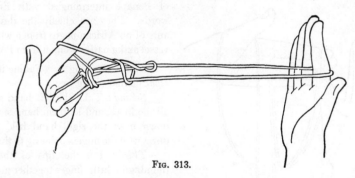

Fig. 313.

ments are the same as the *Second, Third, Fourth* and *Fifth* movements of the "Two Stars," but carried out on the left hand only. The *Seventh* and *Eighth* movements are new ones.

The "Porcupine" appears to be really an Eskimo figure, and one very widely distributed; it is found in Alaska under the name of "Wolf" or "Wolverine" (p. 361), and, as a "Fox," is one of the six patterns from Smith Sound given by A. L. Kroeber in the Bulletin of the American Museum of Natural History, XII, 1899, p. 298.

CHAPTER V

A CAROLINE ISLANDS CATCH

THIS catch was shown to Dr. W. H. Furness in 1902 by a Natik woman, "Emily," who was returning to the Caroline Islands, on the steamer *Oceana*, from Australia, where she had gone from Ponapè as a nurse in an English family. Natik (or Ngatik) is a small island south of Ponapè, with a population of about one hundred and fifty. It has twice been swept by tidal waves and almost all of the inhabitants killed. The natives speak a strange dialect

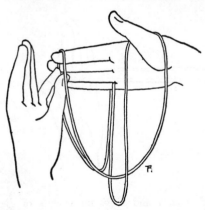

FIG. 314.

of Ponapè intermingled with English words. They are chiefly the descendants of an African negro from a whaling vessel and a native woman from Ponapè.

First: Opening A. (Taking up the *right* palmar string first.)

Second: Take the left hand out of all the loops, and let them hang straight down from the right hand held palm down with the fingers pointing to the left.

Third: Put the tips of the left thumb and little finger together and insert them from the left side into the right index loop (Fig. 314); then separate the left thumb and little finger, and, taking the loop off the right index, draw the

hands apart (Fig. 315). This movement arranges the string on the left hand in the "First Position," and on the right hand puts a twisted loop on the thumb, a twisted loop on the little finger and a string across the palm.

Fourth: With the left index take up from below (as in Opening A) the string on the right palm (Fig. 316) and separate the hands (Fig. 317).

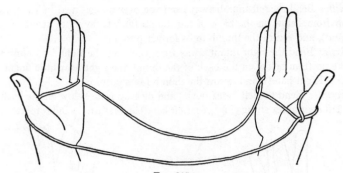

FIG. 315.

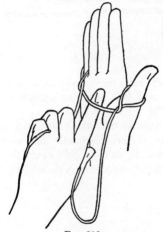

FIG. 316.

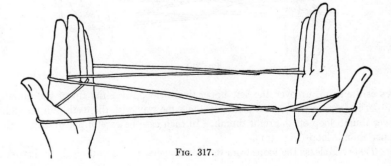

FIG. 317.

Fifth : Bend the left thumb away from you over the left near index string, and take up from below on the back of the thumb the left far index string (Fig. 318, Left hand), and return the thumb to its former position.

Sixth : Bend the right thumb away from you over the right far thumb string, and take up from below on the back of the thumb the right near little finger string (Fig. 318, Right hand), and return the thumb to its position.

Seventh : Bend the left index down, and pick up from below on the back of its tip the left near index string (Fig. 319, Left hand) and return the index to its position.

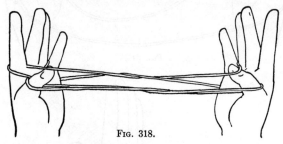

Fig. 318.

Eighth : Bend the right index down, and pick up from below on the back of its tip the right far thumb string (not the string passing across the palm) (Fig. 319, Right hand), and return the index to its position.

Ninth : Keep the strings on the index fingers well up at the tips by pressing the thumb against the index, and bend each little finger over the far little finger string and all three fingers down on the palm to hold down the little finger string (Fig. 320). Then with the teeth pull the lower left thumb loop (the one whose far string

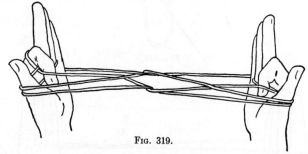

Fig. 319.

crosses the palm) up over the left upper thumb loop, over the tip of the thumb, and let it drop on the palmar side. In the same way with the teeth pull the right lower thumb loop off the right thumb. In each case be careful not to disturb the upper thumb loop (Fig. 321).

Tenth : Release the loops from the little fingers, and extend the figure between the thumbs and the tips of the index fingers. It is not absolutely necessary to turn the palms away from you (Fig. 322). If the figure fails to appear after this last

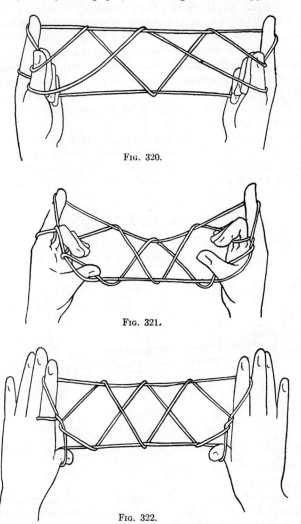

FIG. 320.

FIG. 321.

FIG. 322.

movement, it is because the right thumb loops have become disarranged; it is essential that the right far thumb string form a cross between the right thumb and index.

If a second person put his hand through the middle diamond of the figure, his wrist will be caught in a loop if the strings be dropped from the left hand, and the right hand strings pulled to the right. His wrist will not be caught if the strings be dropped from the right hand and the left hand strings pulled to the left.

This figure is closely related to the Torres Straits catch, the "King Fish." The result produced by the first four movements of the "King Fish" differs from the result of the first four movements of this catch merely in the twist in the left index loop. The opening movements of this figure are very neat, and, so far as I know, are not found in any other string figure. Of course the same result can be obtained, if after Opening A you release the right index loop and give the right thumb and index loops a single twist.

All these catches, whether of wrist or finger, as well as the tricks in which the string is unexpectedly drawn from the hand or neck, possess a great attraction to all natives; it is truly delightful to witness their pleasure when they are successful, and their gratification at the observer's astonishment which it will amply repay him to make very evident.

CIRCLES AND TRIANGLES

Dr. Furness obtained this figure from the same woman who taught him the preceding catch. The native name is *Bur-bur-ani jau,* which has some reference

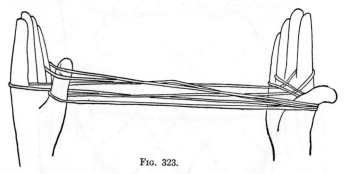

FIG. 323.

to a dog. I have called it "Circles and Triangles" until the translation of the native name can be made.

First : Opening A.

Second : Pass each thumb away from you over the far thumb string and the index loop, and pick up from below on the back of the thumb both strings of the little finger loop (Fig. 323, Left hand), and return the thumb to its position (Fig. 323, Right hand).

Third : Bend each index finger well down into the original thumb loop, the strings of which pass toward the centre of the figure, and move the index away from you (Fig. 324), by turning the palm away from you, and then straighten the index, which thus takes upon its back both strings of the index loop and also the far thumb string (Fig. 325). Slip the thumbs from their loops, and turn the hands

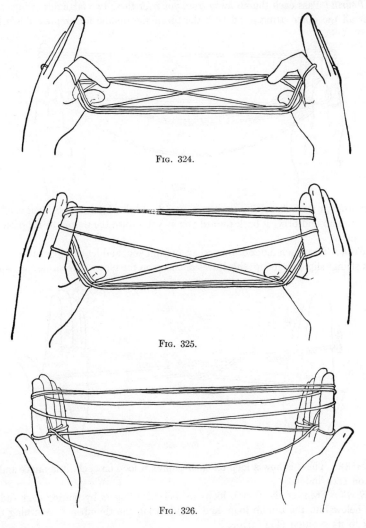

Fig. 324.

Fig. 325.

Fig. 326.

with the palms facing each other (Fig. 326). You now have a loop on each little finger with its strings passing across the palm to the index; and on each index there are three near strings; an upper far string passing from side to side, and two strings which may be called lower far index strings; together they come through a tight loop around the base of the index.

Fourth : Pass each thumb away from you over these two far index strings and under all the other strings, and with the tip of the middle finger press down the

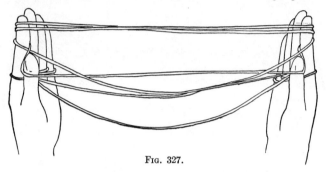

FIG. 327.

upper straight far index string until it is over the back of the thumb, then catch it on the thumb and bring it back toward you as you return the thumb to its position (Fig. 327).

Fifth : Turn each index down and away from you, and let the upper three near index strings slip over its tip; this leaves one loop on the index. Separate the hands

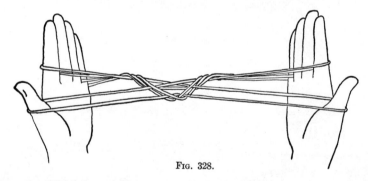

FIG. 328.

(Fig. 328). There is now a loop on each thumb, a loop on each little finger and a loop on each index.

Sixth : Transfer the thumb loops to the index fingers by putting each index from below into the thumb loop, and withdrawing the thumb and returning the index to its position (Fig. 329).

Seventh : Put each thumb from below into the lower index loop, and with the tip of the middle finger press down the upper far index string until it is over the back of the thumb, when you can catch it on the thumb and draw it toward you (Fig. 330, Left hand) as you return the thumb to its position (Fig. 330, Right hand).

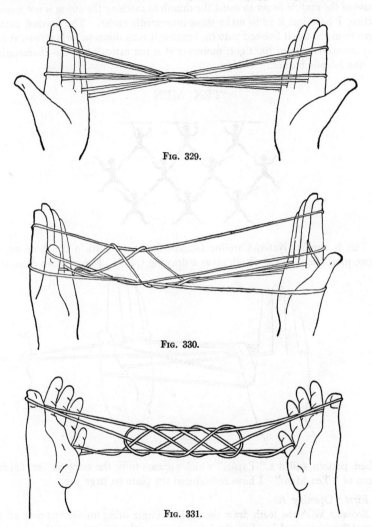

FIG. 329.

FIG. 330.

FIG. 331.

Eighth : Withdraw the index fingers from their loops, turn the hands with the fingers pointing away from you, and extend the figure loosely (Fig. 331). If the strings be drawn tight the pattern cannot be seen.

This is a most interesting and novel figure. The *First* and *Second* movements are unlike anything occurring in other figures. In the *Fourth* and *Seventh* movement, the use of the middle finger to assist the thumb in catching the string is not a native practice; I have put it in to make these movements easier. The finished pattern differs from the usual finished pattern, because it runs down to form a twisted cord if the strings be pulled too tight; moreover it is not extended in the characteristic Caroline Islands fashion.

TEN MEN

This is another Natik, Caroline Islands, figure collected in the same way as the two preceding figures. Roth gives a drawing (pl. VI., Fig. 7) of an Australian

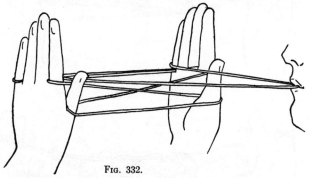

Fig. 332.

finished pattern called a "Turtle," which appears to be the same as the finished pattern of "Ten Men." I have reproduced the plate on page 379.

First : Opening A.

Second : With the teeth draw the far little finger string toward you over all the strings (Fig. 332), and bending the left index over the left string of the loop held by the teeth, pick up from below on the back of the finger the right string of the loop held by the teeth, and return the left index to its position. Bend the right index over to the left, and pick up from below the left string of the loop held by the teeth, and return the right index to its position (Fig. 333). Now release the loop held by the teeth, separate the hands, and draw the strings tight (Fig. 334).

You now have two loops on each index, a loop on each thumb, and a loop on each little finger.

Third: Release the loops from the thumbs, and draw the hands apart.

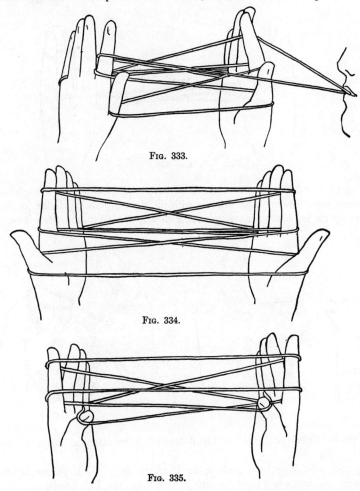

Fig. 333.

Fig. 334.

Fig. 335.

Fourth: Put each thumb away from you, under the index loops, and pick up on the back of the thumb the near little finger string, and return the thumb to its position (Fig. 335).

Fifth : Pass each thumb up over the lower near index string, and put it from below into the upper index loop, and draw the thumb away from the index in order to enlarge the loop now passing around both index and thumb (Fig. 336).

Sixth : With the left thumb and index (or the teeth) pick up the right lower near thumb string close to the right thumb, and draw it over the tip of the thumb

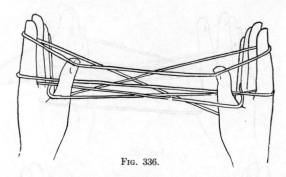

FIG. 336.

(Fig. 337), and let it drop on the palmar side; being careful not to disturb the upper thumb loop.   In the same manner with the right thumb and index (or the teeth) pick up the left lower near thumb string close to the left thumb, draw it over the tip

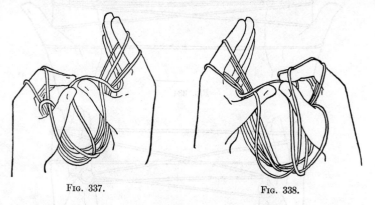

FIG. 337.   FIG. 338.

of the left thumb (Fig. 338), and let it drop on the palmar side.   Separate the hands (Fig. 339).

Seventh : Withdraw each index from the loop which passes around both thumb and index and draw the strings tight (Fig. 340, Left hand).

Eighth : Transfer the thumb loops to the index fingers by putting each index from below into the thumb loop (Fig. 340, Right hand) and withdrawing the thumb (Fig. 341).

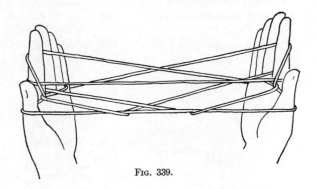

FIG. 339.

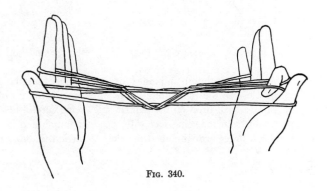

FIG. 340.

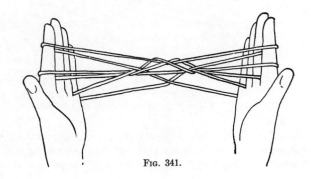

FIG. 341.

Ninth : Put each thumb away from you under the index loops, and pick up on the back of the thumb the near little finger string, and return the thumb to its position (Fig. 342, Left hand).

Tenth : Pass each thumb up over the lower near index string, and put it from below into the upper index loop, and draw the thumb away from the index (Fig.

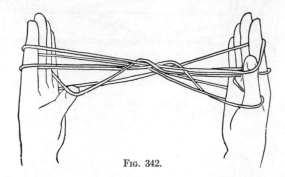

Fig. 342.

342, Right hand) in order to enlarge the loop now passing around both index and thumb (Fig. 343).

Eleventh : With the left thumb and index (or the teeth) pick up the right lower near thumb string close to the right thumb, and draw it over the tip of the right thumb (Fig. 344), and let it drop on the palmar side, being careful not to disturb the upper thumb loop. In the same way with the right thumb and index (or the teeth) pick up the left lower near thumb string close to the left thumb, draw it over

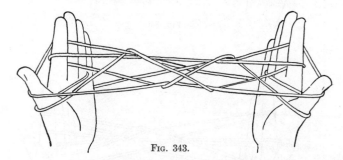

Fig. 343.

the tip of the left thumb (Fig. 345), and let it drop on the palmar side. Separate the hands (Fig. 346).

Twelfth : Bend each middle finger over the upper far index string, and take up from below on the back of the finger the lower near index string (the one passing from index to index) (Fig. 347), and return the middle finger to its position.

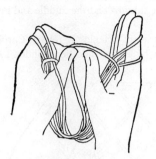

Fig. 344.

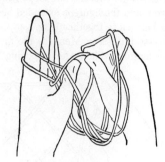

Fig. 345.

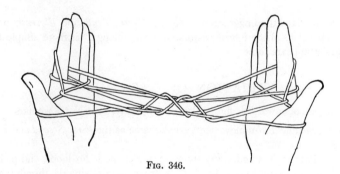

Fig. 346.

Fig. 347.

Thirteenth : Release the loops from the little fingers, and turn the palms away from you, and the figure is extended between the thumbs and the middle and index fingers held close together (Fig. 348).

I have put "Ten Men" as the first of a series of five closely related Caroline Islands figures, which, after Opening A, begin by having additional index loops

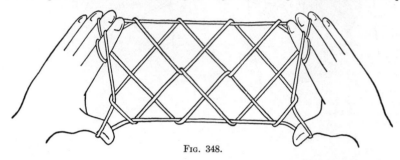

Fig. 348.

formed from the far little finger string. As the *Ninth, Tenth* and *Eleventh* movements are repetitions of the *Fourth, Fifth* and *Sixth,* the figure is more simple than at first sight it appears to be.

A VARIATION OF "TEN MEN"

Dr. Furness obtained this figure also from "Emily," the Natik woman.

First, Second and *Third* movements are the same as the *First, Second* and *Third* of "Ten Men."

Fourth : Pass each thumb away from you under the index loops, and pick up on the back of the thumb the near little finger string, and drawing the thumb toward

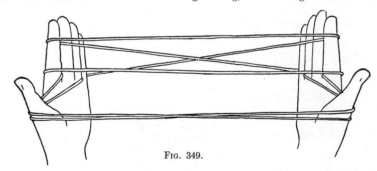

Fig. 349.

you pick up also on its back the lower far index string and return the thumb to its position (Fig. 349).

Fifth : The same as the Fifth of "Ten Men."

Sixth : With the teeth pick up both the right lower near thumb strings close to the right thumb, and draw them over the tip of the thumb, and let them drop on

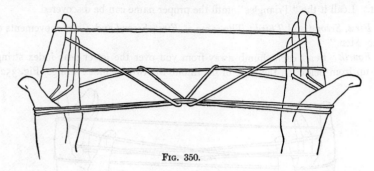

Fig. 350.

the palmar side, being careful not to disturb the upper thumb loop. In the same manner with the teeth draw the two left lower near thumb strings over the tip of the left thumb.

Seventh and *Eighth :* The same as the *Seventh* and *Eighth* of "Ten Men."

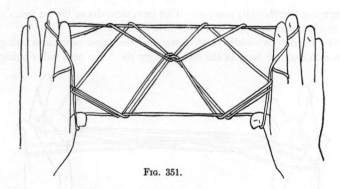

Fig. 351.

Ninth : Repeat the *Fourth* movement (Fig. 350).

Tenth : The same as *Fifth* movement of "Ten Men."

Eleventh : Repeat the *Sixth* movement.

Twelfth and *Thirteenth :* The same as *Twelfth* and *Thirteenth* of "Ten Men" (Fig. 351).

This figure is like "Ten Men"; the difference is produced in the *Fourth* movement, where you draw toward you on the thumb the lower far index string in addition to the near little finger string.

CAROLINE ISLANDS TRIANGLES

The Natik woman, "Emily," who taught Dr. Furness this figure had no name for it. I call it the "Triangles" until the proper name can be discovered.

First, Second and *Third :* The same as *First, Second* and *Third* movements of "Ten Men."

Fourth : Bend each thumb away from you over the lower near index string, pick up from below on the back of the thumb the two far index strings (Fig. 352),

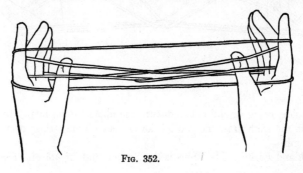

Fig. 352.

and return the thumb to its position. This movement draws the far index strings toward you between the upper and lower near index strings.

Fifth : Bend each middle finger down over the upper near index string, pick up from below on the back of the middle finger the lower near index string (Fig.

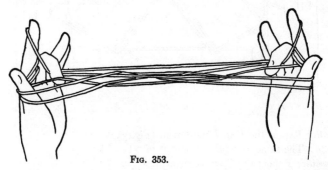

Fig. 353.

353), and return the middle finger to its position. Bend each ring and little finger away from you over the little finger loop, and then down on the palm.

Sixth : Take each thumb out of its loops, and let the loops hang down (Fig. 354). Then pass each thumb away from you through these hanging loops, pick

up from below on the back of the thumb the near index string (Fig. 355, **Left hand**),
which hangs somewhat loosely over the little finger loop, and return the thumb
to its position (Fig. 356).

Seventh : Turn the hands with the palms away from you, and holding **the**
thumbs upright bend the middle fingers over the far middle finger string **and down**

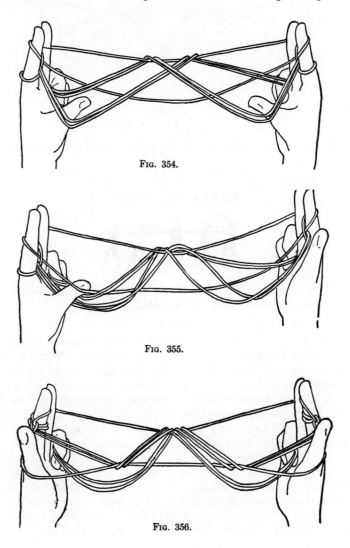

Fig. 354.

Fig. 355.

Fig. 356.

on the palm. Then turn the hands so that the fingers closed on the palms face each other and the finished figure will be formed (Fig. 357).

The only interesting thing about this figure is the method by which the final

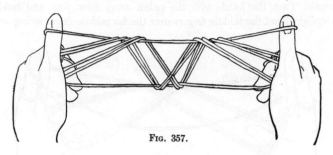

Fɪɢ. 357.

pattern is exhibited; in no other figure is the pattern turned over so that the far side becomes the near side.

CARRYING MONEY

Dr. Furness learned "Carrying Money" from a boy in the Island of Uap, Western Carolines, in 1902. The native name is *Runi-ka-fei*.

First: Form the figure of "Ten Men."

Second: Rest the figure on your lap and slip each thumb out of its loop, and then pick up from below on the back of the thumb, close to the index finger, the string which passed from the thumb to the index (Fig. 358). Gently withdraw each middle finger from its loop, and let the string which passes over each index and thumb slip off the index, and draw the hands apart with the strings on the thumbs and index fingers until the central figure is about two inches in diameter (Fig. 359). Now withdraw the thumbs and index fingers, and let the figure lie flat on the lap, or a table, with the four loops radiating from the central circle.

Third: Without disturbing the figure, pick up with the left thumb and index the far string of the right near loop about two inches from the central figure, and pick up with the right thumb and index the same string about two inches farther to the right; and form a small, flat circle in the string by passing the string held by the right thumb and index under the string held by the left thumb and index; the point where the strings cross should be toward you. Lay the ring down, and with the

STONE MONEY OF UAP, WESTERN CAROLINE ISLANDS.

(From the paper by Dr. W. H. Furness, 3rd, in Transactions, Department of Archæology, University of Pennsylvania, Vol. I, No. 1, p. 51, Fig. 3, 1904.)

DAKOFEL, A UAP GIRL.

(Courtesy of Dr. William Henry Furness, 3rd.)

left thumb and index pick up the end of the right far loop and, without twisting the strings, thread the whole loop from below through the small circle formed on the far string of the right near loop and put the far loop back into its former place.

With the left thumb and index pick up the near string of the right far loop about two inches to the right of the ring through which it has just been threaded, and with

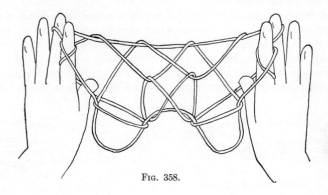

FIG. 358.

the right thumb and index pick up the same string about two inches farther on to the right; in the same way as before, make a similar circle in this string by passing the string held by the right thumb and index *over* the string held by the left thumb and index; in this circle the cross of the strings should be away from you. Pick up

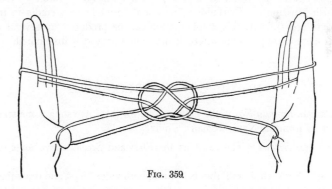

FIG. 359.

with the left thumb and index the right near loop, and, without twisting the strings, thread the whole loop from above and away from you through the circle just formed in the near string of the right far loop, and put it back in its place on your lap.

In the same manner put a similar loop on the far string of the left near loop and thread the left far loop through it; and put a similar loop on the near string of the left far loop, and thread the near loop through it (Fig. 360). The central figure represents a piece of Caroline Islands Money—a large circular slab of stone—and the four little circles are the natives who are carrying the money on a pole passing through the middle of the slab.

This is the only example I am able to give of a final figure which is made by taking the loops from the fingers and then arranging the strings, as it were, artificially.

As this particular figure was shown to Dr. Furness by a young boy, one might reasonably suspect that there is another way of doing it which he did not know; but I have seen an Eskimo make a figure in a similar manner and it is possible that the finished figures (which I give farther on) from the Nauru, or Pleasant, Island of

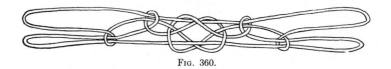

Fig. 360.

the Marshall Islands, were, to some extent, made artificially. Obviously, figures formed in this way are less interesting than those developed entirely on the hands.

The figure produced by the *Second* movement (Fig. 359) occurs among the finished patterns from Australia given by Roth (pl. x, Fig. 1) see page 383; and Edge-Partington figures (pl. 341, 1) a similar pattern from Torres Straits, preserved in the British Museum (A. C. Haddon Collection) entitled "cat's-cradle in the form of a mouth (*good*)." As this simple pattern can be produced by several entirely different methods, it probably will be found to be very widely distributed.

HOUSE OF THE BLOS–BIRD

Palangan-im-mun-blos is the native name for this interesting game secured by Dr. Furness from the Natik woman "Emily."

First and *Second :* The same as the *First* and *Second* movements of "Ten Men."

Third : Put each thumb from below into both index loops, and draw the thumb toward you in order to make the loop wider. Turn the middle, ring and little fingers of each hand away from you down over both strings of the little finger loop, and then, keeping the strings taut, turn the hands with the palms facing each other and then facing upward, to bring these three fingers toward you and up through the two loops passing around the thumb and index.

Let the far index strings slip over the knuckles of the middle, ring and little fingers to the back of the hand; straighten these fingers to release the little finger

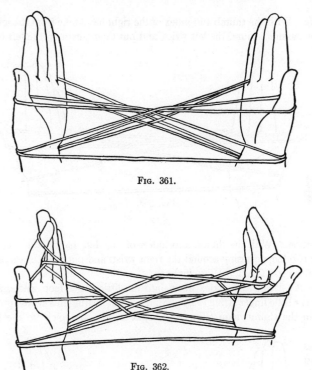

FIG. 361.

FIG. 362.

strings held under them, the loop itself, however, remaining on the little finger. Let the former index loops slip down on the wrists. Draw the strings tight (Fig. 361).

Fourth : Bend each index down into the little finger loop, and draw toward you the near little finger string, then still holding this string put the index down into the thumb loop (Fig. 362, Right hand), and pick up the far thumb string by turning the palm away from you and straightening the index (Fig. 362, Left hand). Separate the hands (Fig. 363).

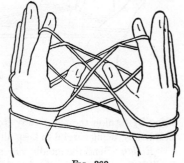

FIG. 363.

Fifth : Withdraw the thumbs from their loops, and transfer each index loop to the thumb by putting the thumb from below into it and withdrawing the index (Fig. 364).

Sixth : With the thumb and index of the right hand take from the left hand the two loops passing around the left wrist, and put them again on the left hand in the

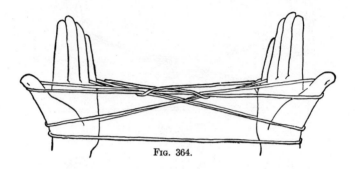

FIG. 364.

First Position.   With the thumb and index of the left hand] take from the right hand the two loops passing around the right wrist, and put them again on the right hand in the First Position (Fig. 365).

Seventh : Bend each index down into the little finger loop, and draw toward you the near little finger string (Fig. 366), then, still holding this string, put the index down into the thumb loop (Fig. 367, Right hand), and pick up the far thumb

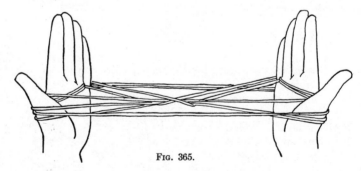

FIG. 365.

string by turning the palm away from you and straightening the index (Fig. 367, Left hand), being careful to keep all the strings on the thumbs.

Eighth : Bend the middle, ring and little fingers of each hand down over all the far little finger strings, and bring the two far little finger strings that pass directly from hand to hand, forward, toward you, until they touch the rest of the figure held extended between the index fingers and the thumbs (Fig. 368).

Ninth : Carefully withdraw each thumb from its loops, and insert it again **into**

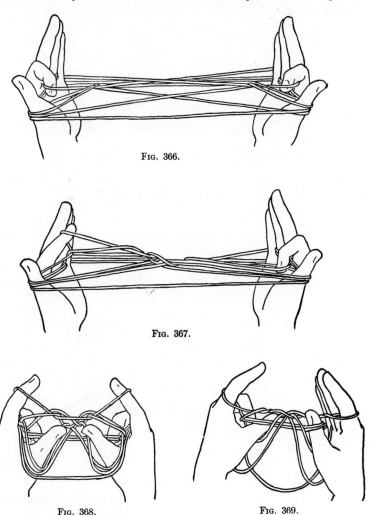

Fig. 366.

Fig. 367.

Fig. 368. Fig. 369.

the loops, but from the near side and away from you, and pick up on the back of the thumb the two straight strings held toward you by the middle finger (Fig. 369,

Left hand), and pull them down through the loops (Fig. 369, Right hand) by restoring the thumb to its original position (Fig. 370).

Tenth : Remove all the loops from the little fingers.   This can be readily done by pushing them off one little finger with the other little finger.

Eleventh : Transfer the index loops to the little fingers by picking up the near index string of one hand with the thumb and index of the other hand, and placing

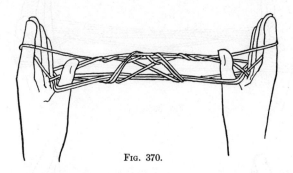

Fɪɢ. 370.

the loop on the little finger, so that, without any twisting, the near index string becomes the far little finger string of the same hand (Fig. 371).

Twelfth : Find the far thumb string which passes directly from thumb to thumb (it often hangs down loosely), and pick it up on the tip of each index finger to form the ridge pole of the "house" (Fig. 372).   The figure is extended between the

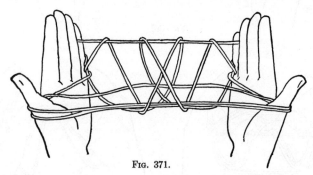

Fɪɢ. 371.

thumbs and the index and little fingers, with the palms facing each other and the fingers directed upward.

Just what a "blos-bird" is, I am unable to say, but it has a house and a very pretty one at that.

The method of transferring the index loops to the wrists, observed in the *Third* movement, is peculiar to this figure; a single index loop is transferred in the same manner in the two figures which follow immediately.

The *Fourth* movement is interesting because of its resemblance to the Torres Straits "King Fish," but in that figure the index is put first into the thumb loop and then into the little finger loop, and the movement is confined to the right hand.

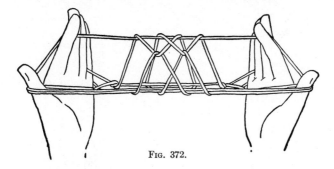

FIG. 372.

We shall see the Torres Straits movement done in the next figure, the "Three Stars," but done with both hands. The *Eighth* and *Ninth* movements are foreshadowed in the *Sixth* movement of the "Triangles." Of course, the *Eleventh* movement can be done by the little fingers; it requires some dexterity.

THREE STARS

Dr. Furness was taught *Dilipi-tuf*, or "Three Stars," by a Uap girl of thirteen, named "Dakofel."

First : Opening A.

Second : Put each thumb from below into the index loop, and draw the thumb away from the index to make the loop wider. Turn the middle, ring and little fingers, of each hand away from you, down over both strings of the little finger loop, then, keeping the strings drawn tight, turn the hands with the palms facing each other and then facing upward, in order to bring these three fingers toward you and up through the loop passing around both thumb and index; let the far index string slip over the knuckles of the middle, ring and little fingers to the back of the hand; straighten these fingers to release the little finger strings held under them, the little finger loop itself remaining on that finger. Let the former index loop slip down on the wrist and draw the strings tight.

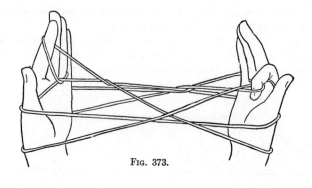

FIG. 373.

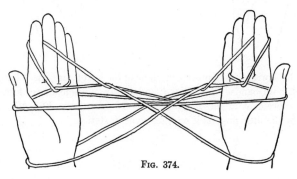

FIG. 374.

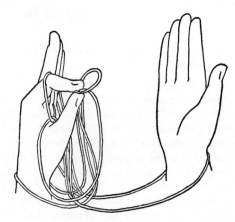

FIG. 375.   FIG. 376.

Third : Bend each index down into the thumb loop, and draw away from you the far thumb string; then put the index, still holding the thumb string, down into the little finger loop (Fig. 373, Right hand), and pick up on its tip the near little finger string, by curving the finger toward you and up to its usual position (Fig. 373, Left hand, and Fig. 374).

Fourth : Turn the right hand with the palm facing you, and with the thumb and index of the left hand pick up together the right near index string and the right far thumb string, just where they cross on the right palm (Fig. 375). Withdraw the right hand from all the loops except the wrist loop (Fig. 376). The left thumb and index are now holding two loops—a long near one (the former right thumb loop) and a smaller far one (the former right index loop). Put the right little finger away from you, and from the near side, through the long loop only (Fig. 377), and put the right thumb above and to the right side of the near string of the loop now on the right little finger, and then toward you, and from the far side, through the smaller loop only (Fig. 378).

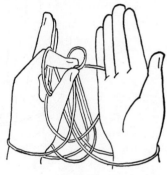

Fig. 377.

Keeping the strings securely on the right hand, turn the left hand with the palm toward you, and with the thumb and index of the right hand pick up together the left near index string and the left far thumb

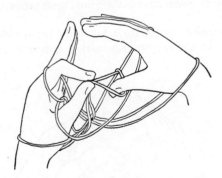

Fig. 378.

Fig. 379.

string, just where they cross on the left palm (Fig. 379). Withdraw the left hand from all its loops except the wrist loop. The right thumb and index are now holding two loops: a long near loop (the former left thumb loop) and a smaller far loop (the former left index loop) (Fig. 380).

Put the left little finger, from the near side, through the long loop (Fig. 381), and put the left thumb above and to the left side of the near string of the loop

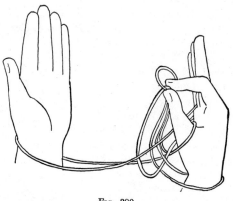

FIG. 380.

now on the left little finger, and then, toward you and from the far side, through the smaller loop (Fig. 382). Separate the hands (Fig. 383).

Fifth : Repeat the *Third* and *Fourth* movements and the figure assumes the appearance shown in Fig. 384.

Sixth : Repeat the *Third* and *Fourth* movements and the central figure becomes more complicated (Fig. 385).

Seventh : Repeat the *Third* movement. Turn the hands perfectly flat with the palms facing upward. You now have a loop on each index, a loop on each

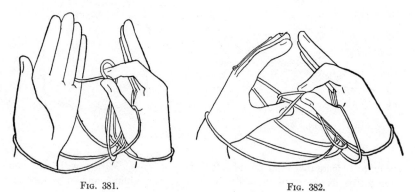

FIG. 381.   FIG. 382.

finger with the loop on each little finger. The movement here is somewhat like that of opening the hand in "Opening A." The effect of drawing the string tight is to free for an instant the little finger loops, permitting the middle three strings to slip on the string of the loop. The string now appears in the manner of Fig. 383.

Then drawing the loops tight, release the thumbs, when the string will

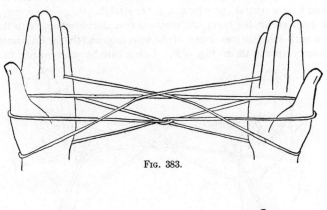

FIG. 383.

assume the form shown in Fig. 384. Finally release the index fingers when

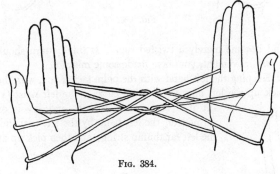

FIG. 384.

the string will be found to have formed the figure of the "three stars," as shown in Fig. 385. It must be confessed, however, that it requires a little fancy to make out the figure. In the accompanying illustration (Fig. 385) the three stars do not show quite as well as they often do. When the string is drawn very tightly, the tips of the little "loops" are drawn together and better represent the stars than in the illustration, where they appear too open.

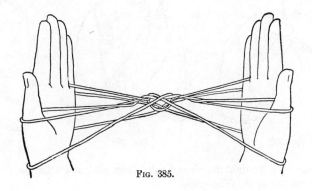

FIG. 385.

thumb and a loop on each wrist. If the movements have been properly performed, you should have a central figure formed of two straight strings (the upper, the common far index string, the lower, the common near thumb string), with three other strings on each side (the two strings of the wrist loop and the far little finger string) looped loosely around them (Fig. 386). Unless care be observed this pattern will

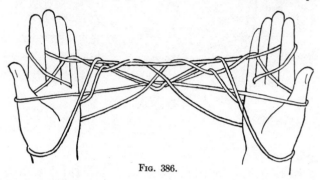

FIG. 386.

slip easily and become merely a twisted rope. If this pattern should not appear after the *Seventh* movement, you have made some mistake.

Eighth : Keeping the left hand with the palm facing you, with the right thumb and index pick up the left near wrist string close to the left wrist (Fig. 387), and lift it over the left thumb, and lay it over the cross formed on the left palm by the left near index string and the left far thumb string; and then pick up at this cross all

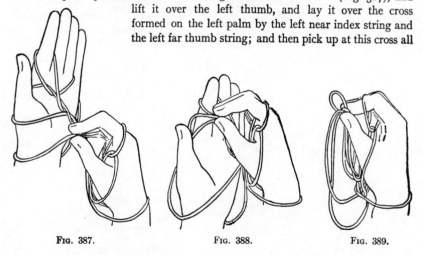

FIG. 387.   FIG. 388.   FIG. 389.

three strings with the right thumb and index (Fig. 388), and withdraw the left hand entirely from the figure (Fig. 389).

The right thumb and index are now holding three hanging loops, a near loop (the former left thumb loop), a middle loop (the former left wrist loop) and a far loop (the former left index loop). Put the left little finger, from the near side,

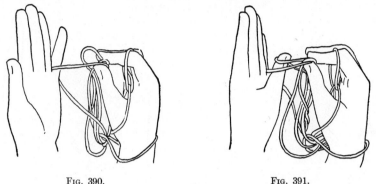

Fig. 390.   Fig. 391.

through the near loop only (Fig. 390), and put the left thumb, from the near side, through the near loop and the far loop, but *not* through the middle loop (Fig. 391). Turn the left hand up to hold the loops on the fingers. Turn the right hand with the palm toward you, and with the left thumb and index pick up the right near wrist string (Fig. 392), close to the right wrist, and lift it over the right thumb and lay

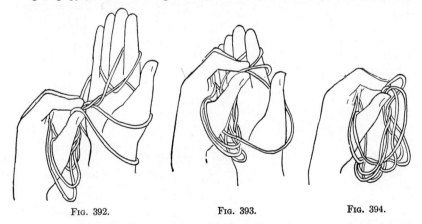

Fig. 392.   Fig. 393.   Fig. 394.

it over the cross formed on the right palm by the right far thumb string and the right near index string, and pick up at this cross all three strings with the left thumb and index (Fig. 393), and withdraw the right hand entirely from the figure (Fig. 394). The left thumb and index are now holding three hanging loops: a near loop (the former right thumb loop), a middle loop (the former right wrist loop) and a far loop (the former right index loop). Put the right little finger through the near loop, from the near side (Fig. 395), and put the right thumb, from the near side,

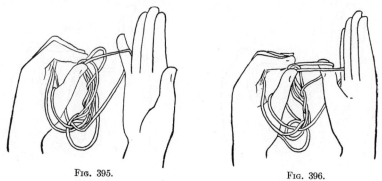

FIG. 395.   FIG. 396.

through the near loop and the far loop, but *not* through the middle loop (Fig. 396). Turn the hands with their palms facing you, but do not draw the strings very tight (Fig. 397).

Ninth : Bend each index down, and take up on the back of the index the far thumb string (not the palmar string) (Fig. 398), and, pressing the thumb against the index to hold the string in place, straighten the index, turn the palm away from

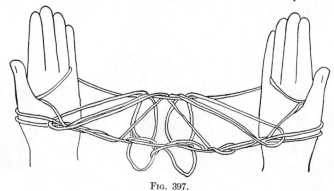

FIG. 397.

you, and press down with the middle, ring and little fingers the far little finger string in order to extend the figure (Fig. 399).

If the "Three Stars" be not at once distinct, they can be worked into shape by alternately turning the palms toward you and away from you, keeping the positions of the strings on the fingers unchanged.

"Three Stars" is one of the longest of all the figures; there is so much repetition, however, that it is really not very difficult. The *Second* movement is similar to the *Third* movement of the "House of the Blos-Bird." The *Third* movement is like a movement in the Torres Straits "King Fish." The *Fourth* and *Eighth* movements

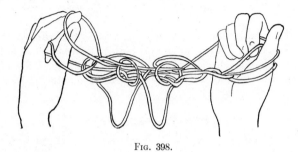

Fig. 398.

are peculiar to this figure; there are, however, analogous movements in the Caroline Islands "Coral."

The final extension of the pattern is found in a number of the Caroline Islands figures ("Three Stars," "Coral," "Two Chiefs," "One Chief," "Diamonds," "Turtle"), and in no others. It is very essential that the thumb be pressed close

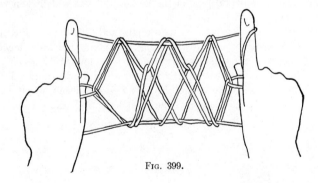

Fig. 399.

to the index, to hold in place the string which passes from the back of the thumb upward, around the tip of the index, otherwise part of the extension by means of the thumb will be lost.

NO NAME

This Natik figure, which I have called "No Name," was shown Dr. Furness by the woman "Emily."

First and *Second*: The same as the *First* and *Second* movements of "Three Stars."

Third: Then follow the *Fourth, Fifth, Sixth, Seventh, Eighth, Ninth* and *Tenth* movements of the "House of the Blos-Bird." Remember that in this figure there is only one loop on each wrist, whereas there are two in the "House of the Blos-Bird," therefore where two loops or strings are referred to in the *Sixth, Eighth* and

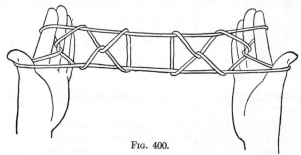

Fig. 400.

Ninth movements of the "House of the Blos-Bird," you will find in this figure only a single loop or string.

The figure is extended between the thumbs and little fingers (Fig. 400). By alternately bringing together and separating the thumb and little finger of each hand, the two parts of the figure can be made to move toward the hands.

This figure reminds us of the "Two Coyotes" of the Navahos. I have been particularly interested in "No Name" because I worked it out myself while trying to make variations on the "House of the Blos-Bird," and before I knew that Dr. Furness had collected it in the Caroline Islands.

CORAL

The native name of this figure is *Melang*. Dr. Furness obtained it from a native woman called "Lemet," who was a "Mispil" (a woman of the long-house) in the village of *Dulukan* in Uap.

First: Opening A.

Second: Turn the hands with the palms toward you, draw the strings tight and close the four fingers on the palm over all the strings except the near thumb

LEMET, A UAP WOMAN.
(Courtesy of Dr. William Henry Furness, 3rd.)

A NATIVE OF PORT MORESBY, NEW GUINEA.
(Courtesy of Dr. A. C. Haddon.)

string (Fig. 401). Now, by turning each hand down and then up toward you under the near thumb string, you can put this string on the backs of the four fingers. Unclose the hands (Fig. 402).

Third : Pass each thumb up on the far side of the string which, passing between

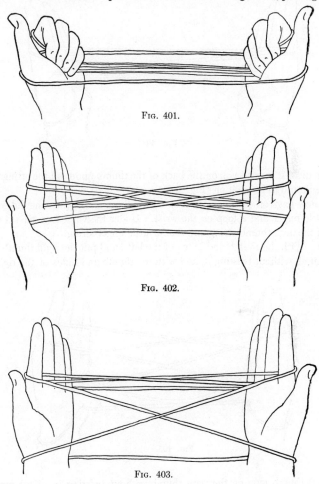

FIG. 401.

FIG. 402.

FIG. 403.

the thumb and index, crosses the back of the four fingers, and let the loop slip down on the wrist (Fig. 403).

Fourth : Incline the hands slightly toward each other, and keeping the strings tight, turn the palms away from you, and pass each thumb under both the near and far wrist strings (Fig. 404), and up into the little finger loop, then catch each far little finger string on the side of the thumb and, turning the palms toward each other

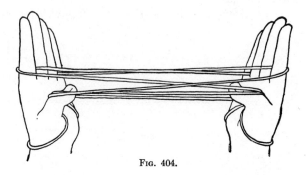

FIG. 404.

(Fig. 405), draw it toward you on the back of the thumb under all the strings as you return the thumb to its position (Fig. 406).

You now have on each hand: a loop on the thumb, a loop on the index, a loop on the little finger and a loop on the wrist. Under the wrist loop passes a string formed of the near thumb string and the far little finger string.

Fifth : With the thumb and index of the left hand put the right thumb loop on the left thumb without twisting it, and with the thumb and index of the right hand

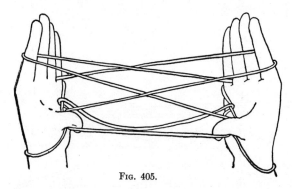

FIG. 405.

put the left thumb loop on the right thumb without twisting it. This movement simply exchanges the thumb loops (Fig. 407).

Sixth : Pass each thumb away from you over the far thumb string and both strings of the index loop, and take up from below on the back of the thumb the near little finger string, and return the thumb to its position (Fig. 408).

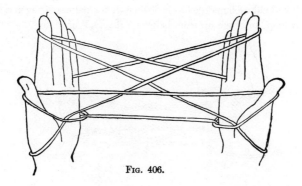

Fig. 406.

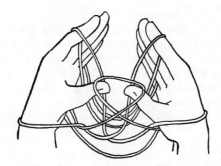

Fig. 407.

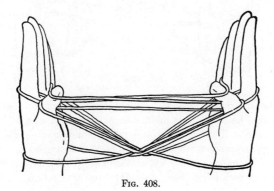

Fig. 408.

Seventh : Bend each middle finger down over the palmar string and both strings of the index loop, and take up from below on the back of the middle finger the far

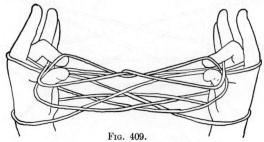

FIG. 409.

thumb string (not the palmar string) (Fig. 409), and return the middle finger to its position (Fig. 410).

Eighth : Release the loops from the thumbs and little fingers˙ and draw the hands apart, but do not draw the strings too tight (Fig. 411).

You should now have a loop high up on each middle finger, a loop around the base of each index and a loop on each wrist. The central figure has the shape of a kite; it should be large or the final figure will not be successful.

Ninth : Turn the hands with the palms up, and with the left thumb and index pick up from the edge of the right wrist the right near wrist string (Fig. 412), and, slipping it out over the thumb and index, place it on the middle finger beside the

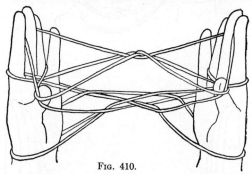

FIG. 410.

near middle finger string (Fig. 413). Now, with the left thumb and index pick up both these strings from the right middle finger, and slip the right hand out of all the loops (Fig. 414). The left thumb and index are now holding two hanging loops; one loop is large and projects farther to the right than the smaller one. Put the right little finger away from you through the wide loop only, and put the right thumb away from you through both loops (Fig. 415), and turn the hand up. You now have a

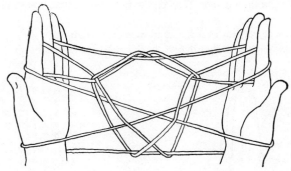

Fig. 411.

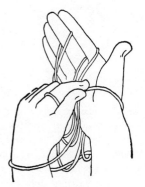

Fig. 412.

Fig. 413

Fig. 414.

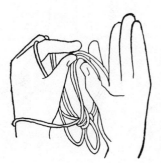

Fig. 415.

loop on the right thumb and a loop on the right hand in the "First Position" (Fig. 416).

In the same way turn the left hand with the palm up, and with the right thumb and index pick up from the edge of the left wrist the left near wrist string and lay

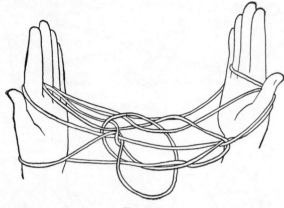

FIG. 416.

it on the side of the left middle finger beside the left near middle finger string. Now with the right thumb and index pick up both these strings, and withdraw the left hand from all its loops. The right thumb and index are holding two hanging loops; put the left little finger away from you through the wide loop only, and put the left thumb away from you through both loops, and turn the hand up, but do not draw the strings tight; only sufficiently to pull out any hanging loops (Fig. 417).

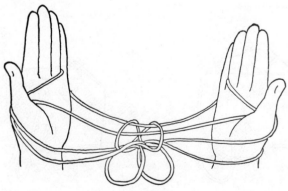

FIG. 417.

Tenth : Bend each index finger down and hold the far thumb string between its first joint and the first joint of the thumb; then pick up from below on the side of the tip of the index the far thumb string (not the palmar string) (Fig. 418). Now, holding the thumb close to the index, curve the index toward you and up, at the same time turning the palms away from you and holding down the far little finger

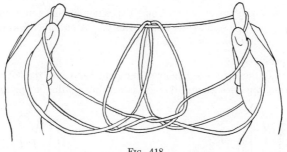

Fig. 418.

string with the middle, ring and little fingers of each hand (Fig. 419). Separate the hands and draw the strings tight.

The final pattern is difficult to form and requires practice. Some working of the strings is usually needed at the end of the last movement to bring out the branching "Coral."

In this figure the *Second* movement is like the movement in the "Leashing of Lochiel's Dogs." The method of catching the far little finger string, seen in the *Third* movement, is peculiar to this figure. You have probably noticed that the

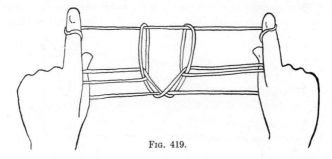

Fig. 419.

thumb loops exchanged in the *Third* movement are not similar to finger loops exchanged in preceding figures, because the same string forms the far string of each thumb loop.

The *Ninth* movement is not very unlike the *Eighth* movement of "Three Stars."

A MAN

I was shown this figure at the St. Louis Exposition in November, 1904, by the two Navaho girls, Zah Tso and her sister, who taught me other Navaho figures. The Navaho name is *Dĕnnĕ*, or *Hastinĕ dĕnnĕ*.

First : Opening A.

Second : With the thumb and index of the right hand turn the left near index string away from you once around the left index, thus putting a ring around that

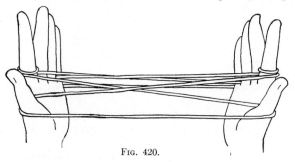

FIG. 420.

finger in addition to the left index loop.   In like manner with the thumb and index of the left hand turn the right near index string around the right index (Fig. 420).

Third : Take up from below on the tip of the right index the ring around the left index and separate the hands (Fig. 421).   Keep the loop just drawn out near

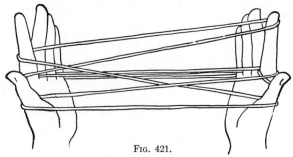

FIG. 421.

the tip of the right index, as it is absolutely necessary throughout these movements to keep the different index loops distinct.   See that on the left index the original

loop (the one with the near string going to the far side of the right thumb) is above
the other loop—about half-way up on the finger; and keep the loops in place by
pressing the side of the left middle finger against the side of the left index.   Now,
take up from below on the tip of the left index the ring around the right index,

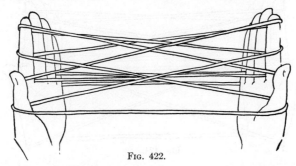

FIG. 422.

and draw the hands apart (Fig. 422).   Keep this new left index loop up at the
tip of the index.   See that the original right index loop (the one with the near
string going to the far side of the left thumb) is placed on the right index half-
way up, and between the other two loops.

You now have a loop on each thumb, a loop on each little finger and three
loops on each index finger; the near strings of these three loops must cross one
another as follows: the near strings of the top loops cross each other to become the

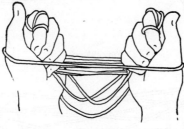

FIG. 423.

near strings of the lower loops; the near strings of the middle loop cross lower
down over the near strings of the lower loop and still lower they cross each other.

Fourth : Keeping the loops in these relative positions on each index, by pressing
the middle finger and index together, carefully turn the hands with the palms
toward you, and close the four fingers down on the palm, over all the strings except
the near thumb string (Fig. 423).   Throw this near thumb string away from you
over the hands and let it fall down on the backs of the hands.   Now return each
hand to its usual position, and put each thumb up under the near string of the

loop you have just put on the back of the hand, and let the whole loop slip down around the wrist (Fig. 424).

Fifth : Pass each thumb away from you under both strings of the wrist loop

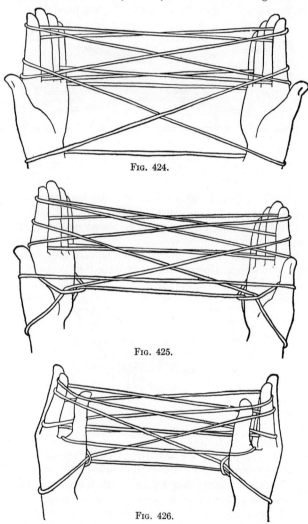

Fig. 424.

Fig. 425.

Fig. 426.

and pick up on the back of the thumb, from the far side, the far little finger string, and return the thumb to its position (Fig. 425).

You now have on each hand, (1) a loop on the wrist; (2) a loop on the thumb formed of a straight near string and a far string crossing the palm under the strings

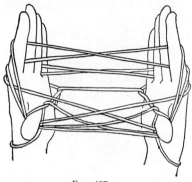

FIG. 427.

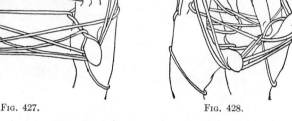

FIG. 428.

of the wrist loop; (3) a loop on the little finger, formed of the palmar string and a near little finger string which becomes the lower far index string; (4) three loops on the index with their six near strings crossing one another as follows: the upper strings cross each other, and then, becoming the strings of the lower loops, run under the middle strings; the middle strings cross over the lower strings, and then cross each other. This arrangement of the near strings of the index loops is essential to the success of the figure.

Sixth : Put each thumb up on the far side of the near string of the middle loop, close to the point where it crosses the same string from the other index, then on the near side of the lower near index string, and then on the far side of the upper near index string (Fig. 426), and separate the thumb from the index to widen out these index loops (Fig. 427).

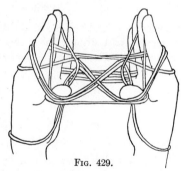

FIG. 429.

Of the three strings now passing around each thumb the two upper form two crosses between the thumbs, and the lower runs directly from thumb to thumb.

Seventh : Bend each middle finger toward you down over all the index strings (not over the strings passing from the back of the thumb to the back of the index), and pick up from below close to the thumb, the lower far thumb string (the string which becomes the palmar string) (Fig. 428), and return the middle finger to its position (Fig. 429). It is necessary to pick the string up at a point between the thumb and the place where it is crossed by the near wrist string.

Eighth : Release the loops from the thumbs, the index fingers, and the little fingers and draw the hands apart (Fig. 430).

I have put this figure next to the "Coral" because, although a Navaho figure, it closely resembles that Caroline Islands figure.

In some respects "Man" is the most difficult of all the games, not because of its length, but because of the necessity of arranging the loops properly on the index fingers, and keeping them so arranged, throughout several very active movements.

The rings placed around the index fingers by the *Second* movement are peculiar to this figure. The transfer of the thumb loops to the wrists is similar to the

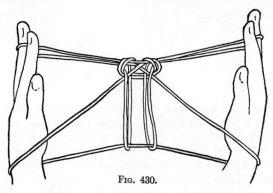

Fig. 430.

transfer in "Coral," as is also the drawing of the far little finger string toward you under the wrist strings; but in this figure the string is picked up from below, not from above. The *Seventh* movement is like the *Seventh* movement of "Coral."

TWO CHIEFS

"Two Chiefs" was secured by Dr. Furness from a man in Uap, probably a native of the village of Dulukan. The native name is *Logaru-pilun.*

First : Put the loop on the hands in the "First Position," but with the two strings between the hands crossed.

Second : Opening A.

Third : With the back of each thumb take up, from below, the near index string, and return the thumb to its former position (Fig. 431).

Fourth : With the left thumb and index lift the right lower near thumb string over the right upper near thumb string, and then over the tip of the right thumb, and let it drop on the palmar side. With the right thumb and index lift the left lower near thumb string over the left upper near thumb string, then over the tip of the left thumb (Fig. 432), and let it drop on the palmar side.

Fifth: Bend each little finger down toward you, and pick up from below on

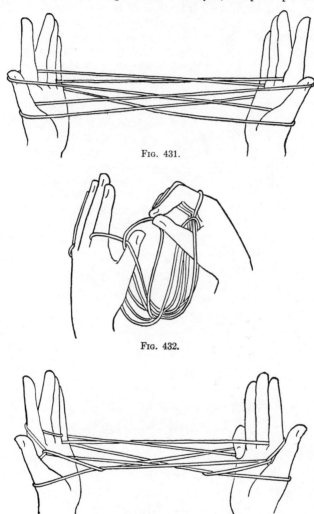

Fig. 431.

Fig. 432.

Fig. 433.

the back of the finger the far index string (Fig. 433, Right hand), and return the little finger to its position (Fig. 433, Left hand).

Sixth : With the left thumb and index lift the right lower far little finger string over the tip of the right little finger, and drop it on the palmar side, without disturbing the upper right far little finger string (Fig. 434). In like manner with the right thumb and index lift the left lower far little finger string over the tip of the

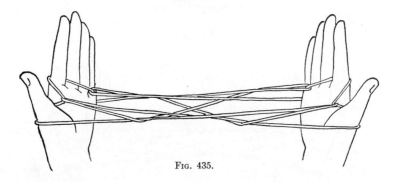

left little finger and let it drop. Separate the hands (Fig. 435).

Seventh : Release the loops from the index fingers. There is now a single loop on each thumb and a loop on each little finger.

Eighth : Bring the hands together with the points of the fingers almost touching, and put the left little finger loop on the right little finger, and put the left thumb loop on the right thumb (Fig. 436), and remove the left hand.

Ninth : Turn the right hand with the palm toward you, and insert the left thumb toward you into both loops hang-

Fig. 434.

ing on the right little finger (Fig. 437), and withdraw the right little finger. Put the hands in their usual positions, the palms facing each other, and let the strings hang loosely between them (Fig. 438).

There are now two loops on each thumb; the upper loop should be near the tip of the thumb, the lower loop down at its base. Take up from below on the tip of

Fig. 435.

each index the upper far thumb string; keep it on the tip of the index (Fig. 439, Left hand), and press down with the other fingers the lower far thumb string.

Then turn the palms away from you, and straighten the index fingers. Hold the upper string which passes from each thumb to the index securely in position,

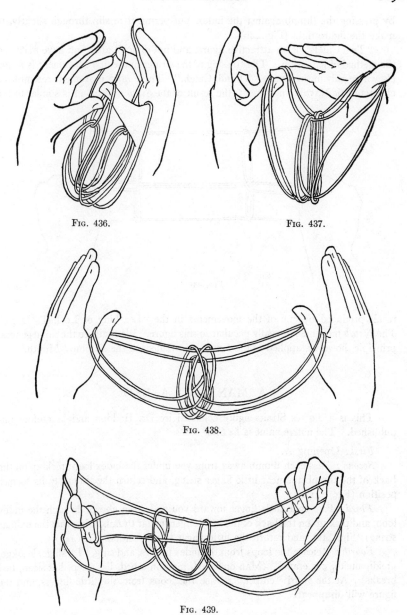

Fig. 436.

Fig. 437.

Fig. 438.

Fig. 439.

by pressing the thumb against the index, but permit it to slip through slightly, to make the figure tight (Fig. 440).

"Two Chiefs" is an attractive figure, and not difficult after you have mastered the method of extension. The crossing of the strings in the first movement is found elsewhere only in the Osage "Thumb Catch." The *Fourth* movement resembles a characteristic Navaho movement; the result of the *Sixth* movement is similar to the

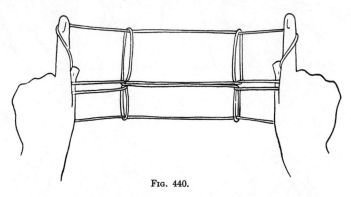

FIG. 440.

result produced by one of the movements in the "Leashing of Lochiel's Dogs." The *Ninth* movement is really peculiar to this figure. We shall see the same general principle, however, applied to the *Seventh* movement of the Eskimo "Mouth."

A MAN AND A BED

This is a Torres Straits figure collected by Dr. Haddon and heretofore un-published. The native name is *Le Sik*.

First : Opening A.

Second : Pass each thumb away from you under the index loop; pick up on the back of the thumb the near little finger string, and return the thumb to its former position (Fig. 441).

Third : Pass each little finger toward you and, from above, through the index loop, and pick up on the back of the little finger the far thumb string (*not* the palmar string) (Fig. 442), and return the little finger to its position (Fig. 443).

Fourth : Release the loops from the index fingers, and sing, "Le sikge, le sikge, uteidi, uteidi, sik erapei" (Man on a bed, man on a bed, lies sleep, lies sleep, bed breaks). At the word "erapei," release the loops from the little fingers, and the figure will disappear.

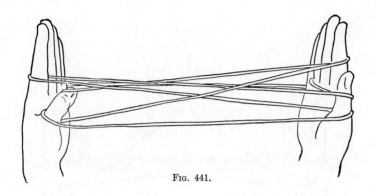

Fig. 441.

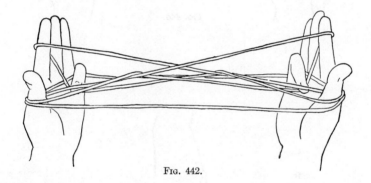

Fig. 442.

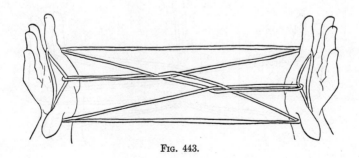

Fig. 443.

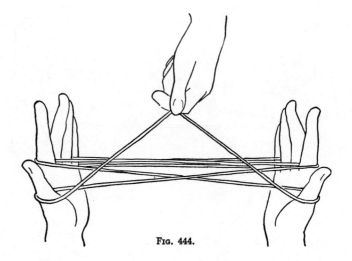

Fig. 444.

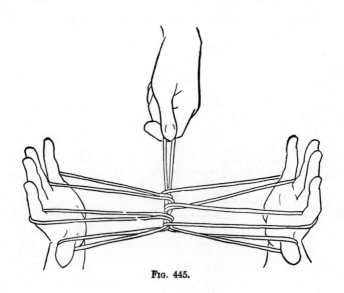

Fig. 445.

A PALM TREE

This is another unpublished Torres Straits figure procured by Dr. Haddon. The native name is *U*.

First : Opening A.

Second : A second person catches the middle of the near thumb string and draws it away from you over all the other strings (Fig. 444).

Third : Exchange the loops on the little fingers, passing the right loop over the left loop.

Fourth : Exchange the loops on the index fingers, passing the right loop over the left loop.

Fifth : Draw the hands toward you to pull tight the loop held by the second person, and work the strings to form the crown of the palm tree (Fig. 445).

In Torres Straits this figure is formed by one person. After Opening A, the four fingers of each hand are passed from above into the thumb loop and closed over all the strings except the near thumb string, to hold them tight. The hands are then turned with the fingers directed away from the body and the *toe* is passed up and put from the far side into the thumb loop to catch the near thumb string and pull it down.

A CANOE WITH TWO MASTS

The native name in Torres Straits is *Nar*. The figure was secured by Dr. Haddon, who has given me his unpublished description of it.

First : Opening A.

Second : A second person passes his hand toward you over the far little finger string and under the crossed far index strings, and picking up the two near index strings where they cross (Fig. 446), pulls them away from you through the figure (Fig. 447).

Third : Bend the right middle finger and pass it from above through the right

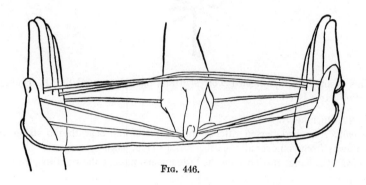

Fig. 446.

ring-like index loop (Fig 448). Then, with the left thumb and index, pull the right near index string to the left, so that you can pick up from below on the back of the

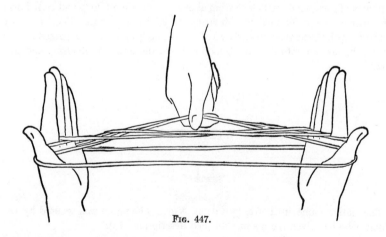

Fig. 447.

right middle finger the right far thumb string (Fig. 449). Return the middle finger to its position and drop the string held by the left thumb and index. In the same

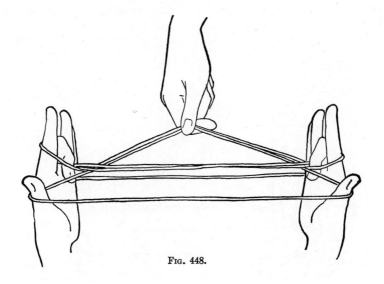

FIG. 448.

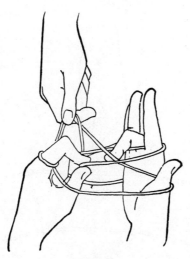

FIG. 449.

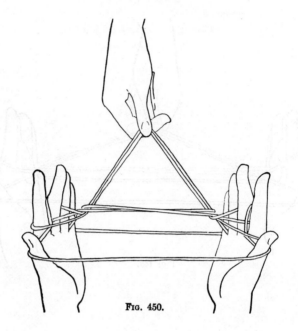

FIG. 450.

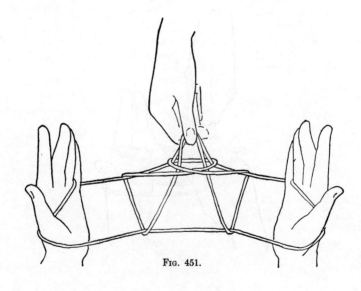

FIG. 451.

manner, bend the left middle finger and pass it from above through the left ring-like index loop. Then with the right thumb and index pull the left near index string to

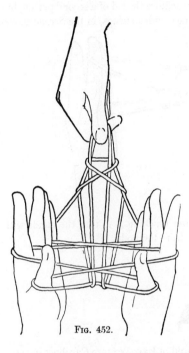

FIG. 452.

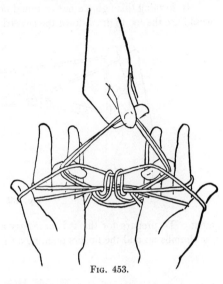

FIG. 453.

the right, and pick up from below on the back of the left middle finger the left far thumb string; return the middle finger to its position and drop the string held by the right thumb and index (Fig. 450).

Fourth: Release the loops from the little fingers, the index fingers and the thumbs. Arrange each middle finger loop on the hand in the "First Position" (Fig. 451). The second person must *not* release the loops he has been holding.

Fifth: From Opening A (Fig. 452).

Sixth: Pass both middle fingers from below into the loops held by the second person, and bending them toward you pick up from below on their backs the near thumb string (Fig. 453); then, by straightening the middle fingers, draw this string away from you and down through the loops held by the second person.

Seventh: The second person now releases the loops he has been holding (Fig. 454)

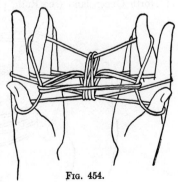

FIG. 454.

and you release the loops from the thumbs and index fingers, and draw the strings tight to extend the figure (Fig. 455)

In forming this figure a native would not require the aid of a second person, but would use the toe to draw down the crossed near index strings, in the *Second* move-

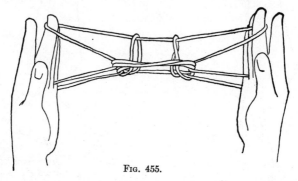

FIG. 455.

ment. To prepare for this it is necessary after Opening A to turn the hands with the thumbs up and the fingers pointing away from the body.

A HOUSE

Dr. Furness collected this figure in the Island of Uap, Western Carolines in 1902, from the same little boy who taught him "Carrying Money." The native name is *Naun*. The pattern is known to the Maoris of New Zealand, and to the blacks of North Queensland (see Roth, plate xii, Figs. 4, 5, reproduced on page 385 of

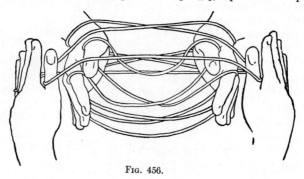

FIG. 456.

this book), but we have no information as to their methods of forming it or that they fully complete the figure by pulling up the ridge-pole.

Two persons (A and B) and two loops of string are required for this figure.

First: Each person takes a loop and proceeds to form Opening A.

Second: They then stand close together facing each other, and each turns his hands with the thumbs up and the fingers directed toward the other person. Then A passes his hands away from him through the index loops of the figure held on the hands of B. B then draws his hands toward him, but leaves his index loops on the wrists of A (Figs. 456, 457).

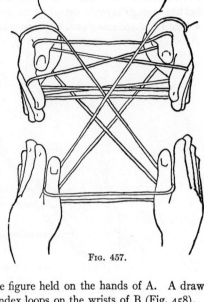

Fig. 457.

Third: B passes his hands away from him through the index loops of the figure held on the hands of A. A draws his hands toward him, but leaves his index loops on the wrists of B (Fig. 458).

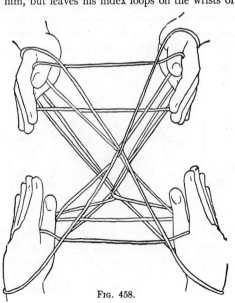

Fig. 458.

Fourth : A now takes his hands entirely out of the figure which he has been holding and, gathering together all the strings running to B's hands, twists them into a rope (Fig. 459), and passes this rope several times around the figure held in B's

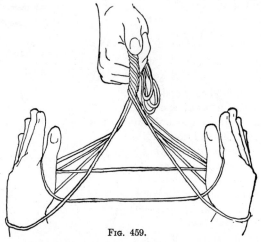

Fig. 459.

hands, under the figure toward B, then up between B and the figure, and finally over the figure toward A, and allows the end to hang down (Fig. 460).

Fifth : A with the right hand now removes the loop from B's left thumb, and with the left hand removes the loop from B's left little finger. B removes his left hand from the wrist loop, and picks up with the left hand the right thumb loop and

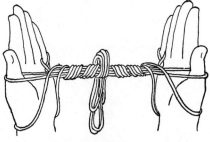

Fig. 460.

the right little finger loop; and removes his right hand from the wrist loop, and then holds in his right hand the right little finger loop (Fig. 461). A and B now draw the hands apart, working the figure until the large square pattern appears (Fig. 462).

Sixth : A and B now sit down opposite each other, crossing the legs tailor-fashion, and each places the loop held by the right hand on the left foot, and the

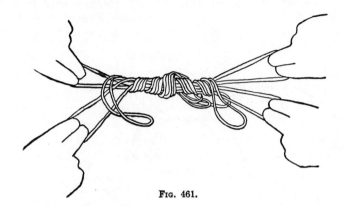

FIG. 461.

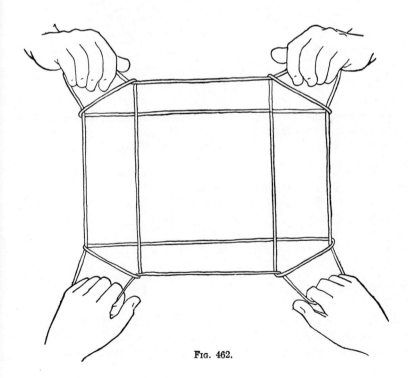

FIG. 462.

loop held by the left hand on the right foot. The feet must be pressed down firmly to keep the loops secure. A now brings together the pair of inner strings

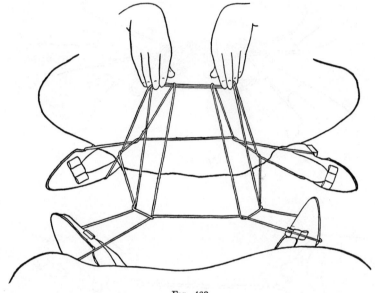

FIG. 463.

which pass at right angles under the other pair of inner strings, and with both hands lifts them up to form the ridge-pole of the house (Fig. 463).

The corner loops held by the feet represent the piles on which the house is built.

This is a pretty figure and the only one—except "Ten Times," in the formation of which two people take equal shares.

I have put it in this place in the series because it is the last of the figures which begin with Opening A.

W

This figure was obtained by Mr. John L. Cox, at Hampton, Virginia, from Wallace Springer, an Omaha Indian.

First: First Position.

Second: Bend each index down and pick up from below, and from the palmar side, the palmar string of the same hand (Fig. 464). Return the index to its position, withdraw the thumbs from the loop and draw the strings tight (Fig. 465).

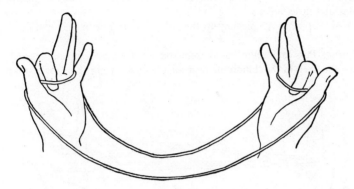

Fig. 464.

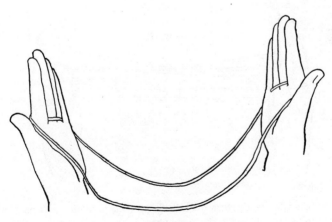

Fig. 465.

You now have on each hand: a near index string, a far little finger string and a string passing across the palmar surface of the middle and ring fingers, and behind the index and little fingers.

Third : Opening A, picking up the palmar strings with the middle fingers (Fig. 466).

Fourth : Pass each thumb away from you over the index loop and take up from below on the back of the thumb the near middle finger string (Fig. 467), and return

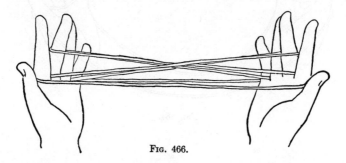

FIG. 466.

the thumb to its position. Release the loops from the little fingers; separate the hands.

Fifth : Pass each little finger toward you over the far middle finger string and far index string, and pick up from below on the back of the little finger the near

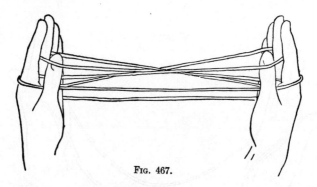

FIG. 467.

index string (Fig. 468), and return the little finger to its position. Release the loops from the thumbs, and draw the strings tight.

Sixth : Pass each thumb away from you over the far index string and the near middle finger string, and pick up from below on the back of the thumb the far middle finger string (Fig. 469). Release the loops from the little fingers and separate the thumbs widely from the other fingers (Fig. 470).

The figure exhibits the "W" when the hands are held in their usual position; it exhibits an M when the hands are turned with the fingers pointing downward.

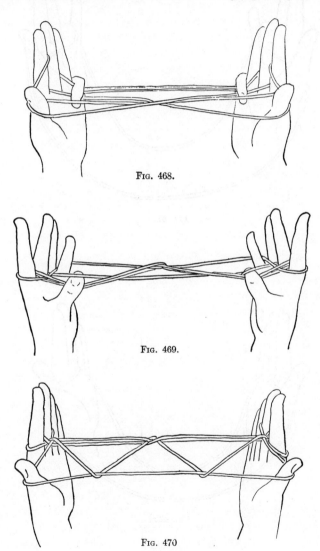

FIG. 468.

FIG. 469.

FIG. 470

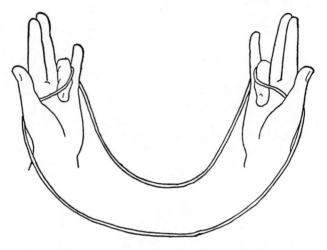

Fig. 471.

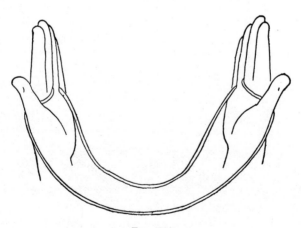

Fig. 472.

M

This is another Omaha figure closely resembling the preceding, and obtained in the same way.

First : First Position.
Second : Pick up with each ring finger, from below and from the palmar side,

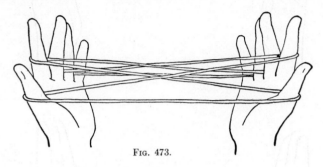

Fig. 473.

the palmar string of the same hand (Fig. 471), and withdraw the little finger (Fig. 472).

Third : Opening A, as usual (Fig. 473).

Fourth : Pass each little finger toward you over the ring finger loop, and pick up from below on the back of the little finger the far index string (Fig. 474), and

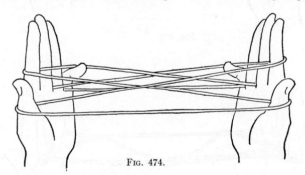

Fig. 474.

return the little finger to its position. Release the loops from the thumbs, and draw the strings tight.

Fifth : Pass each thumb away from you over the near index string and the near ring finger string, and pick up from below on the back of the thumb the far ring

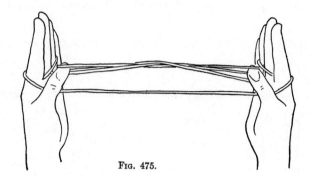

Fig. 475.

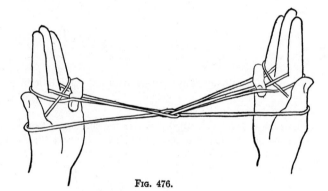

Fig. 476.

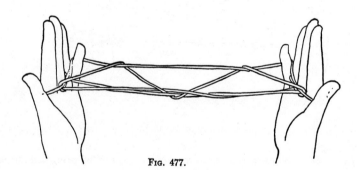

Fig. 477.

finger string (Fig. 475), and return the thumb to its position. Release the loops from the little fingers.

Sixth : Pass each little finger toward you over the near ring finger string and the far index string, pick up from below on the back of the little finger the near index string (Fig. 476), and return the little finger to its position. Release the loops from the thumbs; separate the little fingers widely from the other fingers (Fig. 477). When the hands are held in their usual position the "M" appears; when held with the fingers pointing away from you a W appears.

CHAPTER VI

A BOW

THIS is another of the Navaho figures shown to me by the same two Navaho girls, at the St. Louis Exposition, in November, 1904. The native name is *Atl-ti* = a Bow.

First: Hold the string between the tips of the thumb and index of each hand, so that a short piece passes between the hands and a long loop hangs down. Make

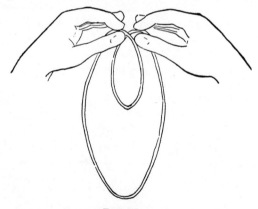

Fig. 478.

a small ring, hanging down, in the short string, putting the right hand string away from you over the left hand string (Fig. 478). Insert the index fingers into the ring downward and toward you (Fig. 479), and, putting the thumbs away from you into the long hanging loop (Fig. 480), separate the hands; and, turning the index fingers

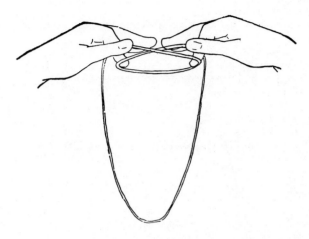

Fig. 479.

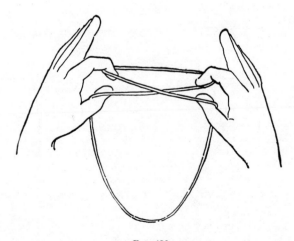

Fig. 480.

upward and outward, with the palms of the hands facing away from you, draw the
strings tight (Fig. 481).

Turn the hands so that the palms face each other, and the thumbs come toward

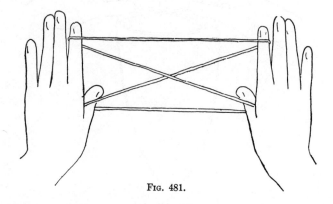

Fig. 481.

you and point upward.   You now have a long crossed loop on each index, a long
crossed loop on each thumb and a single cross in the centre of the figure (Fig. 482).

Second : Pass each thumb away from you over the near index string, and take
up from below with the back of the thumb the far index string, and return the

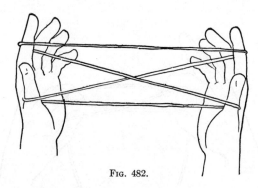

Fig. 482.

thumb to its former position (Fig. 483).   This movement draws the far index string
over the near index string.

Third : Pass each middle finger toward you over the near index string, and
take up from below on the back of the finger the far thumb string (Fig. 484, Left
hand), and return the middle finger to its original position (Fig. 484, Right hand).

Fourth : Turn the palms toward you, and put the ring and little fingers of each hand from below between the near index string and the far middle finger string (Fig. 485, Left hand), and pull down the near index string by closing the ring and little fingers on the palm (Fig. 485, Right hand). Keep the index and middle

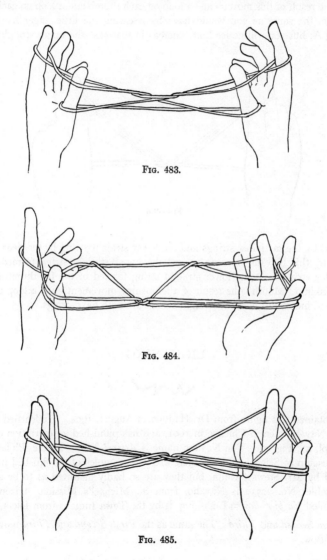

Fig. 483.

Fig. 484.

Fig. 485.

fingers erect; release the loops from the thumbs, and turn the palms away from you, drawing the strings tight (Fig. 486).

The "Bow" is not very interesting; it is the first of a series of six Navaho figures which begin in the same way—by an opening peculiar to the Navahos. At first glance the result of this movement—a loop on each thumb and a loop on each index —appears the same as you would have by releasing the little finger loops after Opening A; but you will notice that, whereas in that case the upper straight string

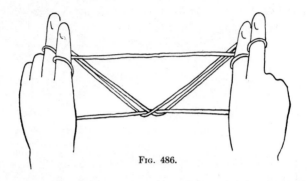

FIG. 486.

is formed by the far index strings and the lower straight string by the near thumb strings, by this Navaho opening we get the upper straight string formed of the near index strings and the lower straight string formed of the far thumb strings. In the Eskimo "Mouth" the result of the opening movement gives a loop on each thumb and index, but here the straight strings are both near strings.

LIGHTNING

I obtained this figure from Dr. Haddon in August, 1904. He learned it from two old Navaho men in Chicago in 1901, and has published a description of it (5, p. 222, pl. xv, Fig. 5). The Navaho name is *Atsinil-klish*. In the Philadelphia Free Museum of Science and Art there are two examples of the finished patterns, collected by Mr. Stewart Culin, but they are so badly distorted as to be scarcely recognizable: No. 22712 is Navaho, from St. Michael's Mission, Arizona; No. 22732 called *Vo-pi-ri-dai* = Lightning, is by the Tewa Indians from Isleta, N. M.

First, Second and *Third :* The same as the *First, Second* and *Third* movements of the "Bow."

Fourth : Bend each ring finger toward you over the far middle finger string and take up from below with the back of the finger the near index string (Fig. 487, Left hand), and return the ring finger to its position (Fig. 487, Right hand).

Fifth : Pass each little finger over the far ring finger string, and take up from

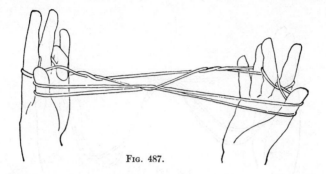

Fig. 487.

below on the back of the finger the far middle finger string (Fig. 488, Left hand), and return the little finger to its position (Fig. 488, Right hand).

You now have two twisted strings passing between the two little fingers, two loose strings passing over the thumbs and two strings laced around the other fingers.

Sixth : Turn the hands with the thumbs upward and the palms facing each

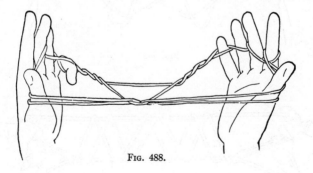

Fig. 488.

other. The little finger strings should be taut, but must not be disturbed. Keep all the fingers close together so that the strings cannot slip; the success of the figure depends entirely upon this precaution. Take the thumbs out of their loops (Fig. 489), and throw these loops away from you over the tightly drawn twisted little finger strings (Fig. 490).

Seventh : Insert each thumb into the small space between the twisted little finger strings, close to the little finger, and lift up the upper of the two strings (which

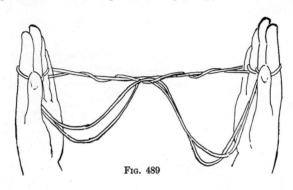

FIG. 489

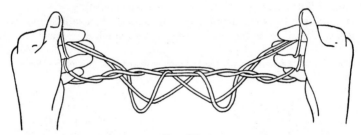

FIG. 490

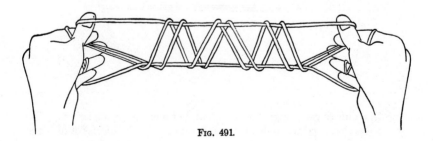

FIG. 491.

is the far ring finger string). Now, if the lower string be kept tightly drawn and the other fingers be kept close together, the loose hanging strings (the original thumb loops) will become wrapped around the twisted little finger strings as these gradually untwist when the upper string is lifted by the thumb. This movement forms the figure, which should be about two inches high (Fig. 491). A better effect is produced if the thumbs lift the upper little finger string just as you toss the hanging loop over; the zigzag lightning will then flash into view.

This is one of the most effective and satisfactory of all the figures, but one in which the novice is very apt to fail owing to his letting the strings slip through the fingers just before its completion. The lacing of the far thumb string and the near index string on the rest of the fingers, which is begun by the middle finger in the "Bow," is carried further in this figure by the ring and little fingers. These movements are peculiar to the "Bow" and to "Lightning."

A BUTTERFLY

I obtained this figure from the two Navaho girls at the St. Louis Exposition. The native name is *Ga-lo-kĭ* or *Ga-hi-kĭ*.

First: The same as the *First* movement of "The Bow."

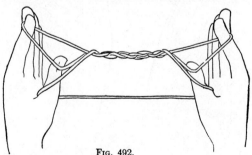

FIG. 492.

Second: Twist each index loop five times by rotating each index down toward you, and up again five times.

Third: Put each thumb from below into the index loop and, without removing the index, separate the thumb from the index (Fig. 492).

Fourth : On each hand in turn, with the teeth slip the lower (the original) thumb loop over the loop passing around both thumb and index, then entirely off the thumb, and let it drop to the palmar side.   Separate the hands (Fig. 493).

Fifth : Bring the hands close together, with the index finger and thumb of the one hand pointing toward the index finger and thumb of the other hand; then

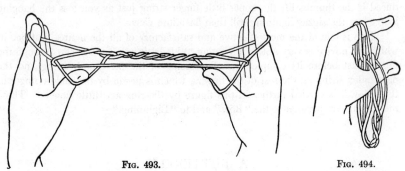

FIG. 493.   FIG. 494.

hang the right index loop on the left index, and the right thumb loop on the left thumb (Fig. 494).   Take up with the right index, from the left side, the loop you have just put on the left thumb, and take up with the right thumb, from the right side, the loop which was originally on the left thumb (Fig. 495); then with the right

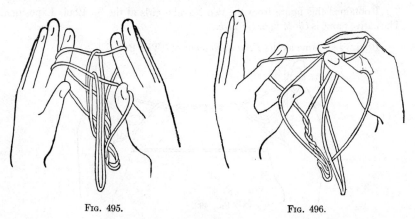

FIG. 495.   FIG. 496.

thumb and index lift both loops from the left index, and put the left index away from you into the loop just hung on the left index, and put the left thumb toward you into the loop originally on the left thumb (Fig. 496).   Now, placing the hands with the thumbs up and the fingers pointing away from you, draw them slowly apart,

and when the strings have partially rolled up in the middle of the figure (Fig. 497),
pull down with the middle, ring and little fingers of each hand the far index string
and the near thumb string (Fig. 498), and the wings of the butterfly will be held up

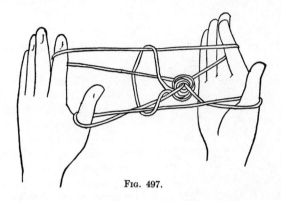

Fig. 497.

by the strings extended between the widely separated thumbs and index fingers,
and the proboscis will appear rolled up on the strings held down by the other fingers.

This is a charming figure, and unlike any of the others. It is very easy to form;
if the *Fifth* movement be done properly, the finished pattern always appears. If

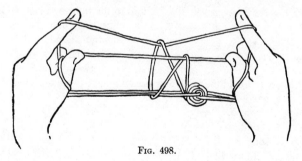

Fig. 498.

you twist the index loops more than five times, the proboscis will not roll up nicely,
if less than four times, it will not be sufficiently large.

The final movement is like "Lightning," in that the twists put on the strings
in the earlier movements, by untwisting assist in the formation of the finished pattern.

A WORM

This is another Navaho figure which I secured from the same Indians who taught me the preceding figure.

First : Hold the string between the thumb and index of each hand so that a short piece passes between the hands and a long loop hangs down. Make a small

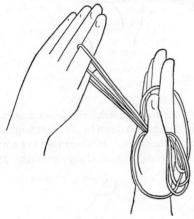

ring, hanging down, in the short string, putting the right hand string away from you over the left hand string.   Insert the index fingers into the ring downward and toward you and with the thumbs in the long hanging loop separate the hands and, turning the index fingers upward and outward, with the palms of the hands facing away from you, draw the strings tight.

Holding the right hand with the palm away from you, move the left hand first to the right between your body and the right hand and then away from you over the right hand, and lay all the left strings, doubled back on the right hand strings, between the right thumb and

Fig. 499.

index (Fig. 499), and hold them there by pressing these two fingers together.   Then,

separating the hands slightly (not enough, however, to pull the strings through the right thumb and index), d r a w the s t r i n g s moderately tight (Fig. 500), and turn the right hand with the palm to the left, and turn the left thumb down and then up toward you, and

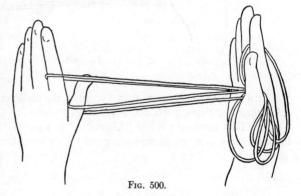

Fig. 500.

point the left index upward (Fig. 501). Now separate the hands, drawing the strings through the right thumb and index, and pull them tight (Fig. 502).

Second : Turn the palms toward you, and put the middle, ring and little fingers of each hand from below into the index loop (Fig. 503, Left hand), and bend these fingers toward you down over the near index string (Fig. 503, Right hand).

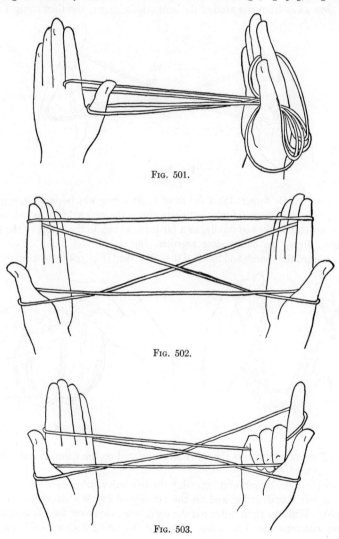

Fig. 501.

Fig. 502.

Fig. 503.

Then, holding this string down with the ring and little fingers, put the middle finger from above into the thumb loop, and close the middle finger down on the palm, holding the string in the bend of the finger as you turn the hands so that the palms face each other (Fig. 504).

You now have on each hand: (1) a near thumb string which passes behind the thumb, then away from you around the bent middle finger, and then straight across

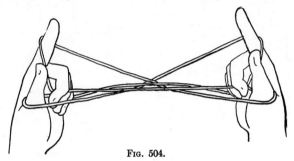

FIG. 504.

to the other middle finger; (2) a far little finger string which passes toward you under the bent little, ring and middle fingers, up on the near side of the index, away from you around its tip and finally, as a far index string, to the centre of the figure.

Third: Bring the hands close together, the thumb and index of one hand pointing toward the thumb and index of the other hand (Fig. 505), and keep through-

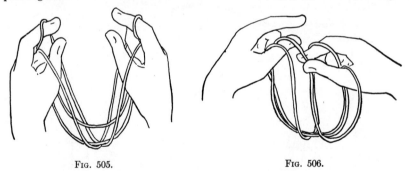

FIG. 505.   FIG. 506.

out the following movements the other fingers closed on the palm, in order to hold their strings securely.

With the right thumb and index lay the left index string over the left thumb beside the left thumb string and on the far side of it. Withdraw the left index (Fig. 506). With the right index put the right index loop over the left thumb (Fig. 507) and withdraw the right index. See that this string is close beside the other two, on the side nearest the tip of the thumb. Put both index fingers toward you under these three strings and withdraw the left thumb (Fig. 508). With the left

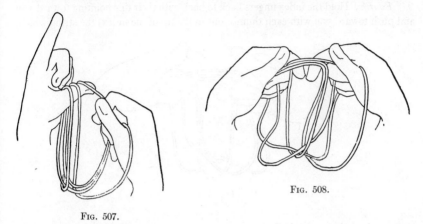

Fig. 507.

Fig. 508.

thumb draw the right thumb string across the index fingers on the near side of the other three strings (Fig. 509).

There are now four strings passing over the sides of the index fingers: On the right hand, the near string passes over the index and middle fingers and out between the middle finger and the ring finger. The two middle strings pass around the

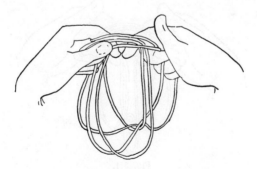

Fig. 509.

index only, and the far string passes around all the fingers closed on the palm; on the left hand, the near string and the far string pass around the index only, and of the two middle strings, the near one passes over both index and middle fingers and out between the middle finger and ring finger, and the far one passes around all the fingers closed on the palm (Fig. 510).

Fourth : Hold the index fingers back to back with their tips pointing toward you and push toward you with each thumb (out to the tip of the index) the string which,

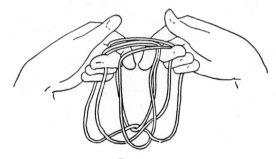

FIG. 510.

crossing the index and middle fingers, passes between the middle and ring fingers (Fig. 511). Hold all the strings on the index fingers by pressing down the thumbs.

Withdraw each middle finger, away from you, entirely out of the hanging loops, and insert it again, toward you, between the other hanging strings and the hanging part of the string held toward you on the tip of the index (Fig. 512). Draw each of these latter strings away from you through the hanging loops by straightening

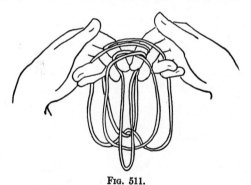

FIG. 511.

the middle finger (Fig. 513). Then pass each thumb away from you, above the ring finger and under the string which is still held to the palm by the ring and little fingers (Fig. 514). The strings are thus released from the index fingers. Release the string held down by each ring and little finger; separate the hands, with

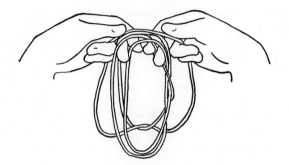

Fig. 512.

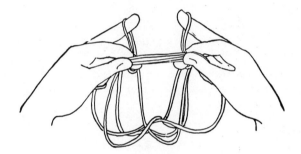

Fig. 513.

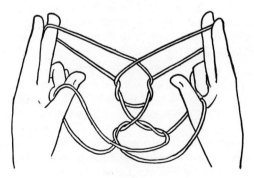

Fig. 514.

the palms turned away from you, and extend the figure between the thumbs and middle fingers (Fig. 515).

This figure has several novel movements; the *Third* and *Fourth* are rather hard to learn, but should present no difficulties in execution. With practice the figure can be formed rapidly and with certainty. The pattern produced by the opening

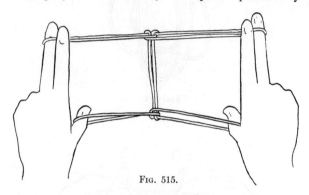

Fig. 515.

movement is very like the pattern produced by the opening movement of the "Bow" but the lower straight string passes on the near side of the near thumb strings, and not on the far side of them.

TWIN STARS

I collected this figure in the same way as the preceding figure. There are two examples of this pattern in the Philadelphia Free Museum of Science and Art, collected by Mr. Stewart Culin; No. 22715 is a Navaho figure, from St. Michael's Mission, Arizona, called *Sono-tsihu* = Twin Stars; No. 22606 is from Zuñi, N. M., called *Pi-cho-wai, wai-lo-lo* = Lightning; it has been artificially distorted.

First : The same as the *First* movement of "The Bow."

Second : Transfer the index loops to the thumbs, by putting each thumb from below into the index loop returning the thumb to its position, and withdrawing the index (Fig 516). Keep the two loops on the thumb well separated; the loop taken from the index up at the tip.

Third : Bend each index toward you and down through the upper thumb loop, and then down to the far side of the lower far thumb string; take up on the back of the finger this lower far string (Fig. 517, Left hand), and lift it up on the tip of the finger as you straighten the latter to its position (Fig. 517, Right hand).

Fourth : Pass each middle and ring finger from below (that is, toward you) through the lower thumb loop, and catch between these fingers the upper near thumb string (Fig. 518), and draw it away from you through the lower thumb loop; then, hooking the middle finger over the string, release the loops from the **thumbs,**

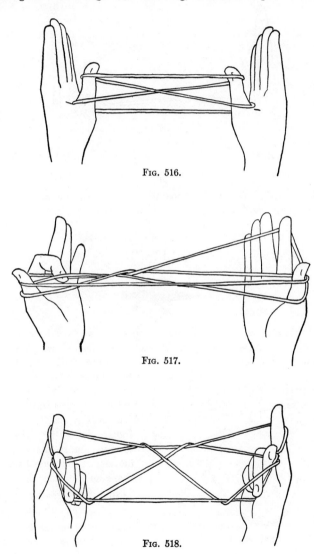

FIG. 516.

FIG. 517.

FIG. 518.

and turn the palms away from you (Fig. 519). The figure becomes extended between the index fingers and the middle fingers closed on the palms.

There is not much to this figure. The final pattern is almost exactly like the "Two Diamonds" of the Osage Indians, if that figure be formed with a single string

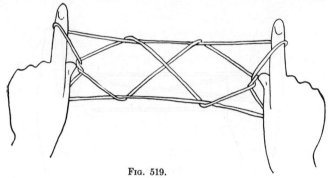

FIG. 519.

loop. The *Fourth* movement is a characteristic Navaho method, which, as we shall see, forms the most important part of the "Storm Clouds."

A LIZARD

This figure also was shown to me by the same two Navaho girls, at the St. Louis Exposition, in November, 1904. An example of the finished pattern collected by Mr. Culin at St. Michael's Mission, Arizona, and preserved in the Philadelphia Free Museum of Science and Art (No. 22721) is labelled *Nashoi-dichizhi* = a Lizard. At Grand Canyon, Arizona, I saw a Navaho Indian form the "Lizard"; he secured the results of the *First* movement, however, by simply exchanging the index loops after the "Bow" Opening.

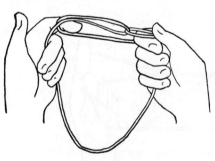

FIG. 520.

First : This movement is a slight modification of the opening movement in "The Bow." Hold the loop between the thumb and index of each hand so that a short piece of string passes from hand to hand and a long loop hangs down. In the short piece make a small hanging ring, by bringing the hands together and putting the part of the string held by the right hand away from you over the part of the string held by the left hand; then give this ring *one twist*, by turning it around away from you from right to left. Put each index finger toward you and downward into the ring, and put the other three fingers toward you into the long hanging loop. Now, pressing

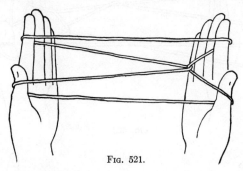

FIG. 521.

your right thumb down on the two right hand strings passing over the right index, to keep them from slipping (Fig. 520), separate the hands.

Put each thumb away from you into the loop held by the middle, ring and little fingers; withdraw these fingers; turn each index away from you and up, and

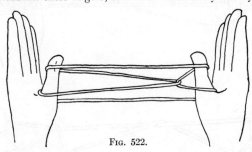

FIG. 522.

turn each thumb up and toward you under the index loop, and place the hands in the usual position (Fig. 521).

You now have a loop on each index and a loop on each thumb; and a loop is formed near the right hand by the left far index string and the left near thumb string passing around the string which runs from the far side of the right index to the near side of the right thumb.

Second : Transfer the index loops to the thumbs, by passing each thumb from below into the index loop and withdrawing the index (Fig. 522)

Third : Pass each index toward you over the upper far thumb string, and then, pulling that string away from you, put the index down on the far side of the lower far thumb string (the far string which passes directly from thumb to thumb), and pick up from below, on the back of the finger, this lower far thumb string,

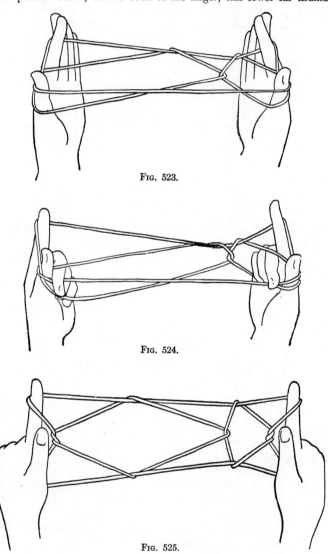

Fig. 523.

Fig. 524.

Fig. 525.

and return the index to its position; thereby drawing the string through the upper thumb loop (Fig. 523).

Fourth : Put the middle and ring fingers of each hand from below through the thumb loop, and catch between them the upper near thumb string (which passes directly from thumb to thumb) (Fig. 523), and pull it down through the loop with the middle finger, and hold it down by closing the finger on the palm, at the same time releasing the loops from the thumbs and drawing the strings tight (Fig. 525). The figure is extended between the ends of the index fingers and the middle fingers closed on the palms. The head of the "Lizard" is at the right end of the figure.

If you do not keep the head of the "Lizard" small by following carefully the *First* movement you will find that the finished figure differs from the preceding "Twin Stars" figure, only by having the central cross strings looped around each other.

LITTLE FISHES

Dr. Haddon taught me this figure in August, 1904. He obtained it in Murray Island, Torres Straits, where it is called *Tup* = a small Fish (Rivers and Haddon, p. 152).

First : Insert the index fingers into the loop of string so that you have a short piece passing from hand to hand as a far index string and a long loop, the near index string, hanging down between each thumb and index (Fig. 526).

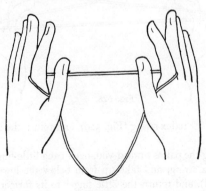

FIG. 526.

Hold the short far index string on each side between the tips of the thumb and index, and form in it a small upright ring by carrying the part of the string held by the left hand toward you, and to the right, over the right hand string. Put the index fingers away from you into this ring (Fig. 527) and separate the hands.

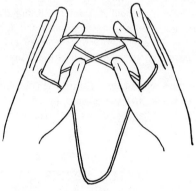

Fig. 527.

You now have two loops on each index, whereof the two far strings cross each other, but the two near strings run straight from index to index (Fig. 528).

Second: Bend each thumb away from you over the lower near index string, and pick up on the back of the thumb the lower far index string, then straighten each thumb, bend it over the upper near index string, and pick up on the back of

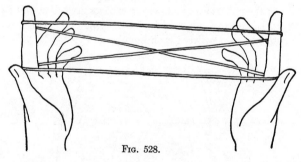

Fig. 528.

the thumb the upper far index string (Fig. 529), and return the thumb to its original position.

Third: Turning the palms toward you, bend each little finger toward you over the upper near index string, and take up from below the lower near index string (Fig. 530, Left hand), and return the little finger to its former position (Fig. 530, Right hand).

Fourth: Bend each index down into the large triangle formed by the upper near index string and the lower near index string (the string passing from the index

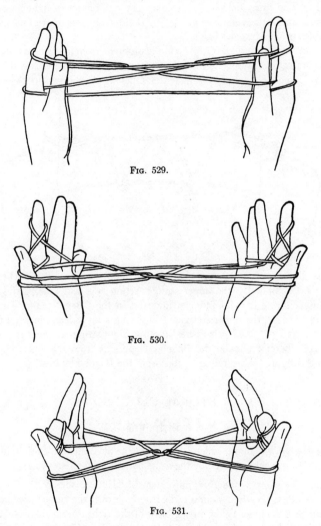

FIG. 529.

FIG. 530.

FIG. 531.

behind the little finger and continuing as the far little finger string), and pick up on the back of the index (Fig. 531), by curving it toward you and then upward, the upper near index string.

Fifth : Turning the palms away from you, release the loops from the thumbs, and the figure is extended between the tips of the index fingers and the little fingers (Fig. 532). The string held by the little fingers may be drawn tight by closing the middle, ring and little fingers over it. Dr. Haddon says there are four fishes—the four double strings arranged like a W.

The opening movement of this figure is different from any we have had so far, and it occurs again only in the following "Storm Clouds" of the Navaho Indians. In the two Bagobo Diamond figures, after Opening A, the two loops become ar-

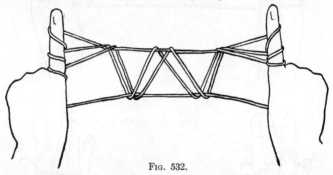

FIG. 532.

ranged on the index finger, but not in the same manner as in "Little Fishes," for in the "Bagobo Diamonds" the upper straight string is a near index string and the lower straight string is a far index string; and in the "Bagobo Two Diamonds" it is just the reverse, the upper straight string being a far index string and the lower a near index string. In "Little Fishes" both straight strings are near index strings. You cannot, therefore, make the Bagobo Diamonds from this opening, nor can you form this figure by beginning as you begin the Bagobo figures.

STORM CLOUDS

This is a Navaho figure which I learned at the St. Louis Exposition, in November, 1904. It was shown to me by the same two Navaho girls.

First : The same as the *First* movement of "Little Fishes."

Second : Pass the right thumb away from you over the right lower near index string, and pick up from below on the back of the right thumb the right lower far index string, and return the right thumb to its position (Fig. 533, Right hand).

Third : Pass the left thumb away from you over the left lower index loop and pick up on the back of the left thumb the left upper far index string, and return the left thumb to its position (Fig. 533, Left hand).

Fourth : Pass the middle, ring and little fingers of the right hand from below into the right upper index loop; and pass the middle, ring and little fingers of the left hand from below into the left lower index loop (Fig. 534). Bend the middle, ring and little fingers of each hand toward you over the upper near index string, and pull this string down by closing the three fingers down on the palm (Fig. 535).

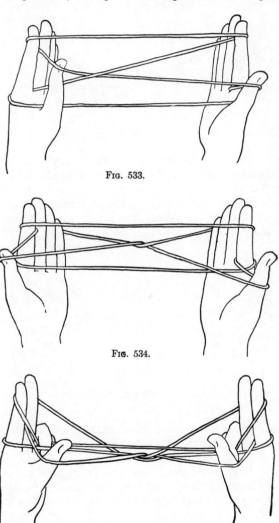

FIG. 533.

FIG. 534.

FIG. 535.

Fifth : Holding the string down with each ring and little finger, bend the middle finger toward you over the lower near index string (Fig. 536), and pull it in the bend of the finger away from you over the upper near index string; release the upper near index string from under the ring and little fingers (Fig. 537), and put the ring

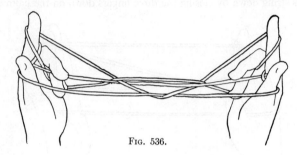

Fig. 536.

and little fingers toward you beside the middle finger to assist in holding down the lower near index string; then release the loops from the thumbs and draw the strings tight (Fig. 538).

You now have one "storm cloud" extended between the index fingers and the other fingers closed on the palms. The central figure is symmetrical; it is a triangle, crossed by a straight horizontal string and sending, on each side, two

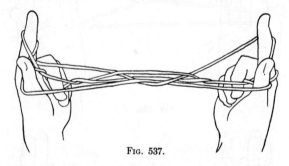

Fig. 537.

diagonal strings to the index finger. The strings are differently arranged, however, on the two index fingers: On the right index, the upper far string forms the straight string at the top of the figure, and then becomes the lower far string on the left index; and the lower far string forms the right upper diagonal string. On the left index, the upper far string is continued toward the centre of the figure as the left upper diagonal string. On each side, the lower diagonal string is the upper near index string, and the string held down by the middle, ring and little fingers is the lower near index string.

Sixth : Pass each thumb away from you under the lower diagonal string, then between the two diagonal strings (Fig. 539), and bending the thumb away from

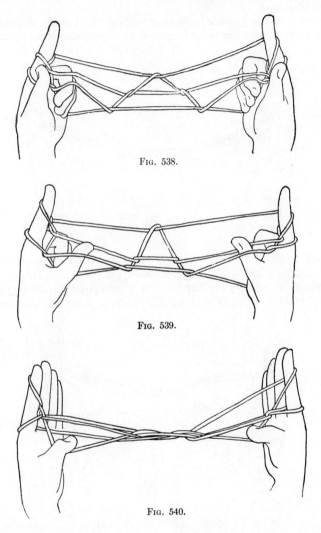

Fig. 538.

Fig. 539.

Fig. 540.

you over the upper diagonal, draw it down toward you in the bend of the thumb under the lower diagonal. Release the string held down by the middle, ring and little fingers (Fig. 540).

Put the middle, ring and little fingers of each hand toward you through the loop held by the thumb and withdraw the thumb, and close the fingers down on the palm (Fig. 541).

Seventh : Pass each middle finger up on the near side of the two diagonal strings, and then up away from you to the far side of the upper string of the figure (formed

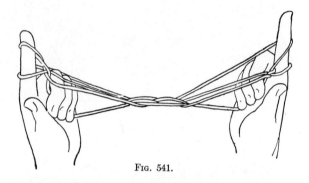

FIG. 541.

of the right upper far index string and the left lower far index string) (Fig. 542), and, bending the finger toward you, pull this upper string down through the loop held down to the palm by the ring and little fingers; then slip the ring and little fingers out of the loop they have been holding (Fig. 543), and put them toward you

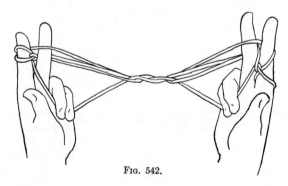

FIG. 542.

into the loop held by the middle finger, and close all three fingers down on the palm (Fig. 544).

Eighth : With each index pick up from the far side at some distance from the index the straight transverse lower near index string, and straighten the index to loop the string around its tip (Fig. 545). The lower near index string can be found by following it carefully from the index toward the centre of the figure. The figure

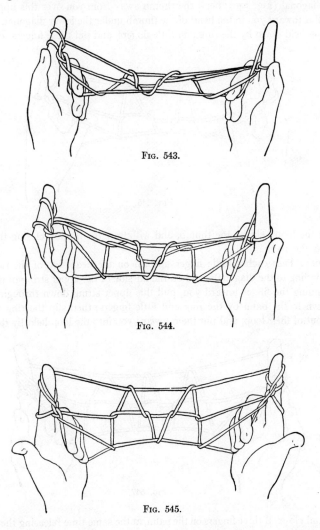

Fig. 543.

Fig. 544.

Fig. 545.

now has a top string and a bottom string extending two triangles—the two "storm clouds"—and two strings on each side corresponding with the former diagonal strings.

Ninth : Put each thumb away from you and up on the far side of the lower diagonal, and then on the near side of the straight string corresponding to the upper diagonal (Fig. 546); bend the thumb away from you over this upper string, and pull it toward you in the bend of the thumb under the lower diagonal. Release the string held down by the ring and little fingers, and put these fingers toward you

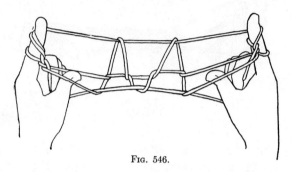

Fig. 546.

through the loop held by the thumb, and withdraw the thumb, closing the fingers down on the palm.

Tenth : Pass each middle finger upward on the near side of the two strings corresponding to the diagonals, and on the far side of the upper string of the figure, and, bending the finger toward you, pull this upper string down through the loop held down to the palm by the ring and little fingers; then slip the ring and little fingers out of their loop, and put them toward you into the loop held by the middle

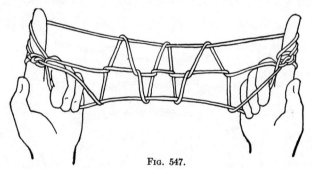

Fig. 547.

finger, and close all three fingers on the palm, at the same time releasing the top loop from each index.

Eleventh : With the right index pick up from the far side the right upper far index string; and with the left index pick up on the far side the left lower far index string, and straighten the index fingers. This movement puts a loop around the tip of each index (Fig. 547).

You now have three "storm clouds"—three triangles between the upper and lower strings—and two strings on each side running to the index.

Twelfth: By repeating the *Sixth* and *Seventh* movements, releasing the top loops on each index, and then repeating the *Eighth* movement, four "clouds" can be formed.

Thirteenth: By repeating the *Ninth* and *Tenth* movements, releasing the top loop on each index, and then repeating the *Eleventh* movement, five "clouds" can be formed.

Fourteenth: By repeating the *Twelfth* movement, six "clouds" can be formed.

Fifteenth: By repeating the *Thirteenth* movement, seven "clouds" can be formed.

I regard this figure as the most difficult of all, because of the complication, introduced at the outset, by the two thumbs picking up different strings and because of the subsequent difficulty of finding the proper strings to pick up owing to the tight twists which grow around the index fingers.

The Indian notion of "storm clouds" can be seen in the small drawing placed at the beginning of the game; this is copied from a Moki pictograph of "clouds with rain descending" (see Garrick Mallery, p. 238, Fig. 164). The same design occurs on the Navaho blankets of the present day.

ONE HOGAN

I obtained this figure from Dr. Haddon, who has published a description of it (**5**, p. 220). He learned it in Chicago in 1901, from the old Navaho men who taught him the other Navaho figures. *Hogan* is the native name for a tent.

First: Hold the left hand with the fingers pointing upward and the palm slightly toward you. With the right hand arrange a part of the loop upon the left hand so that it crosses the backs of both index and middle fingers, and passes to the palmar side between the middle and ring finger, and between the index and thumb; let the rest of the loop hang down on the palm (Fig. 548. In this and some of the following drawings the hanging loop is represented as quite short, to save space).

FIG. 548.

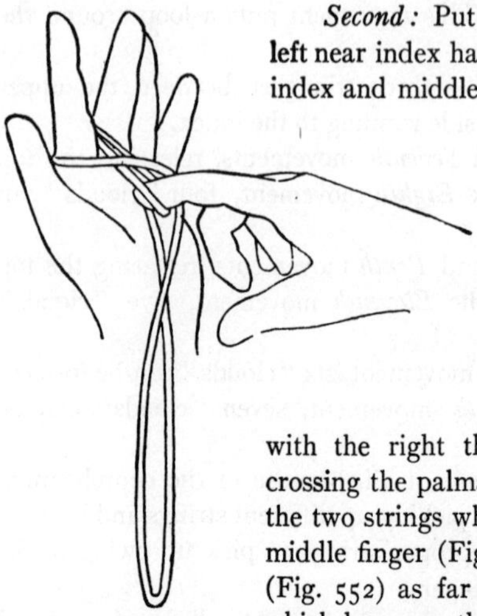

Second : Put the right index from the near side under the left near index hanging string, and then through between the index and middle finger, and with the ball of the finger pick up the cross string which is on the backs of the left index and middle finger, and pull it through between these fingers (Fig. 549), and then out to the full extent of the string (Fig. 550).

Third : Letting the loop hang down on the left palm, put the whole right hand from the near side under the near string and into the hanging loop. Then with the right thumb and index catch, above the string crossing the palmar surfaces of the index and middle finger, the two strings which come from between the left index and middle finger (Fig. 551), and draw them out to the right (Fig. 552) as far as possible. In this movement the loop which hung on the right wrist slips over the right hand and along the two strings just drawn out, until it reaches the palm.

FIG. 549.

You now have on the left hand a loop on the index and a loop on the middle finger, both loops knotted together lower down on the palm (Fig. 553). Arrange the four strings which hang down on the palm below the knot so that they lie side by side evenly and uncrossed, with the two which pass up through the knot and between the index and middle finger lying in the middle between the other two.

You will observe that the near string runs up to the knot, passes from the front around a cross string, comes forward, and passes to the far side as a second cross string over all four hanging strings; it then passes from behind around the back cross string, a n d hangs down in front as the far string of the four.

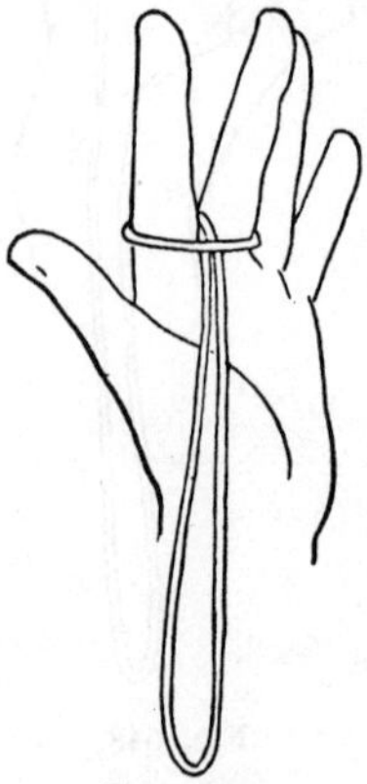

Fourth : With the thumb and index of the right hand pick up, below the knot,

FIG. 550.

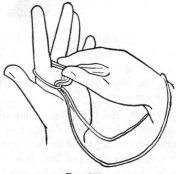

FIG. 551.

the near hanging string, and put it behind the left thumb; in like manner pick up the far hanging string, and put it behind the little finger (Fig. 554).

Fifth : With the right thumb and index pick up that straight string of the knot which passes in front of the four hanging strings (Fig. 555), and pull the loop out as far as possible; then lifting the right hand sweep the left hand down, with the palm up and the fingers

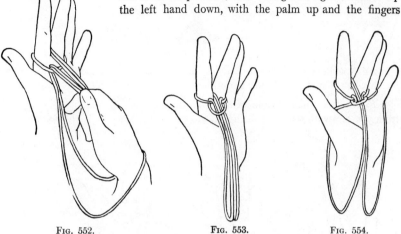

FIG. 552.   FIG. 553.   FIG. 554.

pointing to the right, and draw the strings moderately tight, and you get a hogan, or tent, with the two sticks coming through its peak (Fig. 556).

This interesting figure belongs to the class wherein the movements consist chiefly of one hand arranging the strings on the other hand.

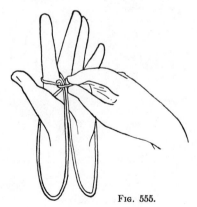

FIG. 555.

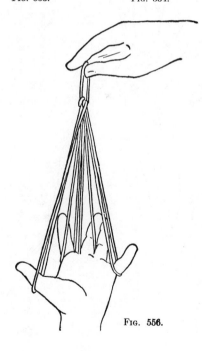

FIG. 556.

AN APACHE TEEPEE

An Apache woman named Darcia Tafoya, from Jicarilla, New Mexico, taught me this figure at the St. Louis Exposition.

First : Hold the left hand with the fingers pointing obliquely upward and away from you and with the palm facing toward you and upward.   With the right hand

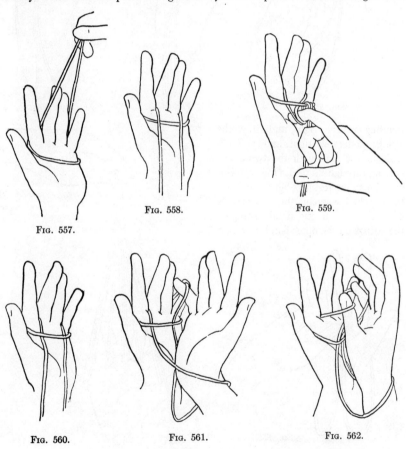

Fig. 557.

Fig. 558.

Fig. 559.

Fig. 560.

Fig. 561.

Fig. 562.

DARCIA TAFOYA, A JICARILLA APACHE.
(Courtesy of Mr. S. C. Simms.)

UAP CHILDREN PLAYING THE "TURTLE."
(Courtesy of Dr. William Henry Furness, 3rd.)

lay a part of the loop across the palm, and let it hang down on the left side, between the thumb and index, and on the right side from the right side of the palm. With the right thumb and index pick up together near the back of the left hand the two hanging strings, and bring them up toward you to the palm of the left hand, by passing the left string between the left index and middle finger, and the right string between the left ring finger and little finger (Fig. 557); and let the two strings hang down on the palm. Observe that they cross *over* the palmar string (Fig. 558).

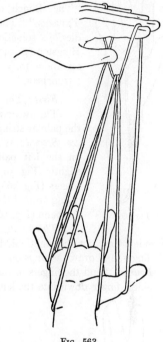

Second : Pass the index of the right hand under the left palmar string, and hook the end around the two hanging strings, and draw them down under the palmar string (Fig. 559); let them hang down on the left palm. Observe that now the palmar string crosses *over* the hanging strings (Fig. 560).

Third : Put the right hand from the left through the far side of the hanging loop, and keep the loop on the right wrist. Put the little finger of the right hand, from the right side, under the right hanging string, above the palmar string (Fig. 561); and put the right thumb, from the left side, under the left hanging string, also above the palmar string (Fig. 562).

Draw these strings out on the right thumb and little finger, keeping the loop still on the right wrist (Fig. 563). The "Teepee," or tent, is formed by swinging

FIG. 563.

the right hand down, palm upward, with the fingers pointing away from you; and by elevating the left hand, and turning the palm down and pointing the fingers to the right.

In this figure the hand which arranges the strings on the other hand in the end takes up some of the strings to form the most important part of the finished pattern.

TALLOW DIPS

Dr. Haddon taught me this game. It is well known in Great Britain; and the Rev. John Gray (p. 117, figs. 1, 2 and 3) has published a description of it as played by the children of the Cowgate in Edinburgh. He gives the different movements of the figure as separate figures, namely, "The Bunch of Candles," "The Chair," "The Pair of Trousers," "The Crown." In Ireland "The Bunch of Candles" is sometimes called "The Broom." Miss Margaret A. Hingston (p. 147) gives the story which was current in Somerset about forty years ago; the "tipstaff" is here called the "truncheon."

First: The first movement of the "Apache Teepee."

The two strings now hang down from the left hand over the palmar string (Fig. 564).

Second: With the right thumb and index pick up the string on the left palm, between the hanging strings, pull it out slightly (Fig. 565), and put it over the left middle and ring fingers (Fig. 566). There is now a ring around the left index, a ring around the left little finger, and a loop hanging down on the palm (Fig. 567).

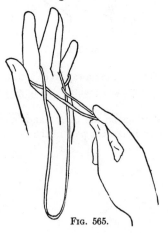

FIG. 564.

Third: Put the right index from above into the ring on the left index; and put the right middle finger from above into the ring on the left little finger, and draw the rings out to the right (Fig. 568) as far as possible.

Fourth: Bend the fingers of the left hand down on the palm as follows: The left middle finger down into the left index loop, the left ring finger down into the

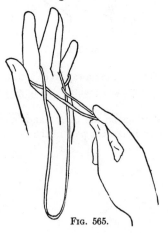

FIG. 565.

FIG. 566.

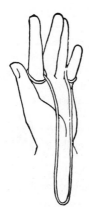

FIG. 567.

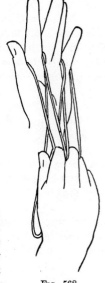

FIG. 568.

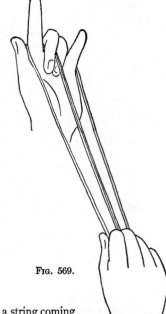

FIG. 569.

left little finger loop
(Fig. 569), the left
little finger over the
left far little finger
string, and the left
index over the left
near i n d e x string.

When the left fist is thus closed, you have a string coming
out between the index and middle finger, two strings coming
out between the middle and ring fingers, and a string coming
out between the ring and little fingers. Over the backs of the fingers, at their
bases, there is a string around the index finger, a string around both the middle and
ring fingers, and a string around the little finger (Fig. 570).

Fifth : With the thumb and index of the right hand pull
up slightly the string on the backs of the left middle and ring
fingers, and p a s s
through this loop to
the back of the hand
the four strings com-
ing out between the
fingers of the left fist
(Fig. 571); let the
strings, pulled entirely
through, hang down
on the back of the
left hand (Fig. 572).

FIG. 570.

FIG. 571.

FIG. 572.

Sixth : With the right thumb and index pull this same loop crossing the backs of the left middle and ring fingers (through which you have just passed the four strings) over the knuckles of the middle and ring fingers (Fig. 573), and to the palm

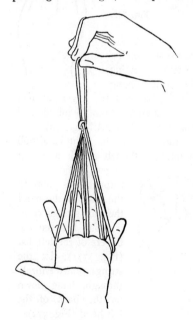

of the left hand; then draw it out to the right as far as possible, but carefully, and not too hard, at the same time unclosing the left fist, and (with some stretch of the imagination) you get the four tallow dips on the left hand (Fig. 574).

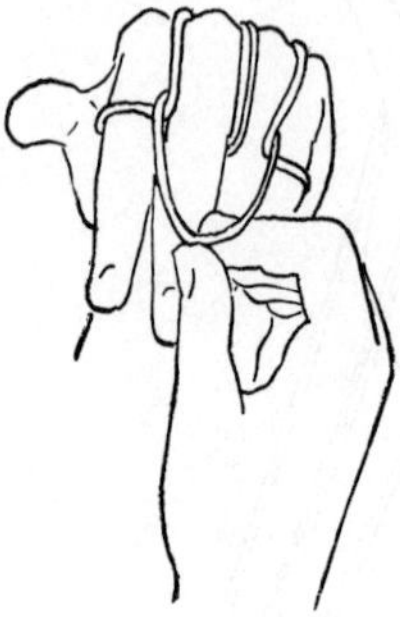

The story of the tallow dips is as follows: "A man stole a pound of tallow dips, and bringing them home hung them on a peg."

Seventh : At this point, place the loop held by the right thumb and index over the left thumb and, being careful not to twist it, let it hang down (Fig. 575).

"And being very tired he sat down on a chair and went to sleep."

FIG. 573.

Eighth : Now, pointing the right index and middle fingers downward, over the back of the left hand held palm down with the fingers pointing to the right, take up from the left side on the ball of the right index, the

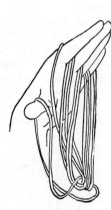

FIG. 575.

FIG. 574.

loop on the back of the left middle finger, and
take up on the ball of the right middle finger the
loop on the back of the left
ring finger (Fig. 576 seen from
above), and draw the loops
out as far as possible to the
right. Turn the left
hand with the palm
u p w a r d, and "the
chair" is formed, the
back, by the loops
held up by the right
hand, the seat by the loop
around the left thumb, and
the four legs by the strings of
the loops held by the left
index and little finger (Fig.
577).

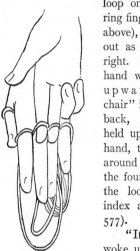

FIG. 576.

"It was dark when he
woke up, so he got a pair of
shears to cut off a tallow dip."

Ninth : Release the loop
from the left thumb, and you
have the "shears" (Fig. 578).

"While he was cutting off
the dip a constable came to arrest him, bringing
along his tipstaff."

Tenth : Release the loop on
the left index finger, and draw the hands gently apart to produce the long tipstaff,

FIG. 577.

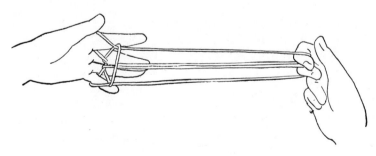

FIG. 578.

with the crown at the end formed by the small crossed loops on the right index and middle finger (Fig. 579).

"The constable put handcuffs on the thief and marched him off to prison."

Eleventh : Release the loop from the right index, and put the right hand through the right middle finger loop; put the left hand through the loop 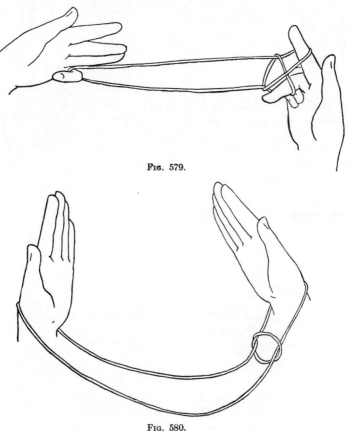 held by the left little finger. Separate the hands (Fig. 580) and draw the strings tight. This movement puts a loop on the left wrist and a slip noose on the right wrist.

In principle, "Tallow Dips" is like the two preceding figures. It is one of the most important of all string figures, because of the story which goes with it. A careful study of its distribution in Great Britain, its varieties, and the different stories told while it is being played would, I am sure, be extremely interesting.

Fig. 579.

Fig. 580.

ONE CHIEF

In Uap, in the Caroline Islands, this figure is called *Pilun* = a Chief. Dr. Furness obtained it in 1902, from the native woman "Lemet."

First : First Position.

Second : With the thumb and index of the right hand wrap the left near thumb string, toward you, once around the left thumb (Fig. 581), and separate the hands.

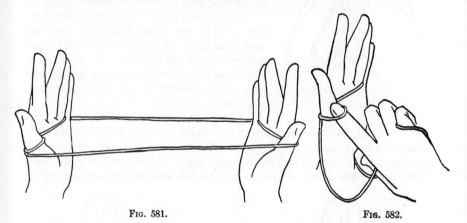

FIG. 581.   FIG. 582.

Third : With the right index take up, from below, on the back of the finger, the ring formed on the left thumb (Fig. 582), and separate the hands (Fig. 583).

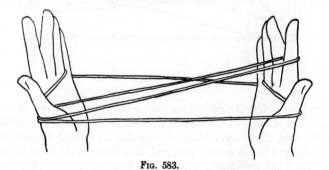

FIG. 583.

Fourth : Proceed with "Opening A," beginning by taking up the string on the right palm with the left index, putting the left index between the strings of the loop on the right index (Fig. 584); separate the hands (Fig. 585); and then take up with the right index the left palmar string also between the strings of the left index loop (Fig. 586). Separate the hands.

You now have a loop on each little finger, a loop on the left index and a loop on the right thumb, and two loops on the left thumb, and two loops on the right index (Fig 587). Be sure that the upper right index loop is the one formed by the left near little finger and far thumb strings.

Fifth : Take the left hand entirely out of the figure, and let the strings hang down from the right hand held with the palm down and the fingers pointing to the left (Fig. 588. In this, and in some of the following drawings the hanging loops are represented as very short, in order to save space).

FIG. 584.

With the thumb and index of the left hand pull up slightly from the back of the right index that right index loop which is nearest the tip of the finger, and, removing the left thumb and index, hold it up by pressing the right thumb and middle finger against the sides of the right index. Then put the left thumb and index, from the left, through this loop, and pull up

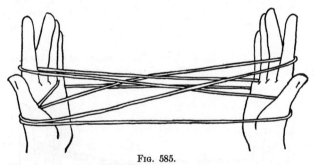

FIG. 585.

slightly, and to the left, the right index loop which is near the base of the finger, so that it comes through the loop already pulled up (Fig. 589); and hold it up by pressing the right thumb and middle finger against the sides of the right index.

The left hand is still entirely free, and, in addition to the loops hanging from the right thumb and little finger, there are two loops standing up about two inches

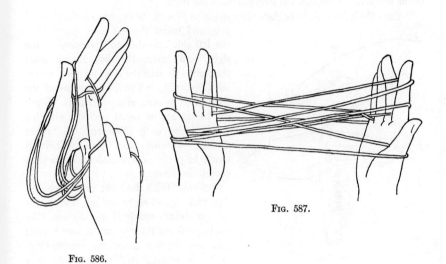

FIG. 587.

FIG. 586.

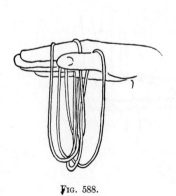

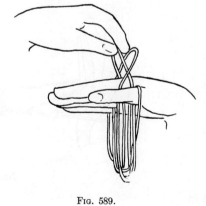

FIG. 588.

FIG. 589.

from the back of the right index, and crossing, so that the original right loop points to the left and the original left loop points to the right.

Place the left hand above these right index loops with the fingers pointing toward

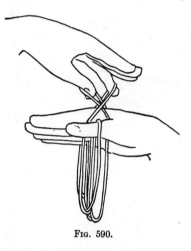

Fig. 590.

you, and insert the left little finger from the left side into the loop pointing to the right, and insert the left thumb from the right side into the loop pointing to the left (Fig. 590), and pull both loops off the right index by separating the hands. Turn the hands to the usual position with the palms facing each other and the fingers directed upward (Fig. 591). There is now a loop on each thumb and a loop on each little finger.

Sixth: With the right thumb and index pick up, close to the left thumb, the left far thumb string (Fig. 592), and take the loop off the thumb, turn it over toward you, and replace it on the thumb (Fig. 593); the original left far thumb string is

Fig. 590.

now the left near thumb string.

In the same way pick up with the left thumb and index the right far thumb string (Fig. 594), take the loop off the right thumb, turn it over toward you, and replace it on the right thumb (Fig. 595). Separate the hands (Fig. 596). The thumb loop may be so reversed by using the index of the same hand.

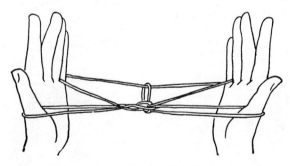

Fig. 591.

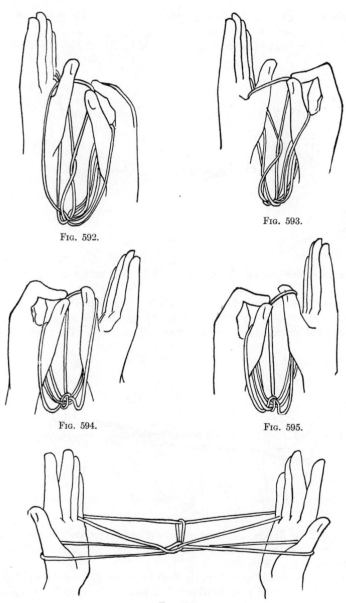

Fig. 592.

Fig. 593.

Fig. 594.

Fig. 595.

Fig. 596.

Seventh : Bend each thumb away from you over the far thumb string, and take up, from below, the near little finger string (Fig. 597, Left hand), and return the thumb to its former position (Fig. 597, Right hand). There are now on each

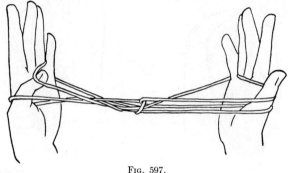

Fig. 597.

hand, a lower loop on the thumb and a higher loop arranged as in the "First Position."

Eighth : Take up with the tip of each index, from below, the far thumb string (not the string crossing the palm), keeping the near thumb strings on the thumb (Fig. 598), and return the index to its position. Then, holding the index strings out

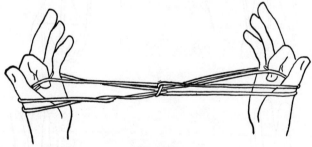

Fig. 598.

on the tips of the fingers, and keeping the strings between the thumbs and index fingers in position (but so that they can slip slightly) (Fig. 599), turn the hands with the palms away from you.

This movement will draw tight the little finger strings, and if the strings held between each thumb and index be slightly loosened, the figure will be formed (Fig. 600).

The finished pattern is not unlike the pattern in "Two Chiefs," but the two figures are done by entirely different methods. With the exception of the *Seventh* and *Eighth* movements, all the others are peculiar to this figure.

The opening of "One Chief" is a modification of Opening A and produces additional loops on the left thumb and the right index. We have already observed

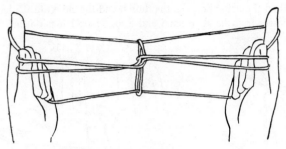

Fig. 599.

that it is not uncommon, at some stage in the formation of a figure, for all the loops to be dropped from one hand and then new loops to be taken up again (for example in the Caroline Islands "Catch," "Two Chiefs," "Three Stars," and "Coral," the Eskimo "Mouth," the Navaho "Butterfly"); the method, however, by which this is done in the *Fifth* movement of "One Chief" is entirely novel. It is not usual

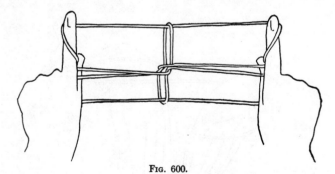

Fig. 600.

to find a finger loop merely turned over in such a simple way as we see it done in the *Sixth* movement. There is another Caroline Islands figure in which "Three Chiefs" are formed, but the native man who attempted to show it to Dr. Furness was so old and so shaken with palsy that he could not succeed in teaching it.

CAROLINE ISLANDS DIAMONDS

Dr. Furness did not get the native name for this figure, so I have called it "Diamonds." It is a Natik figure obtained from "Emily," the native who taught Dr. Furness the "Catch."

First : Hold the string between the thumb and the index of each hand so that a short piece passes from hand to hand and a long loop hangs down. In the short

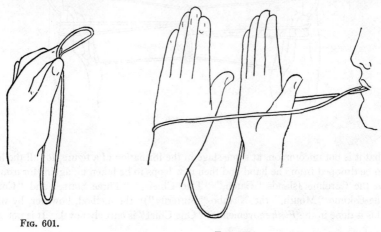

FIG. 601.

FIG. 602.

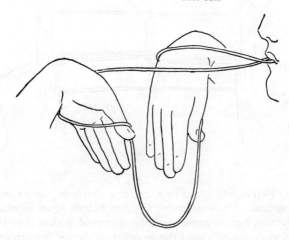

FIG. 603.

piece make a small upright ring, by passing the part of the string near the right hand toward you over the part near the left hand. Hold the cross of the ring

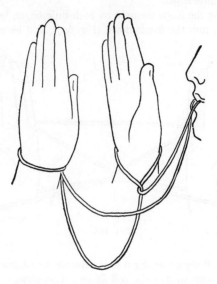

Fig. 604.

between the thumb and index of the left hand (Fig. 601). Then take between the teeth the upper part of the ring, and put both hands away from you through the long hanging loop, of course below the cross forming the bottom of the ring (Fig. 602). Now turn each hand down away from the other, then toward you around the hanging string of the same side (Fig. 603), and finally up between the hanging string and your body (but not away from you through the hanging loop) (Fig. 604); then putting the little fingers toward you into the ring held by the teeth (Fig. 605), catch the sides of the ring in the bend of each little finger, and releasing the strings from the teeth,

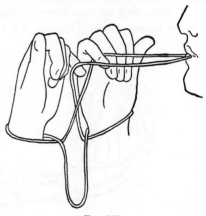

Fig. 605.

separate the hands; turn the palms toward each other, and straighten the little fingers. Draw the strings tight (Fig. 606). You now have a loop on each wrist and a loop on each little finger.

Second: Holding the loops securely on each little finger, by bending the four fingers on the palm, turn the hands down (Fig. 607), and let each wrist loop slip

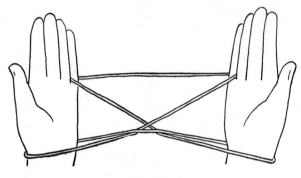

FIG. 606.

off the wrist, and, as it slips, transfer it to the thumb, by catching with the back of the thumb the near wrist string (Fig. 608 as seen from above). Put the hands in the usual position.

Third: Bend each thumb away from you over the far thumb string, and pick up from below, on the back of the thumb, the near little finger string (Fig. 609), and return the thumb to its position.

Fourth: Pick up from below, on the tip of each index, the far thumb string (not the palmar string) (Fig. 610), and straighten the index. Press each thumb

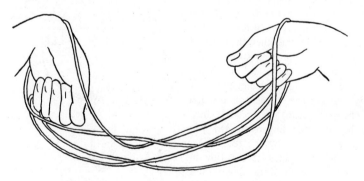

FIG. 607.

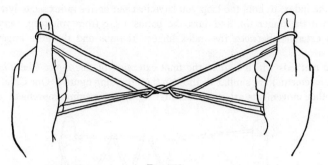

FIG. 608.

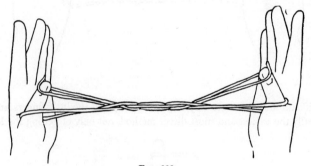

FIG. 609.

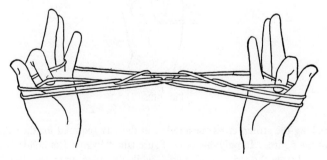

FIG. 610.

against the index, to hold the loop you have just put on the index securely and well out toward the finger tip, and turn the palms away from you (Fig. 611). The figure is extended between the index fingers, thumbs and the little fingers (Fig. 612).

The methods which lead to the final extension of this figure (the *Third* and *Fourth* movements) are similar to those in the preceding figure ("One Chief "), but all the other movements are new. At first sight, the opening movement appears

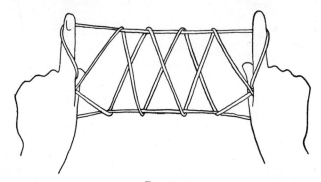

FIG. 611.

to be a difficult and elaborate way of putting loops on the little fingers and wrists, but it is really the easiest and most direct method, not only of getting the loops, but

FIG. 612.

also of making the strings cross one another in the way required for the subsequent success of the figure. In only one other figure (the "Pygmy Diamonds") are the loops dropped from the wrists, and caught, while dropping, upon the thumbs.

A TURTLE

This Caroline Islands figure was shown to Dr. Furness by the young Uap girl "Dakofel."

First : Put the string around the upright finger of a second person, and then holding the strings untwisted in your right and left hands, take a second turn around the other person's finger with the right string.

Second : Put both hands from below through the long loop (Fig. 613); then swing each hand over and to the outside of the string of the same side, around the string, up toward you and again through the loop (Fig. 614). This movement

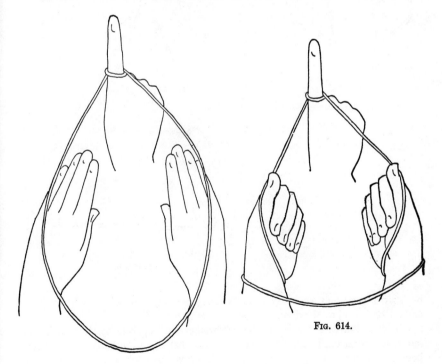

Fig. 613.

Fig. 614.

puts a turn on each wrist. With the thumb and index fingers of both hands catch the ring which is around the finger of the second person (Fig. 615), and pull it toward you, and by separating the hands, the cross string of the loop, thus formed, comes under the original right and left strings (Fig. 616). Now let the loop slip off

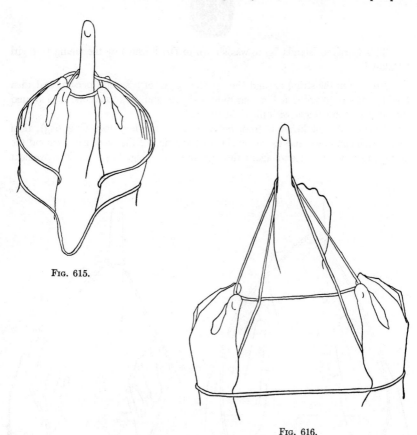

FIG. 615.

FIG. 616.

both wrists, and you get a second cross string over the two right and left strings, and a loop is held by the thumb and index of each hand (Fig. 617).

Third: Put each hand from below through the loop held by the thumb and index, and with each little finger take up from below, in the bend of the finger, between the finger of the other person and the cross strings, the outside string of the two strings passing to the other person (Fig. 618). With the thumbs take up,

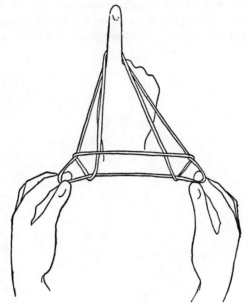

Fig. 617.

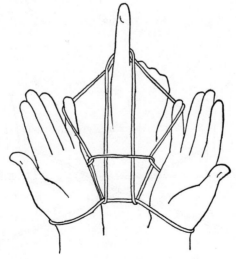

Fig. 618.

from the near side, the far cross string (the string crossing over the four strings passing to the other person) (Fig. 619). Then the second person withdraws the finger, and you separate the hands, put them in the usual position, and draw the

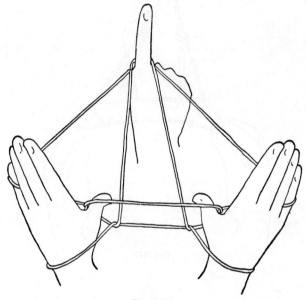

FIG. 619.

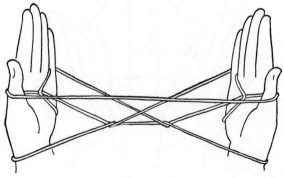

FIG. 620.

strings tight (Fig. 620).   You now have a loop on each wrist, a loop on each thumb
and a loop on each little finger.

Fourth: Holding the loops securely on the thumbs and little fingers, turn the

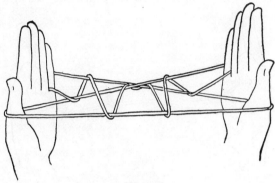

Fig. 621.

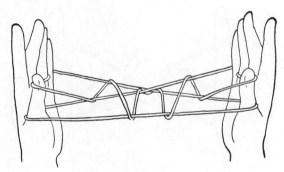

Fig. 622.

hands with the fingers pointing down, and shake the wrist loops off the hands.
Separate the hands, and restore them to their usual position (Fig. 621).

Fifth: Pass each thumb away from you over the far thumb string, and pick
up from below on the back of the thumb the near little finger string, and return the
thumb to its position (Fig. 622).

Sixth : Pick up from below on the tip of each index the far thumb string (Fig. 623), and pressing the thumb against the index, straighten the latter, and hold the string high on its tip. Turn the palms away from you (Fig. 624).

Seventh : Swing the left hand down so that the palm is toward you and the fingers are directed to the right, and at the same time swing the right hand so that

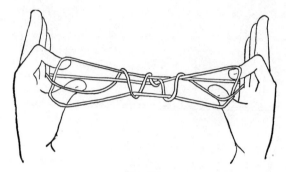

Fig. 623.

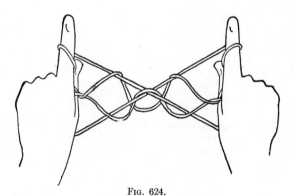

Fig. 624.

the palm faces away from you and the fingers point to the left. Draw the strings tight (Fig. 625).

The "Turtle" has the same final pattern as the "Bagobo Diamonds" and it is likewise extended vertically. If the next figure, "Ten Times," be formed from the "Bagobo Diamonds" it will eventually come back to the "Turtle," with simple loops on the thumbs and index fingers. The opening movements, although resem-

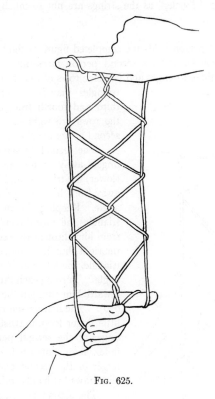

FIG. 625.

bling the opening movements of the "Pygmy Diamonds," are found only in this figure; the later movements are like those in the two preceding figures.

TEN TIMES

This game is really only a continuation of the "Turtle," but I have made it a separate figure, provisionally, because I saw the Philippine Linao Moros at the St. Louis Exposition form it from another figure which I could not record, but I think it was the same as "Bagobo Diamonds." Subsequently I learned the figure, as a part of the "Turtle," from Dr. Furness, who collected it in the Caroline Islands from the Uap girl "Dakofel."

Two persons are required for this figure, which is formed from the completed figure of either the Caroline Islands "Turtle" or the "Bagobo Small Diamonds," preferably from the "Turtle," as the strings are not so much twisted about the fingers.

First: The first person holds the completed figure of the "Turtle" in front of him, vertically of course, and the second person faces him. The figure consists of a central row of three lozenges and two side rows of four triangles each. These

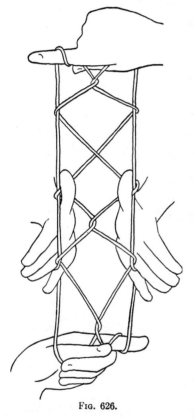

FIG. 626.

triangles may be numbered first, second, third and fourth from below upward, and the rows are right and left as seen by the second person.

The second person directs his left little finger away from him through the first (lower) left triangle, and his right little finger away from him through the first right triangle. Keeping the little fingers in these triangles, he now directs the thumbs away from him through the second side triangles, the right thumb of course through the right triangle, the left thumb through the left triangle. Turning each thumb up he directs it toward him through the third triangle (Fig. 626). The first person now places his right little finger loop, untwisted, on the left little finger of the second person, and his right index loop, untwisted, on the right little finger of the second person (Fig. 627), and withdraws his hands entirely from the figure.

The second person now puts his hands in the usual position and draws the strings tight. He has two loops on each thumb and two loops on each little finger.

Second: The first person now puts his right thumb from below into the left thumb loops of the second person, and his left thumb from below into the left little finger loops of the second person, and takes these loops away from the second person on his thumbs. The second person puts his left thumb from below into the loops which are on his right thumb, and removes the right thumb, and puts his right thumb from below into the loops which are on his right little finger, and removes the right little finger. The figure is now drawn tight on the four thumbs (Fig. 628). It consists of a central lozenge, the sides of which form the bases of the triangles held by the thumbs.

Third: Each person now puts the index and middle finger of each hand, from below, into the triangle extended by the thumb, and then away from him over the

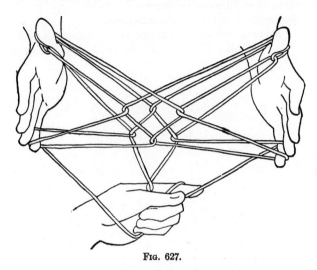

Fig. 627.

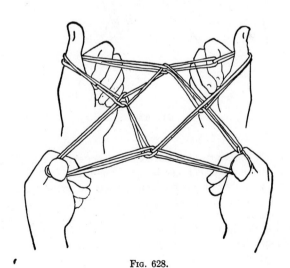

Fig. 628.

strings forming the base of this triangle (the corresponding side of the central lozenge) (Fig. 629), and pulls these strings down and toward him, letting the loops slip off the thumb (Fig. 630).

Each person now puts each thumb from below into the loop held by the index and middle finger and withdraws these fingers.

Fourth: Repeat the *Third* movement nine times.

Fifth: The figure is now laid down, and all the fingers are withdrawn. If you are careful, the top half of the figure can now be lifted up and opened out like

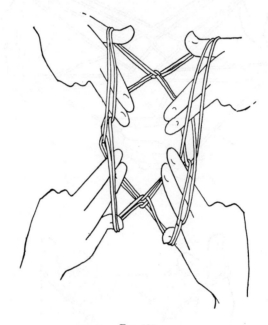

FIG. 629.

a book, when it will be seen that you have again the original "Turtle" figure (Fig. 631), from which these movements can be again repeated.

The Moros, who showed me this figure, appeared to take great delight in doing it; and they were much surprised to see Dr. Furness form it from the "Turtle." They always repeated the *Third* movement nineteen times, so we might more properly call the figure "Twenty Times," but in the Caroline Islands it is universally done ten times. As a matter of fact the figure will succeed if the movement be done *any even* number of times.

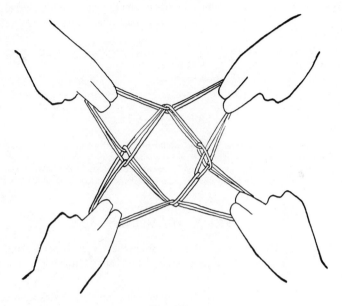

Fig. 630.

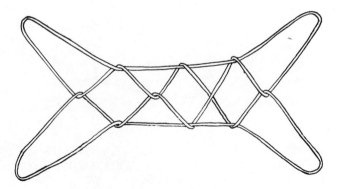

Fig. 631.

CHAPTER VII

PYGMY DIAMONDS

AMONG the African Batwa Pygmies, from the Congo Kasai Valley, at the
St. Louis Exposition, was a bright little man, "Ottobang," who taught
me this figure.

First: Put both hands through the loop of string, up to the wrists, and take up
between the thumb and index of each hand a short piece of the upper wrist string.
Then make a small hanging ring in this string, by passing the string held by the right

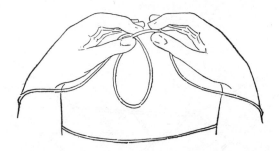

Fig. 632.

hand toward you over the left hand string (Fig. 632). Turn this ring up, and
put first the right thumb (Fig. 633) and then the left thumb (Fig. 634) away from
you into the ring, and separate the hands (Fig. 635).

Second: Get another person to take between the thumb and index the cross
formed in the centre of the figure by the far thumb and near wrist strings, and

276

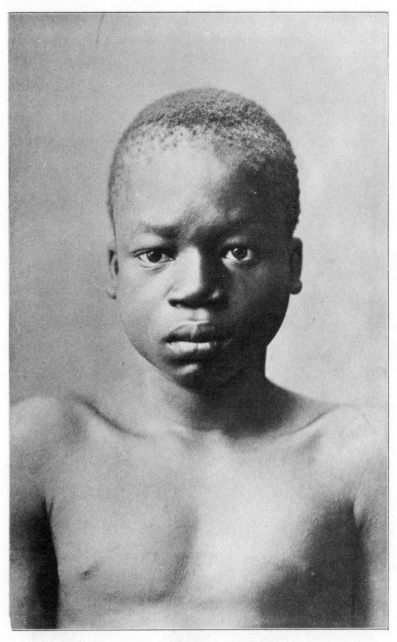

OTTOBANG, A CANNIBAL PYGMY, KASAI VALLEY, CONGO, AFRICA.

(Courtesy of Mr. S. C. Simms.)

CHIEF ZAROFF, AN ALASKAN ESKIMO.

Turning the palms toward you, let them move away from you (Fig. 633); then, as the right hand passes over the upper far string, let the far string slide to 46 47.

TENTH: Insert each thumb from below into the far thumb loop, and draw it away from the near thumb loop, which is released from each thumb (Fig. 634).

ELEVENTH: Straighten the hands (Fig. 635).

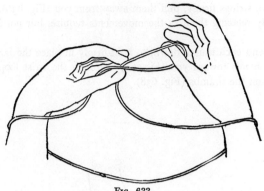

Fig. 633.

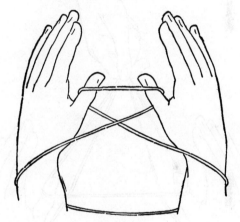

Fig. 634.

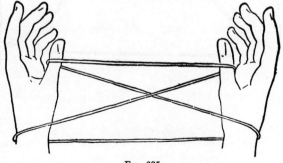

Fig. 635.

holding the two strings firmly, pull them away from you (Fig. 636), keeping them taut, or slightly relaxing them as the movements require, but not letting go until told to do so.

Third: Bend each thumb down, to hold firmly in place the far thumb string, and draw the hands toward you (Fig. 637) through the wrist loops, keeping the loops securely on the thumbs (Fig. 638).

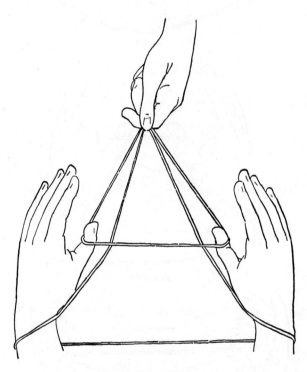

FIG. 636.

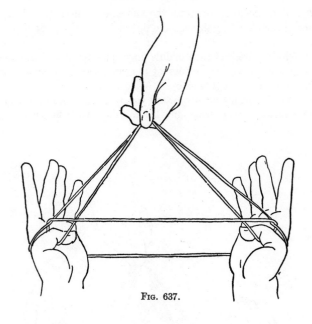

FIG. 637.

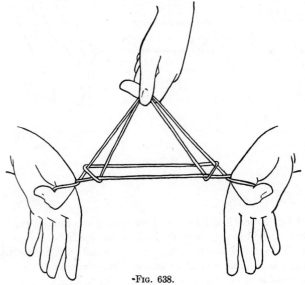

-FIG. 638.

Fourth : Turn the hands up with the palms away from you (Fig. 639, **Left** hand), and slip each hand up through the thumb loop to the wrist (Fig. 639, **Right** hand).

Fifth : With the back of each middle finger pick up, from below, the oblique string passing around the two strings of the wrist loop, and return the **middle** finger to its former position (Fig. 640).

Sixth : Turn the palms slightly toward you, and bend each middle finger down over the near middle finger string, and holding the middle finger loop (Fig. 641,

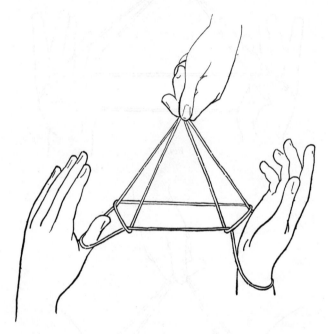

FIG. 639.

Left hand) tightly in position, draw each hand toward you through the wrist loop, which should be caught in passing on the back of the thumb.

Seventh : Turn the palms toward each other; pull each middle finger loop further through the thumb loop, and turning the palm upward, straighten the middle finger outside of the thumb loop (Fig. 641, Right hand).

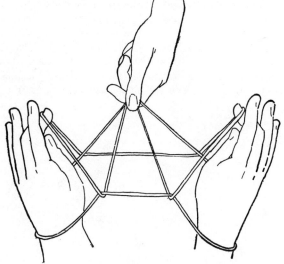

Fig. 640.

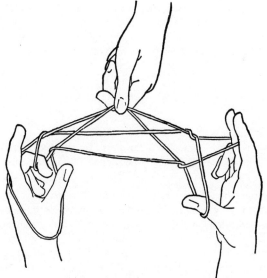

Fig. 641.

Eighth : The figure is extended by spreading the thumbs and middle fingers widely apart and separating the hands (Fig. 642). The strings held by the second person are now released.

So far as I know, this figure is the first African string game that has ever been described. The nature of the Batwas and their isolation in the heart of Africa would not lead us to expect to find among them a relatively complicated figure, and make any resemblances which this figure may bear to other figures doubly

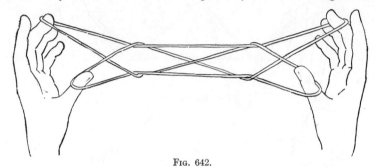

FIG. 642.

interesting. We see at a glance that it has much in common with the "Caroline Islands Diamonds" and the "Turtle." The finished pattern is identical with the pattern formed after the *Sixth* movement of the Eskimo "Mouth"; hence you can go on and finish the "Mouth" from the finished pattern of the "Pygmy Diamonds." This is the only case, in my experience, where the finished pattern of one figure occurs as a stage in the development of another entirely different figure.

A MOUTH

I obtained this figure from Chief Zaroff, a Topek Eskimo from Alaska, in the Eskimo Village at the St. Louis Exposition. The native name is *Rote* = a Mouth.

First : Put the loop on the hands in the First Position.

Second : Pass the right index from above behind the string crossing the left palm, and as you draw the loop out, turn the right index away from you and upward (Fig. 643), to put a cross in the loop, and also bend the left index down, and pick up from below on the back of the finger the left near little finger string, and return the index to its position (Fig. 644). Release the loops from the little fingers (Fig. 645). You now have a loop on each index and a loop on each thumb.

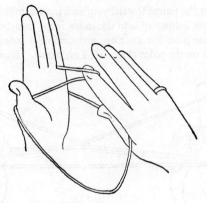

FIG. 643.

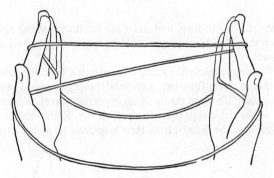

FIG. 644.

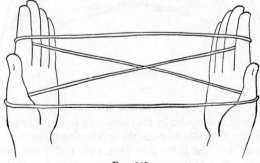

FIG. 645.

Third : Turn the palms toward you, and put the middle, ring and little fingers of each hand, from below, up into the index loop; then bend these fingers toward you down over the near index string, and draw the string down and hold it by closing the fingers on the palm (Fig. 646, Left hand). Now put each middle finger

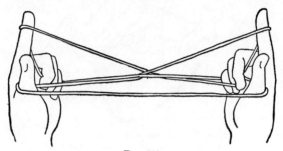

FIG. 646.

from above into the thumb loop, and draw the far thumb string against the ring finger, closed on the palm, by closing the middle finger also down on the palm (Fig. 646, Right hand).

Fourth : Keeping carefully the string on each index, bend the index toward you over the near thumb string (Fig. 647, Left hand); then, by moving the index away from you and upward, lift up on the tip of the finger this near thumb string, while the string already on the index slips over the tip (Fig. 647, Right hand).

Fifth : Withdraw the thumbs from their loops, and let go the string held down

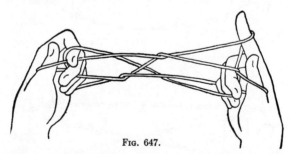

FIG. 647.

by each middle finger (Fig. 648). You now have on each hand a loop around the index and a loop held to the palm by the closed ring and little fingers.

Sixth : Transfer the index loops to the middle fingers, by putting each middle finger, from above, into the index loop (Fig. 649, Left hand), withdrawing the index, and returning the middle finger to its position (Fig. 649, Right hand).

Seventh: Bring the palms close together, and hang the right middle finger loop, without twisting it, over the left middle finger; and hang the loop held on the

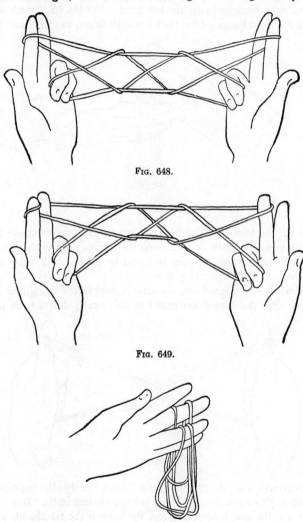

Fig. 648.

Fig. 649.

Fig. 650.

right ring and little fingers, without twisting it, on the left ring and little fingers; withdraw the right hand (Fig. 650).

Then put the four fingers of the right hand to the left, through the two loops hanging from the left ring and little fingers (Fig. 651), and closing the right fingers on the palm, take these loops off the left hand. Put the left thumb away from you into the two loops hanging from the left middle finger, and withdraw the middle

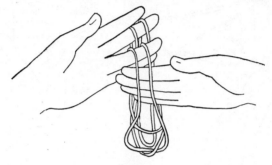

FIG. 651.

finger; now put the four fingers of the left hand toward you into these loops, and close the fingers on the palm, withdrawing the thumb. Draw the strings apart. The "Mouth" can be made to open and shut by rotating the wrist alternately away from you and toward you (Fig. 652).

As I have already pointed out, the arrangement of the string into index and thumb loops, after the *Second* movement of this figure, differs from the almost

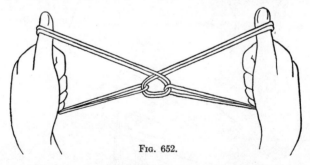

FIG. 652.

similar arrangement after the opening in the "Bow," in that the two straight horizontal strings in this figure are both near strings, whereas in the "Bow" the upper straight string is the near index string and the lower is the far thumb string. If, after Opening A, you release the little finger loops, you get a similar figure, but the upper straight string is the far index string and the lower is the near thumb string. I do not yet know of an instance in which, in a similar figure, both straight strings are far strings.

TWO LITTLE BOYS RUNNING AWAY

This figure was obtained by Mr. John L. Cox, at Hampton, Virginia, from Emma Jackson, the Klamath Indian from Oregon.

First: The loop of string is doubled and used throughout as a single string. Put the thumbs into the loop, and separate the hands. Insert the

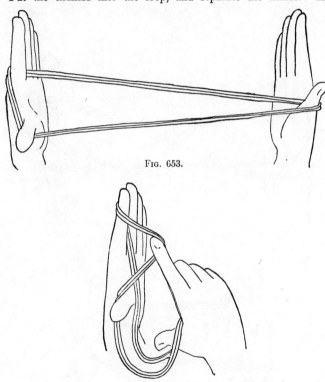

FIG. 653.

FIG. 654.

left index from below into the loop, and separate widely the left thumb and index (Fig. 653). Put the right index, from above, down behind the strings which pass from the left thumb to the left index (Fig. 654), and draw the

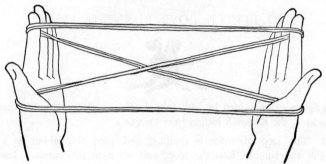

Fig. 655.

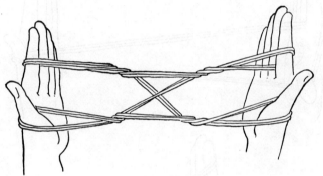

Fig. 656.

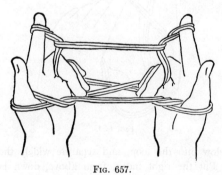

Fig. 657.

loop out, at the same time turning the right index away from you and up to its usual position (Fig. 655).

Second : Give the index loops one twist, by rotating each index toward you, down, away from you, and up again.

Third : Give the thumb loops one twist, by rotating each thumb away from you, down, toward you, and up again (Fig. 656).

Fourth : Put the middle, ring and little fingers of *both* hands toward you through the upper triangle at the centre of the figure, then over the cross strings and down into the lower triangle (Fig. 657), and finally close these fingers down on the palms (Fig. 658).

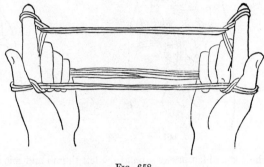

FIG. 658.

Fifth : Put the left thumb from below into the left index loop and enlarge the loop slightly. Bring the left thumb and index close to the right index, and pick up the right near index string between the tips of the left thumb and index (Fig. 659), and, without remov-

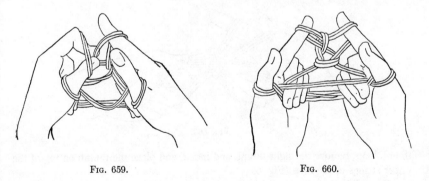

FIG. 659.   FIG. 660.

ing the right index, draw it through the loop passing around the left thumb and index, which is now allowed to slip off these fingers. Insert the left index away from you through the loop which you have been holding between the tips of the left thumb and index, remove these fingers and leave the loop on the left index (Fig. 660).

Sixth : Repeat the same movement on the thumb loops by putting the left middle finger from below into the left thumb loop, and then, with the tips of the left thumb and middle finger, drawing the right near thumb string (Fig. 661) through

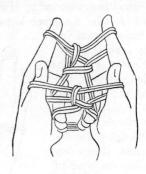

FIG. 661.

FIG. 662.

the loop which passes around the left thumb and middle finger, allowing this loop to slip off these fingers, but keeping the right thumb in its loop. Now insert the left thumb away from you into the loop you have been holding between the tips of the left thumb and middle finger, and draw the hands apart, still keeping the strings held to the palms (Fig. 662).

Seventh : Take all three fingers of the right hand out of the loop they are holding to the palm, and put them toward you into both the right index loop and right

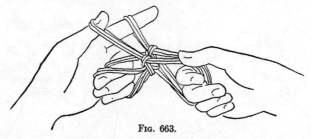

FIG. 663.

thumb loop; remove the right thumb and index, and place the thumb on top of the upper strings of the loop (Fig. 663).

The "little boys" are made to run by pulling on the upper right hand strings.

This is a curious and not very interesting figure although some of the movements are novel. The result produced by the *First* movement is the same as that produced by the opening movement of the Eskimo "Mouth." If the "boys" appear too near the left hand they must be pushed to the right so that their "flight" to the left may be a little longer.

A LITTLE FISH THAT HIDES IN THE MUD

This is another Klamath figure secured by Mr. John L. Cox, from Emma Jackson, of Oregon.

First: The same as the *First* movement of the "Two Little Boys Running Away."

Second: Holding the fingers of the right hand close together, turn the right hand so that the finger tips sweep down toward you under the figure (Fig. 664),

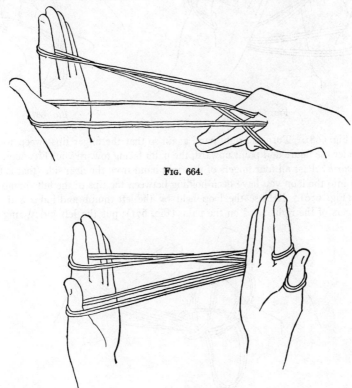

FIG. 664.

FIG. 665.

and the whole hand comes on the near side of the figure, the finger tips pointing upward and the palm facing toward you (Fig. 665).

Third: Pass all four fingers of the right hand up on the near side of the left thumb loop and put them from below into the left index loop, so that the left near index string becomes a palmar string on the right hand (Fig. 666); remove the left index. With the left thumb and index take hold of the palmar string of the loop which is on the right index (above the right palmar string) (Fig. 667), and, keeping the loop on the right thumb, withdraw the right hand from all the other

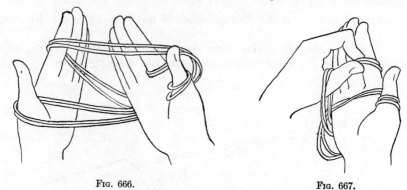

FIG. 666.   FIG. 667.

loops (Fig. 668). Turn the right hand again so that the finger tips sweep toward you under the figure and point upward, the palm facing toward you (Fig. 669).

Fourth : Pass all four fingers of the right hand from the near side (that is from below) into the loop you have been holding between the tips of the left thumb and index (Fig. 670). Release the loop held by the left thumb and index and close the fingers of the right hand on the palm (Fig. 671); put the left index, ring and

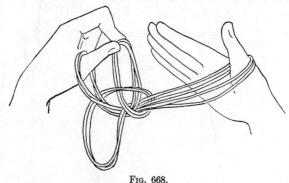

FIG. 668.

middle fingers (below the other strings of the figure) toward you into this loop beside the fingers of the right hand (Fig. 672).

Fifth : Remove the right fingers from this lower loop, and hold the loop by bending the fingers of the left hand down on the palm; then sweep the right hand

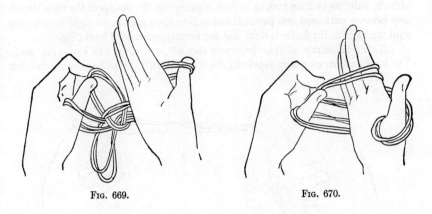

FIG. 669.   FIG. 670.

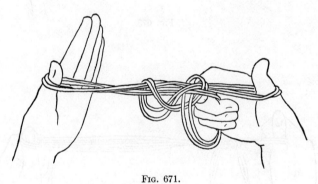

FIG. 671.

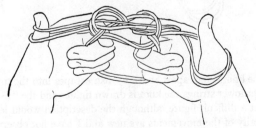

FIG. 672.

with the palm away from you, or in such manner that the strings of the right thumb loop become untwisted and parallel, and pull to the right on the right thumb loop until the twist in the figure is tight, but not formed into a hard knot (Fig. 673).

Sixth : Withdraw all four fingers of the left hand from the loop (Fig. 674). The knot and hanging loop represent the "little Fish"; by pulling on the two left

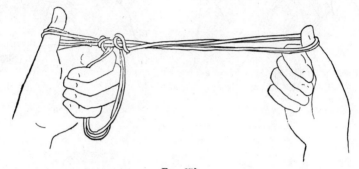

Fig. 673.

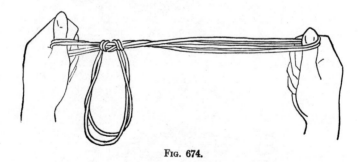

Fig. 674.

lower strings the knot comes apart and the "fish escapes into the mud"; by pulling on the two right lower strings the knot is drawn tighter and the "fish is caught."

This is not a difficult figure, although the description would lead one to think so. The majority of the movements are new and I have not observed them in any other figure.

A LITTLE BOY CARRYING WOOD

This also is a Klamath Indian figure, obtained in the same way as "Two Little Boys Running Away."

First : With the right thumb and index turn one string of the loop toward you about ten times, loosely, around the last joint of the left thumb. Then put the left index and the right thumb into the rest of the loop and separate the hands. Now put the right index, from above, behind the string which passes from the left thumb

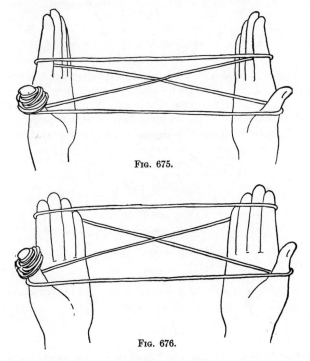

Fig. 675.

Fig. 676.

to the left index, and pull the loop out, at the same time turning the right index away from you and up to its usual position (Fig. 675).

Second : Pass the middle, ring and little fingers of each hand from below into the index loop (Fig. 676), and draw the near index string down on the palm, then bring the hands together and pass the left middle finger to the far side and the left index to the near side of the right far index string (Fig. 677), and draw this string to the left, between the fingers, through the left index loop and put it around the

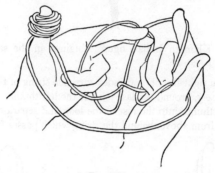

FIG. 677.

tip of the left index by turning the left hand with the palm away from you. During this movement the original left index loop slips from the finger (Fig. 678).

Third : Release the loop from the right index. With the right thumb and index take hold of the two strings of the left index loop (close to the index), and lift the loop from the finger; then thread this loop from above downward through the turns

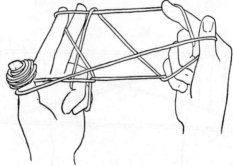

FIG. 678.

on the left thumb (Fig. 679), and put it back on the left index, withdrawing the left thumb from the turns (Fig. 680).

Fourth : Transfer the right thumb loop to the right index, by picking up from below on the back of the index the near thumb string, returning the index to position and withdrawing the thumb (Fig. 681).

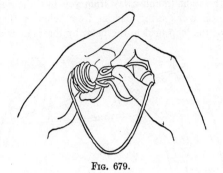

Fig. 679.

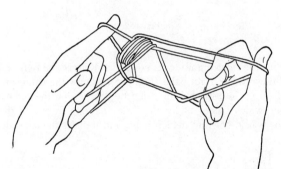

Fig. 680.

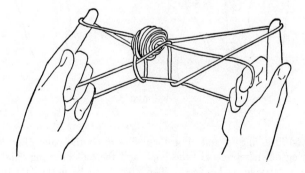

Fig. 681.

Fifth : Pass the right thumb away from you into the right index loop, and, pulling down the near index string, pick up from below on the back of the thumb the upper string of the loop held to the palm by the right middle, ring and little

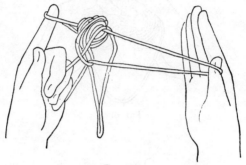

Fig. 682.

fingers. Return the right thumb to its position. Release the right index loop and the loop held down to the right palm (Fig. 682). Draw the hands apart, and pull the hanging loop up into the ball of string by drawing on the right lower thumb string (the one which passes under the little and ring fingers of the left hand). Release the loops held down to the left palm, and transfer the left index loop to the

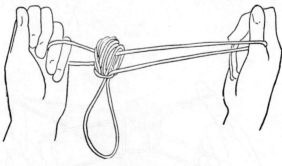

Fig. 683.

left ring and little fingers, and close these fingers on the palm (Fig. 683). The loop hanging down represents "the boy" and the ball of string "the bundle of wood" he is carrying on his head. The "boy" can be pushed far to the right, and then made to walk to the left by pulling on the right upper thumb string.

A SECOND WORM

The two Navaho girls at the St. Louis Exposition who taught me most of the other Navaho figures taught me this one also.

First: Put the thumbs through the untwisted loop and separate the hands.

Second: Bend each index toward you down into the thumb loop (Fig. 684, Right hand), and pick up from below on the tip of the index the near thumb string and return the index to its position (Fig. 684, Left hand).

Third: Bring the hands together, and pick up from below on the back of the right thumb the string which passes from the left thumb to the left index (Fig. 685), and draw out the loop by separating the hands (Fig. 686).

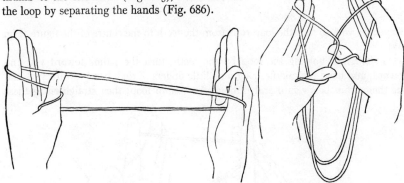

Fig. 684.   Fig. 685.

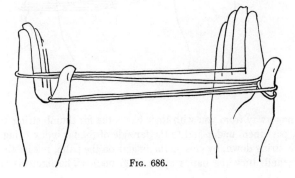

Fig. 686.

Fourth : With the teeth pick up, on the back of the right thumb, the right lower thumb loop, and draw it over the tip of the right thumb; then draw the hands

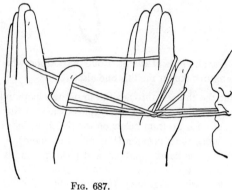

FIG. 687.

away from you, so that the loop runs from the teeth to the centre of the figure (Fig. 687).

Fifth : Still holding the loop by the teeth, turn the palms toward you and upward, and bend the middle, ring and little fingers of each hand toward you, and put them from below into and through the thumb loop; then straightening these

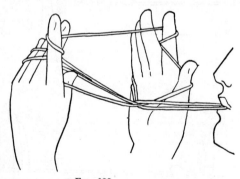

FIG. 688.

fingers, pushing away from you with their backs the far thumb string and the near index string, pass them under and to the far side of the far index string (Fig. 688). Now pull this string down, by closing the fingers on the palm, release the loops held by the teeth, and draw the hands apart (Fig. 689). The figure is extended by separating widely the loops held by each thumb and each index, at the same time holding down the lower string with the other fingers closed on the palm.

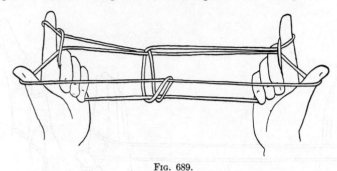

Fig. 689.

The first four movements of this figure are entirely new; the last is a characteristic Navaho movement.

A BRUSH HOUSE

This figure was obtained by Mr. John L. Cox, at Hampton, Virginia, from a Pueblo Indian, Antonio Abeita, from Isleta, New Mexico. He called it *Nathu* = a Hut. Mr. Cox tells me that it is also known to Emma Jackson the Klamath Indian, who taught him the other Klamath figures. There is a finished pattern of this figure preserved in the Philadelphia Free Museum of Science and Art, collected by Mr. Stuart Culin at Zuni, New Mexico. It is numbered 22607 and labelled *Pi-cho-wai, ham-pun-nai* = a Brush House.

First : Put the untwisted loop on the index fingers only, and separate the hands. Pass each thumb from below into the index loop (Fig. 690, Left hand), bend it over the far index string and sweep it down, toward you, and up again (Fig. 690, Right

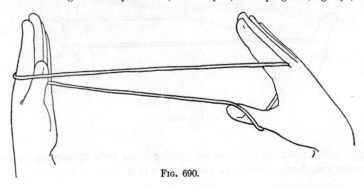

Fig. 690.

hand). In this way you put crossed loops on the thumbs and index fingers (Fig. 691). You now have, on each hand, a far thumb string and a near index string,

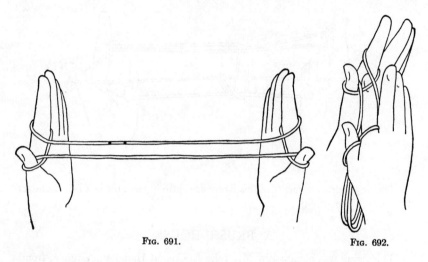

FIG. 691.   FIG. 692.

and a palmar string passing from the near side of the thumb to the far side of the index.

Second: Put the right index from below under this left palmar string, between the far thumb string and the near index string (Fig. 692), and draw the loop out on

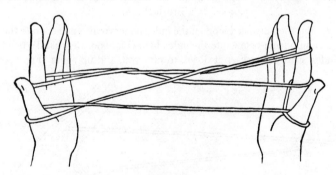

FIG. 693

the back of the index, at the same time giving it one twist by rotating the index away from you, down, toward you, and up again (Fig. 693).

Third: Put the right thumb from below into the right upper index loop, and separate the thumb from the index in order to make the loop wider (Fig. 694). Now pass the left index from above through this upper loop extended on the left

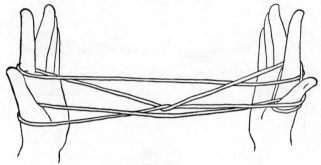

Fig. 694.

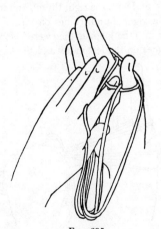

Fig. 695.

thumb and index, and pick up, from below (between the lower near index string and the lower far thumb string) on the back of the left index the right palmar string (Fig. 695), and draw the loop out and give it one twist by rotating the left index away from you, down, toward you, and up again.

Fourth : Pass the left thumb from below into the upper left index loop, and separate the thumb from the index in order to make the loop wider (Fig. 696).

Fifth : Bend the right middle, ring and little fingers toward you over all the loops on the right hand, and close these fingers on the palm to hold the strings in

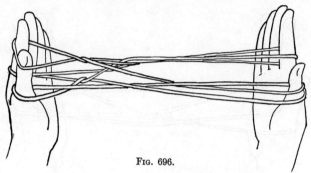

Fig. 696.

place while you gather together, close to the left hand, between the right thumb and index all the loops on the left hand, by putting the right thumb below the loops and closing the right index down on them (Fig. 697). Now withdraw the left hand from all the loops, and with the right thumb and index turn the loops over, away from you (so that the right thumb comes on top of the loops), and put the left thumb and index back into the loop, as they were before (Fig. 698), except that now the left thumb loop goes on the left index and the left index loop goes on the

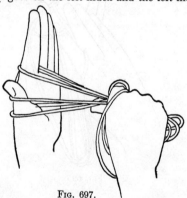

Fig. 697.

left thumb and the loop common to both thumb and index is now the lower loop. Draw the hands apart and repeat the same movement on the right hand, as follows: Bend the left middle, ring and little fingers toward you over all the loops on the left hand, and close these fingers down on the palm to hold the strings in place while you gather together, with the left thumb and index, close to the right hand, all the loops on the left hand, putting the left thumb below the loops and closing the left index down on them. Now withdraw the right hand from all the loops and with the left thumb and index turn the loops over, away from you (so that the left thumb

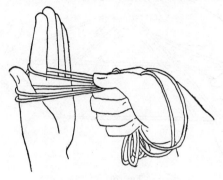

Fig. 698.

comes on top of the loops), and put the right thumb and index back into the loops as they were before, except that now the right thumb loop goes on the right index, the right index loop goes on the right thumb and the loop common to both right thumb and index is now the lower loop.

Separate the hands and draw the strings tight (Fig. 699). The figure now consists of an upper string which is a single straight near index string passing on

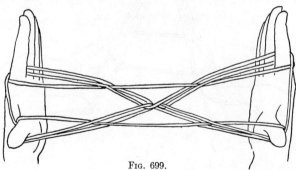

Fig. 699.

either side between the two far index strings; a lower string which is a single straight far thumb string passing, on each side, between the two near thumb strings; and double near thumb and far index strings twisted together in the centre.

Sixth: A second person now pulls upward the twisted strings in the centre of the figure, while you bend each index down toward you, over the near index string and each thumb away from you over the far thumb string (Fig. 700), and, holding these strings down, you let the other strings slip off the thumbs and index fingers.

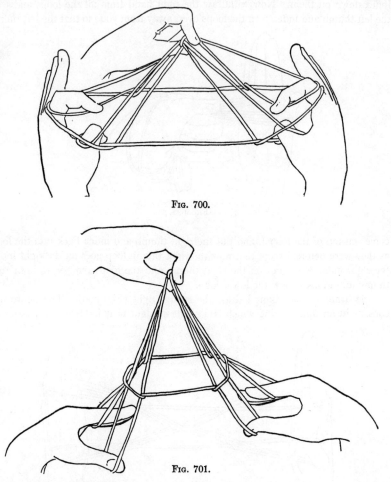

Fig. 700.

Fig. 701.

Now turn the hands with the palms down, and separate the thumbs widely from the index fingers, and the "Brush House" is formed (Fig. 701).

This is a very pretty figure and many of the movements are novel; the *Sixth* is of particular interest because it is just the reverse of the usual "Navaho movement," the thumb and index loops being drawn through the loop common to both thumb and index.

A SIX-POINTED STAR

Mr. Cox also secured this figure from the Pueblo Indian, Antonio Abeita, from Isleta, New Mexico. It is known to the Klamath Indians. A finished pattern preserved in the Philadelphia Free Museum of Science and Art (No. 25730), collected by Mr. Stuart Culin from the Tewas at Isleta, is labelled *pah-rhu-la* = a Star.

This figure is formed from the "Brush House," by the second person releasing the loops which he has been holding up, and pulling out in opposite directions the straight strings at the sides of the figure (Fig. 702).

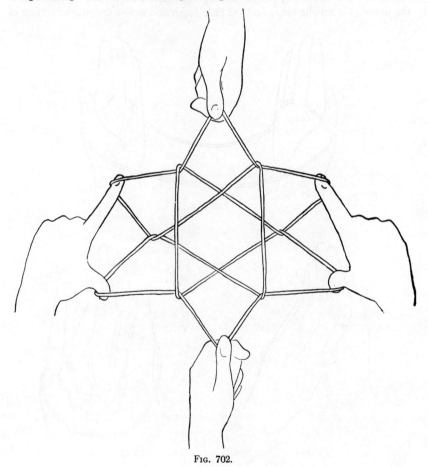

Fig. 702.

THE BREASTBONE AND RIBS

I learned this figure from the same Eskimo, Chief Zaroff, who showed me the "Mouth." The native name is *Grut* = the Breastbone and Ribs.

First : Lace the string between the fingers of each hand, so that it passes behind the thumb, the middle finger and the little finger and across the palmar surface of

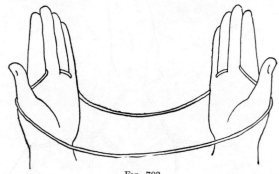

FIG. 703.

FIG. 704.

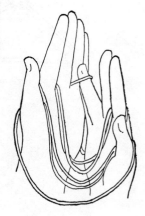

FIG. 705.

the index finger and of the ring finger. The near thumb string and the far little finger string pass straight from hand to hand (Fig. 703).

Second: With the right index take up, from below, the string on the palmar surface of the left index (Fig. 704) and separate the hands. With the left index

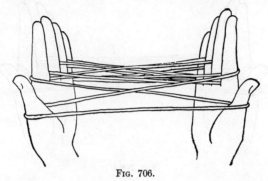

FIG. 706.

take up from below, between the strings of the right index loop, the string on the palmar surface of the right index and separate the hands.

Third: With the right ring finger take up, from below, the string on the palmar surface of the left ring finger (Fig. 705) and separate the hands. With the left

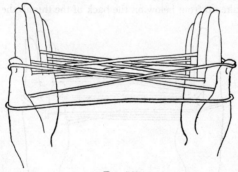

FIG. 707.

ring finger take up, from below, between the strings of the right ring finger loop, the string on the palmar surface of the right ring finger and separate the hands. There is now a loop on every finger of each hand (Fig. 706).

Fourth: Put each thumb from below into the index loop, and separate the thumb from the index (Fig. 707). With the teeth draw the original thumb loop, of each hand in turn, up over the loop passing around both thumb and index, and, slipping it entirely off the thumb, let it drop on the palmar side (Fig. 708).

Fifth : Pass each thumb away from you over the far thumb string and both strings of the index loop, and take up from below, on the back of the thumb, the

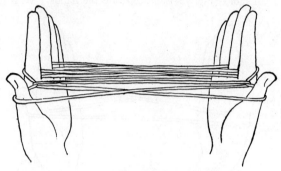

FIG. 708.

near middle finger string and return the thumb to its position (Fig. 709). With the teeth draw the lower thumb loop, of each hand in turn, up over the loop just taken on the thumb, and, slipping it off the thumb, drop it on the palmar side (Fig. 710).

Sixth : Pass each thumb away from you over the thumb, index and middle finger loops, and take up from below on the back of the thumb the near ring finger

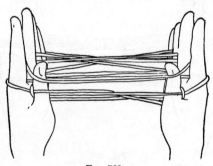

FIG. 709.

string, and return the thumb to its position (Fig. 711). With the teeth draw the lower thumb loop, of each hand in turn, up over the upper thumb loop (the loop you have just taken on the thumb), and, slipping it off the thumb, drop it on the palmar side (Fig. 712).

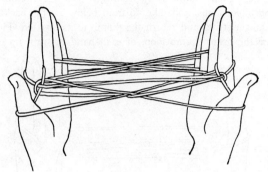

FIG. 710.

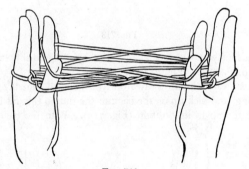

FIG. 711.

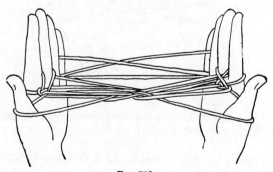

FIG. 712

Seventh : Pass each thumb away from you over the thumb, index, middle finger and ring finger loops, and take up from below, on the back of the thumb, the near little finger string and return the thumb to its position (Fig. 713). With the teeth draw the lower thumb loop, of each hand in turn, up over the upper

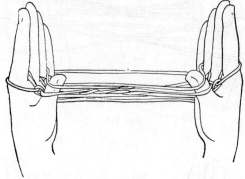

FIG. 713.

thumb loop (the loop you have just taken on the thumb), and slipping it off the thumb drop it on the palmar side (Fig. 714).

Eighth : Pass each thumb away from you over all the strings except the far little finger string, and pick up on the back of the thumb this far little finger string and return the thumb to its position (Fig. 715). With the teeth draw the lower

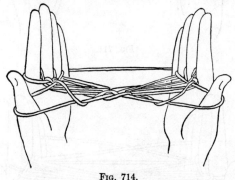

FIG. 714.

thumb loop, of each hand in turn, up over the upper thumb loop (the loop you have just taken on the thumb), and slipping it off the thumb drop it on the palmar side (Fig. 716).

Ninth : Transfer the thumb loops to the little fingers, by bending each little finger toward you and putting it from above down into the thumb loop; and then, picking up on the back of the finger the near thumb string (Fig. 717, Right hand) return the little finger to its position as you withdraw the thumb (Fig. 717, Left hand).

Tenth : Pick up with the teeth the middle of the nearest straight string which runs from hand to hand (it usually hangs down, and is the lower of the two strings

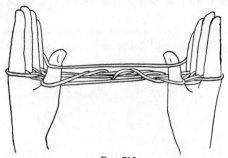

Fig. 715.

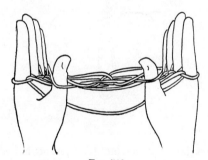

Fig. 716.

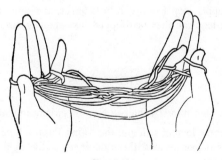

Fig. 717

which, on each side, form a loop around the near index string). Draw this string toward you, and still keeping the loop between the teeth, extend the figure by drawing the hands away from you, with their palms toward each other and the fingers directed away from you.

I have found it more convenient, after the figure has been extended, to release the loop held by the teeth and hold it between the tips of the extended thumbs (Fig. 718).

In this Eskimo figure, the movement which we have regarded as the most characteristic "Navaho movement" (slipping a lower loop over an upper loop and

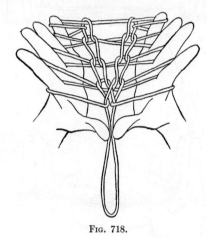

Fig. 718.

then off the finger) reaches its maximum development; indeed there is little else in this figure than a constant repetition of this movement.

To take the string off the hands without tangling it, release the loop held by the teeth, remove the upper loop from each little finger, and draw the hands forcibly apart. The simple loop can then be dropped from the fingers.

A BIRD'S NEST

This figure was shown me by the two Navaho girls from Gallup, New Mexico.

First : Arrange the loop of string in the "First Position" on the left hand, and as a single, uncrossed loop around the little finger of the right hand. Draw the strings tight (Fig 719).

Second : Put the thumb and index of the right hand, from above, behind the string crossing the left palm, and draw the loop out to the right (Fig. 720), at the same time by widely separating the right thumb and index, and turning the hand up to its usual-position, you put a crossed loop on each of these fingers (Fig. 721).

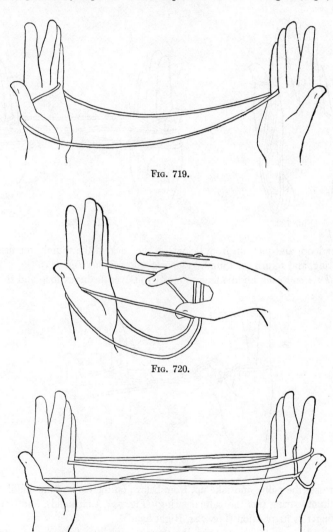

FIG. 719.

FIG. 720.

FIG. 721.

Third : With the left index pick up from the right index, from below and on the far side of the right near index string, the right far index string (which passes to the near side of the right thumb) (Fig. 722), and separate the hands.

Fourth : Bend each thumb away from you over the far thumb string and over

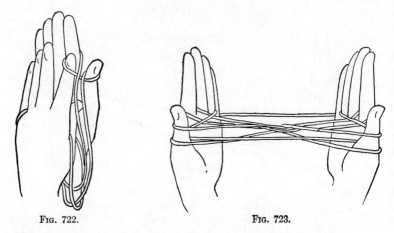

Fig. 722.   Fig. 723.

the index loop, and pick up from below, on the back of the thumb, the near little finger string, and return the thumb to its original position (Fig. 723).

Fifth : Bend each middle finger toward you over the index loop and the string

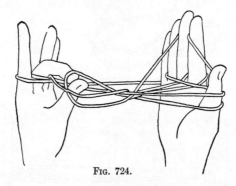

Fig. 724.

which crosses the palm, and take up, from below, on the back of the middle finger, the far thumb string (*not* the palmar string) (Fig. 724, Left hand), and return the middle finger to its position (Fig. 724, Right hand).

Sixth : Release the loops from the thumbs and little fingers, and extend the figure by keeping the middle finger loops up on the tips of those fingers, and by pulling each far index string down to the palm with the ring and little fingers, at the same time drawing each near index string toward you with the thumb (Fig. 725).

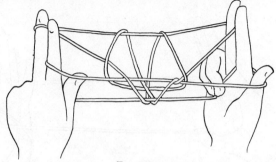

FIG. 725.

The first three movements of this figure are new, and do not occur in any other figure; of these the *Second* is particularly interesting.

TWO BOYS FIGHTING FOR AN ARROW

The Klamath Indian, Emma Jackson, who taught Mr. John L. Cox the other figures, also showed him this one.

First : Put each hand completely through the untwisted loop. Bend each little finger down toward you, and pick up from below on its back the near wrist string, and return the little finger to its position (Fig. 726). Bend each thumb away from

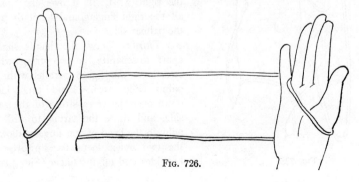

FIG. 726.

you, and pick up from below on its back the far wrist string, and return the thumb to its position (Fig. 727). With the right index pick up, from below, both strings

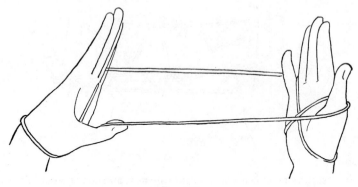

FIG. 727.

on the left palm just where they cross (Fig. 728), and separate the hands; with

FIG. 728.

the left index pick up, from below, both strings on the right palm just where they cross, and separate the hands (Fig. 729).

Second: With the right thumb and index pick up the string on the back of the left wrist, lift it over the tips of all the left fingers, and let it drop on the palmar side. With the left thumb and index pick up the string on the back of the right wrist, lift it over the tips of all the right fingers, and let it drop on the palmar side.

Third: Draw the hands slightly apart to separate the two strings which cross over the figure parallel with the palms (Fig. 730). Bend each index down over the cross string of the same side, and draw the string toward the palm in the bend of the finger; allowing the two index loops to slip over the knuckles and off the finger (Fig. 731).

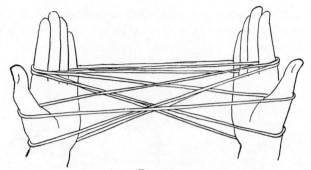

Fig. 729.

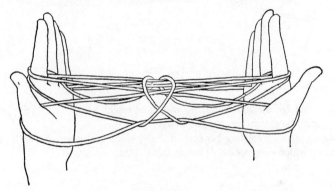

Fig. 730.

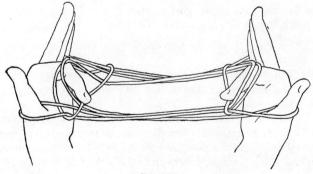

Fig. 731.

Fourth : A second person now holds lightly a small piece of stick (a match for example) down into the centre of the figure (Fig. 732); if you now quickly let go

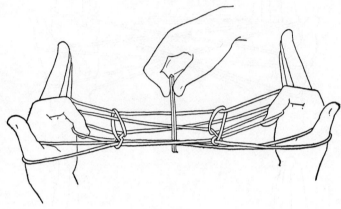

FIG. 732.

the loops held by the index fingers, which represent the "boys," the stick, or "arrow," may be caught or snapped away.

This figure is interesting because of the opening movement, a modification of Opening A, which does not occur in any of the other figures.

FLINT AND STEEL

In the Caroline Islands this figure is called *Nifi* = Flint and Steel. Dr. Furness obtained it from a Uap boy named "*Gumaun.*"

First : First Position, with the loop doubled and used throughout as a double string.

Second : Put the right thumb, from above, behind the strings on the left palm (Fig. 733), and separate the hands, turning the right thumb toward you, and upright (Fig. 734).

Third : Pass the left thumb away from you, and pick up from below on its back the near little finger strings, and return the thumb to its position (Fig. 735).

Fourth : Bend each index down, and pick up from below the far thumb strings (*not* the palmar strings), and hold them up on the back of the last joint of the index (Fig. 736).

TWO UAP BOYS. THE ELDER IS GUMAUN.
(Courtesy of Dr. William Henry Furness, 3rd.)

TWO NATIVES OF MURRAY ISLAND. THE YOUNGER IS JIMMIE RICE.
See Haddon's *Head Hunters: Black, White and Brown*.
(Courtesy of Dr. A. C. Haddon.)

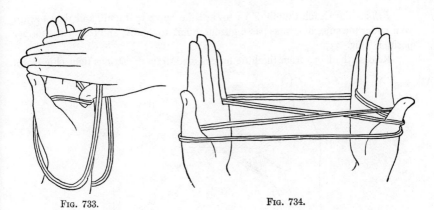

FIG. 733.   FIG. 734.

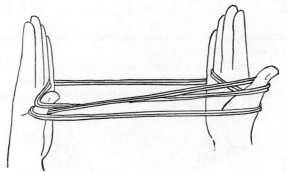

FIG. 735.

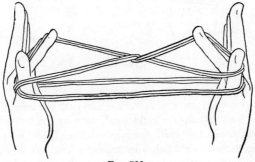

FIG. 736.

Fifth : Turn each thumb down toward the opposite thumb, and then toward you, under the straight strings passing from thumb to thumb, and back to its former position (Fig. 737).

Release the loops from the little fingers, and draw the strings tight (Fig. 738).

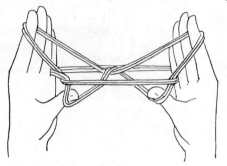

FIG. 737.

The hands are now in their usual positions; the thumbs, separated from the index fingers, are directed toward you.

Sixth : Keeping the loops securely on the fingers, turn the right hand so that the right thumb passes under the figure; the palm is directed away from you, the fingers pointing upward; now turn the left hand with the palm away from you,

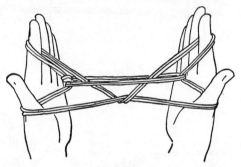

FIG. 738.

and move it so that the finger tips sweep away from you, down (Fig. 739), and then under the figure toward you and upward. Carry the left hand to the right as far as possible, without moving the right hand, crossing the left wrist over the right wrist draw the strings tight with the hands having their backs directed toward each other (Fig. 740), the right palm directed to the left, the left palm directed to the right, and the thumbs pointing upward. This movement should be done quickly.

The "fire" is supposed to lie between the thumb and index of the left hand. If a native were doing the figure, he would tell you to blow out the fire, and when you did so, bringing your head near his left hand, he would bring the thumb and index of each hand together quickly; the fire would surely be out, but your nose would be in—between his left thumb and index.

In this figure we have a new opening and a new method of extension. The finished pattern closely resembles the pattern of the "Osage Two Diamonds"; there are slight differences, however, in the crossing of the strings.

In the fifth volume of the Reports of the Cambridge Anthropological Expedition to Torres Straits, page 17, Dr. Haddon gives a legend which is of interest in connection with this game.

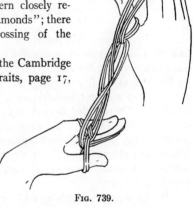

FIG. 739.

"THE ORIGIN OF FIRE

"Eguon, described as a large bat, is fabled to have introduced fire to Mawata. A legend goes that a tribe once inhabited Nalgi (Double Island), one of whose members showed fire to come from the left hand, between the thumb and forefinger, whereupon dissension arose and the people were all transformed into animals, birds, reptiles, fish

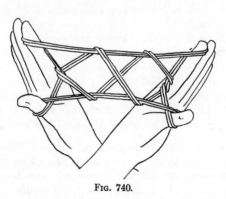

FIG. 740.

(including dugong and turtle). Eguon found his way to Mawata, the others to different places in the Straits and New Guinea. There appears to have been some friendly arrangement among the snakes whereby some took to the land and others to the water. This legend was originally published by Mr. E. Beardmore, in his paper on 'The Natives of Mowat, Dandai, New Guinea' (*Journal of the Anthropological Institute*, xix, 1890, p. 462). I have quoted this as it is primarily a Torres Straits tale. The plucking of the first fire from between the thumb and forefinger is a widely spread myth in the Straits."

REAL CAT'S–CRADLE

As Dr. Haddon has pointed out, the familiar game of cat's-cradle probably had its origin in Asia whence it was introduced into Europe; it has also spread to some extent among the Asiatic islands. It is well known in China, Korea, Japan, the Philippines and Borneo; and it may be known in Java, Celebes, and Australia. It is apparently unknown in Micronesia, Melanesia, Polynesia, and to the Amerinds. In Europe it is recorded from Austria, Germany, the Netherlands, Denmark, Sweden, Switzerland, France, and England. From France it has spread into Northern Africa, for Dr. W. H. Furness found several little Arab girls in the tapestry school in Algiers who played it exactly as we do; they learned it in a French school. Of course it is probably known in all parts of the world which have felt the influence of European culture.

We have not been able to find any record of the time or manner of its introduction into England, but this must have happened within comparatively recent years as there are no references to it in the older literature. Moreover, no satisfactory explanation of the name "cat's-cradle" has ever been given; its other name, "cratch-cradle," may refer to the two important stages of the game: the "manger" (a cratch) and the "cradle."

In Southern China cat's cradle is known as *Kang sok* = Well rope ; in Swatow the name means "Sawing wood." In Korea it is called *Ssi-teu-ki* = Woof-taking ; and in Japan, *Aya ito tori* = Woof pattern String-taking. In Germany it has various names : *Abheben* = Taking-off, *Faden-abheben* = Taking-off strings, *Fadenspiel* = String game, *Hexenspiel* = Witch's game, and *Auf- und Abnehmen* = Picking-up and taking-off. In Holland it is known as *Afpakken : Dradenspel* = Taking-off : String game ; in France and Algeria as *la scie*.

Two persons and one loop of string are required for the game of " Real Cat's-Cradle," which is played by the persons alternately taking the string off each other's hands to produce eight definite figures which have been given distinctive names, as follows: 1, Cradle; 2, Soldier's Bed; 3, Candles; 4, Manger; 5, Diamonds; 6, Cat's Eye; 7, Fish in a Dish; 8, Clock. For convenience in describing the game the players will be called " A " and " B." The terms " near," " far," " right," and " left " describe the position of the strings as seen by the person from whose hands the figure is being taken.

(1) CRADLE

Synonym: *Sang-tou-tou-ki* = cover for a hearse (Korea) ; *le berceau* (France) ; *Wasser* (Brabant).

First : "A" takes the string and passes the four fingers of each hand through the untwisted loop, and separates the hands; then with the thumb and index of the right hand he turns the left near string away from him across the left palm, and then toward him across the back of the left hand, bringing the string to the right between

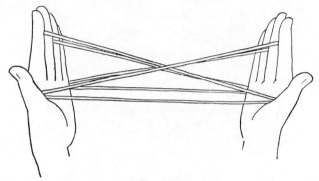

Fig. 741.

the left thumb and index. In the same manner, he turns the right near string once around the right hand. There are now two strings across the back of each hand and a single string across each palm.

Second : Opening A (picking up the palmar string with the middle finger). There is now a loop on each middle finger and two strings across the back of each hand; the "Cradle" being formed by a straight near string, a straight far string, and the crossed strings of the middle finger loops (Fig. 741).

(2) SOLDIER'S BED

Synonyms: *Pa-tok-hpan* = chess board (Korea); *nekomata* = a mountain cat into which a domestic cat is supposed to transform itself (Japan); *die Schere* (Brabant); *les ciseaux* (France) ; church window (England); fish pond (America).

"B" puts his left thumb away from "A" under the right near middle finger string and his left index away from "A" under the left near middle finger string, and then, by bringing the thumb and index together, picks up between their tips the two near middle finger strings just where they cross at the near side of the figure. In the same manner he picks up the two far middle finger strings, by putting the right thumb toward "A" under the right far middle finger string, and the right index toward "A" under the left far middle finger string, then bringing the thumb and index together to hold the two strings where they cross at the far side of the figure. Now separating his hands, drawing the right hand away from "A" and the left hand toward "A" (Fig. 742) he carries the thumb and index of each hand, still holding the strings, around the corresponding side string of the

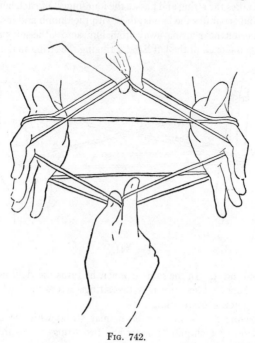

Fig. 742.

figure and up into the centre of the figure (Fig. 743); then by drawing his hands apart and separating the index fingers widely from the thumbs he removes the figure from "A's" hands and extends the "Soldier's Bed" (Fig. 744). There is a loop on each thumb, a loop on each index, and a string passing across the backs of the thumb and index of each hand. The figure is formed of the four finger loops crossing in the middle, a straight near string and a straight far string.

(3) CANDLES

Synonyms: *Tjye-ka-rak* = chopsticks (Korea); *Koto* = a musical instrument, or *geta no ha* = the two pieces of wood under the sole of clogs (Japan); mirror (Denmark); *les chandelles* (France); *die Geige* (Brabant).

"A" inserts his left index from above into the left thumb loop, near the centre of the figure, and his left thumb from above into the right thumb loop and then, bringing the thumb and index together, picks up between their tips the near thumb strings just where they cross. In like manner, by inserting the right thumb from

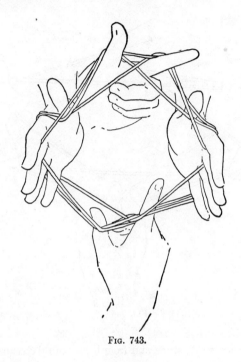

Fig. 743.

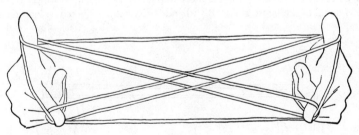

Fig. 744.

above into the right index loop and the right index from above into the left index loop, he picks up the two far index strings where they cross. He then separates the hands—drawing the right hand away from "B" over, and past, the far straight string, and the left hand toward "B" over, and past, the near straight string (Fig. 745); and finally puts the thumb and index of each hand (still holding the strings)

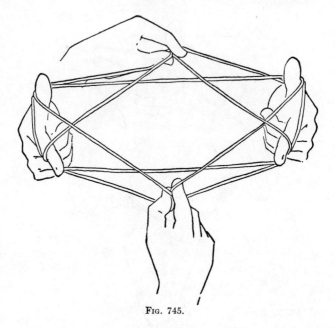

Fɪɢ. 745.

under the corresponding side string and from below into the centre of the figure, when, by drawing the hands apart and separating the index fingers widely from the thumbs he takes the figure from "B's" hands (Fig. 746).   There is a loop on each

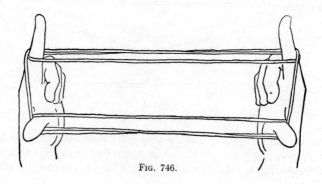

Fɪɢ. 746.

thumb, a loop on each index, and a string passing across the backs of the thumb and index of each hand; the "Candles" being formed by a straight single far thumb string, a straight single near index string, and straight double far index and near thumb strings.

(4) MANGER

Synonym: The inverted cradle (England); *die Wiege* (Brabant).

"B" turns his left hand with the palm facing upward, and takes up in the bend of the little finger the near index string, and draws it over the strings toward "A";

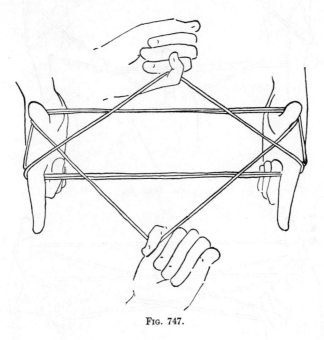

FIG. 747.

then turning his right hand with the palm up he takes up in the bend of the right little finger the far thumb string, and draws it over the other strings away from "A" (Fig. 747). Closing the little fingers on the palms, he passes the left thumb and index from the near side under the two near thumb strings and up on the far side of them, and at the same time passes the right thumb and index from the far side under the two far index strings and up on the near side of them (Fig. 748). Then, drawing the hands apart, and separating the index fingers widely from the thumbs, he takes the figure from "A's" hands (Fig. 749). He now has two strings passing

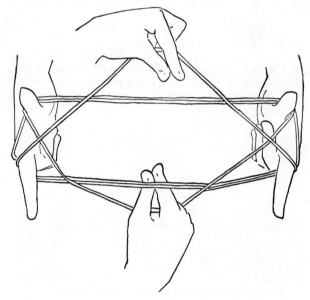

Fig. 748.

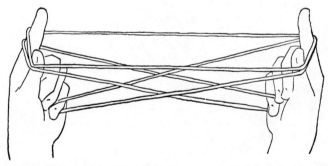

Fig. 749.

across the backs of the thumb and index of each hand and a loop held to the palm by each little finger. The form of the "Manger" is the same as that of the "Cradle" only inverted.

(5) Diamonds

Synonym: Soldier's Bed again (England); *les carreaux* (France).

"A" now takes the "Manger" from "B's" hands in the same way as "B" took the "Cradle" from his hands, but the thumb and index of each hand (holding between their tips the two crossed strings) are brought up around the corresponding

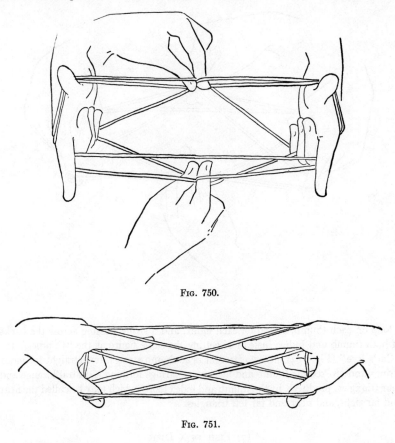

Fig. 750.

Fig. 751.

side string and down into the centre of the figure (Fig. 750); then, when the hands are drawn apart and the thumbs and index fingers widely separated, he forms a figure exactly like the "Soldier's Bed" but it is held with the fingers pointing downward (Fig. 751).

(6) CAT'S EYE

Synonyms: *Soi-noun-kal* = Cow's Eyeball (Korea); *umano me* = Horse-eye (Japan); diamonds (England).

"B" takes the figure from "A's" hand in the same way as "A" took the "Soldier's Bed" from "B" to form the "Candles" (Fig. 752); but, although he has

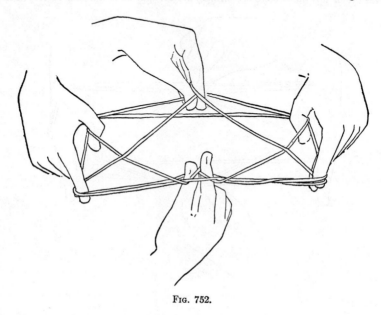

FIG. 752.

a loop on each thumb, a loop on each index, and a string passing across the backs of both thumb and index, instead of getting the same figure as the "Candles," the "Cat's Eye" (Fig. 753) has two straight near thumb strings, two straight far index strings and crossed far thumb and near index strings forming a central lozenge and four triangles, produced by the thumb and index loops, which may be called the near and far right, and near and far left triangles.

(7) FISH IN A DISH

Synonyms: *Tjyel-kou-kong-i* = Rice-mill Pestle (Korea); *tsuzumi* = a Musical Instrument (Japan).

"A" inserts the right index from above into the far left triangle, and his right thumb from above into the far right triangle, his left index from above into the near left triangle and his left thumb from above into the near right triangle; then turning the thumbs and index fingers up into the central lozenge (Fig. 754), he draws his hands apart, separates the index fingers widely from the thumbs, and takes the

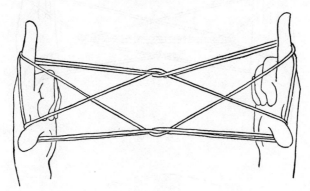

FIG. 753.

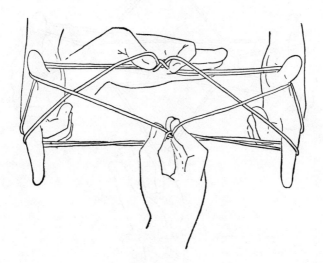

FIG. 754.

In the middle out the left thumb loop a piece into the over right loop the after finger in the present and now presses out into the overhead loop to get Fig. 755. The finger off right again presses the under loop to get over the overhead loop and takes the

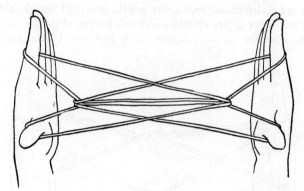

Fig. 755.

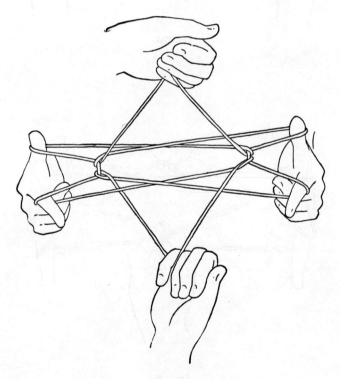

Fig. 756.

figure from "B's" hands (Fig. 755). The "Fish in a Dish" consists of a large central lozenge, divided lengthwise by two straight strings; and right and left near and far triangles. There is a loop on each thumb and a loop on each index, but no string passing across the backs of both thumb and index.

(8) CLOCK

My father, Dr. Horace Howard Furness, tells me that as a child he ended the game of Cat's-cradle by forming the "Clock" from the "Fish in a Dish," in the following manner:

First: "B" arranges the two strings which pass from side to side through the central lozenge so that, uncrossed, they can easily be separated into a near string and a far string.

Second: "B" now turns his left hand with the palm facing upward, and picks up in the bend of the left little finger the *near* string which passes through the central lozenge, and draws it over the other strings toward "A"; then turning the

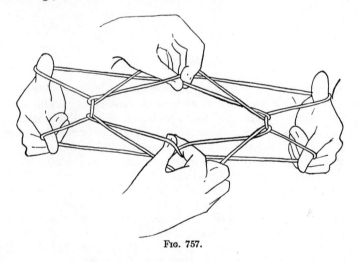

FIG. 757.

right hand with the palm facing upward he picks up in the bend of the right little finger the *far* string which passes through the central lozenge, and draws it over the other strings away from "A" (Fig. 756). Putting the right thumb from above into the right far triangle, the right index from above into the left far triangle, the left thumb from above into the right near triangle, and the left index from above into the left near triangle, "B" turns the thumb and index of each hand toward the centre of the figure and up into the central lozenge (Fig. 757), when, by drawing the hands apart, and separating the thumbs widely from the index fingers, he takes the figure from "A's" hands (Fig. 758).

When the figure is held vertically it is supposed to represent a tall clock.

The "Real Cat's-cradle" is capable of some variation: The Philippine Linao Moros at the St. Louis Exposition always passed from the (6) "Cat's Eye" back to the (4) "Manger" without any intervening steps, as follows: The "Cat's Eye" is on "A's" hands. "B" picks up in the bend of his right little finger the string

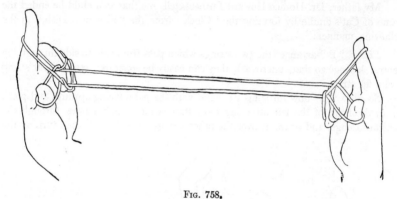

FIG. 758.

which passes between "A's" left thumb and index, and lifts that string off "A's" *left index only;* in like manner he picks up in the bend of his left little finger the string which passes between "A's" right thumb and index, and lifts that string off "A's" *right thumb only;* then, still holding each string in the bend of the little finger, "B" puts his right thumb and index (held close together) down into the figure, near "A's" left hand, and then up into the central lozenge, and thus picks up from below on these fingers the crossed strings of that side; in the same way "B" puts his left thumb and index down near "A's" right hand and then up into the central lozenge, and thus picks up from below on these fingers the crossed strings of that side. The figure is now taken off "A's" hands and extended as the "Manger." This may be the way that the Koreans, according to Dr. Weir, pass from the (6) "Cat's Eye" to the (3) "Candles." Apparently the Japanese and Koreans pass from the (3) "Candles" to the (6) "Cat's Eye" (see Culin, 2, p. 30), but I do not know how it can be done without an intervening figure. It is possible to jump from the (l) "Cradle" to the (3) "Candles" by picking up the crossed strings as if for the "Soldier's Bed," but putting the fingers down into the figure, and separating the hands; then the "Candles" are held of course with the fingers pointing downward. We can pass directly from the (2) "Soldier's Bed" to the (6) "Cat's Eye" by picking up the crossed strings from below, bringing them around the side strings and down into the centre of the figure, and then separating the hands.

CHAPTER VIII

TRICKS AND CATCHES—A TORRES STRAITS LIZARD—HANGING—THE MOUSE—A DRAVIDIAN TRICK—A
FINGER CATCH—A FLY ON THE NOSE—A THUMB CATCH—WILL YOU HAVE A YAM?—THREADING
A CLOSED LOOP—A SAW-MILL.

A TORRES STRAITS LIZARD

THIS trick I got from Dr. Haddon, who has published a description of it (see Rivers and Haddon, p. 152). In Murray Island, Torres Straits, it is known as *Monan* = a Lizard; in Mabuiag as *Maita* = Intestines of a Turtle. It was shown to Dr. Furness in the Caroline Islands by the Uap boy, who showed him "Carrying Money."

First: Hold the left hand high with the palm down and the fingers pointing away from you, and with the right hand place the loop of string over the back of the left hand, and let it hang down in front of you.

Pass the right hand away from you through the hanging loop, with the fingers pointing downward (Fig. 759); then turn the right hand around the right hanging string, by pointing the fingers to the right, then toward you, and finally upward (Fig. 760). Now pass the right hand to the left, between the hanging strings and

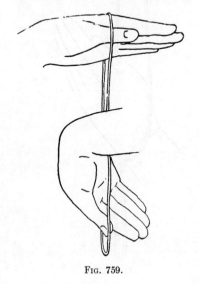

Fig. 759.

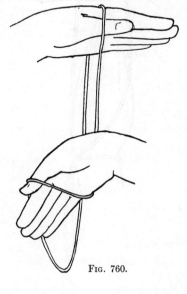

Fig. 760.

337

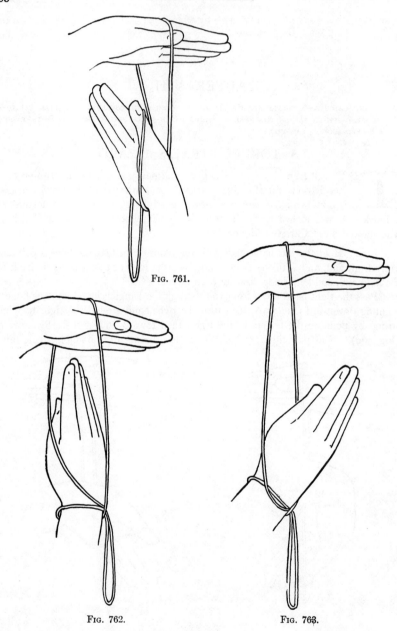

Fig. 761.

Fig. 762.

Fig. 763.

your body, beyond the left hanging string (Fig. 761), then away from you, then to the right around the left string (Fig. 762), and finally toward you back through the hanging loop (Fig. 763).

Draw the right hand down and to the right, and it will come free from the noose around the wrist.

This trick is rather hard to learn and it can be done only in the one way I have described. Of course you will observe that you take your right hand out of the loop when you finally bring it toward you apparently through the loop.

HANGING

I call this trick with the string "Hanging" merely because it is done around the neck. I saw it done by the Filipinos of the Linao Moro and Negrito tribes. Dr. Furness was shown it in the Caroline Islands by the girl "Dakofel."

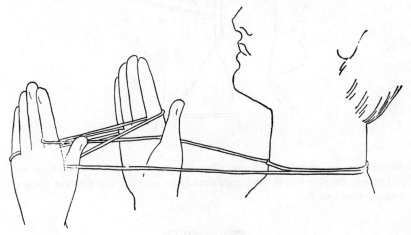

Fig. 764.

First: Put your head through the loop of string, and let the rest of the loop hang down in front of you.

Second: Pass the right string around the neck from the left side, draw the loop tight, and let it hang down in front of you.

Third: Put the hanging loop on the hands and form Opening A, taking up the left palmar string first (Fig. 764).

Fourth : Pass the index loops over the head (Fig. 765) (you may release the loops from the little fingers to increase the size of the index loops), and remove the hands from the other loops.

Fifth : A loop now hangs down in front of you, and if you pull on it, or on either string of it, all the strings will come off the neck.

The reason for the strings coming off the neck, after you have apparently

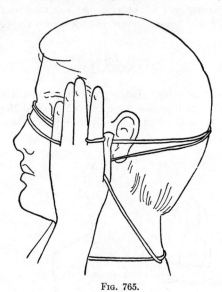

Fig. 765.

wound them on securely, is because when you put the index loops over the head you reverse the direction of the strings already on the neck and they are no longer wound around on it.

THE MOUSE

This figure is probably the most widely distributed of all the string figures. I have seen it done by the African Batwa Pygmies, the Philippine Negritos and Linao Moros, and American Indians of the Chippewa, Osage, Navaho and Apache tribes. Dr. Haddon gives it as an Omaha string trick (**5,** p. 218) and says it is known to the Japanese. I have been told that it is well known in Ireland. Dr. Haddon also met with it in Torres Straits; in Murray Island it is known as *Kebe Mokeis* = the Mouse (Rivers and Haddon, p. 152); quite recently it has been reported from the Wajiji in British East Africa, and from the Alaskan Eskimos.

First : Hold the left hand with the palm facing the right and the fingers pointing away from you. With the right hand place the loop of string over the edge of the left thumb, and let it hang down over the palm and back of the left hand (Fig. 766).

Second : Pass the right index on the near side of the left palmar string, between the left thumb and index, and catch the string on the back of the left hand (Fig. 767), and pull it to the right between the left thumb and index and on the near side of the hanging string (Fig. 768). Do not pull the loop entirely out, but with the

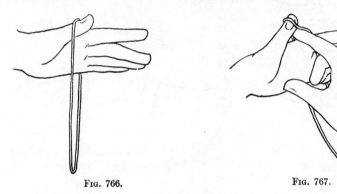

FIG. 766.   FIG. 767.

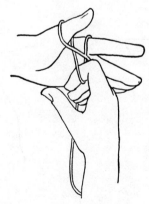

FIG. 768.

right index give it one twist away from you (Fig. 769), and put it on the left index (Fig. 770).

Pull down the two hanging strings, in order to hold tight the loops on the thumb and index.

Third : In the same way pass the right index on the near side of the hanging string (Fig. 771), between the index and middle finger, catch the string on the back of the hand, and draw it through between the index and middle finger, on the near side of the hanging string (Fig. 772). Give the loop one twist away from you (Fig. 773), put it on the middle finger (Fig. 774), and pull the hanging strings tight.

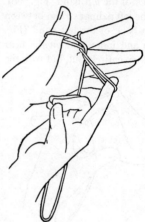

FIG. 769.

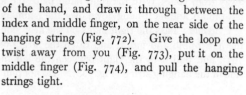
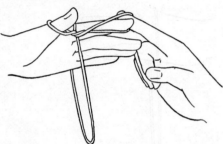

FIG. 770.

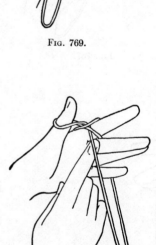

FIG. 771.

FIG. 772.

Fourth : In the same way put a loop on the ring finger.

Fifth : In the same way put a loop on the little finger (Fig. 775).

Sixth : With the right thumb and index take the loop off the left thumb, and place it between the tips of the left thumb and index (Fig. 776), which should now hold it lightly. With the right hand pull down the string which hangs from the palmar side of the left hand, letting go the loop held

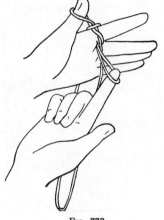

FIG. 773.

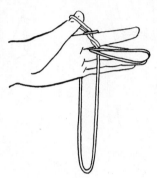

FIG. 774.

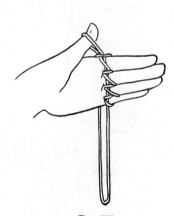

FIG. 775.

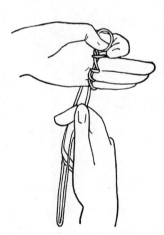

FIG. 776.

by the left thumb and index, and the entire string will come off the hand; make a squeaking noise as "the mouse (the thumb loop) escapes from the cat."

Fig. 777.

Fig. 778.

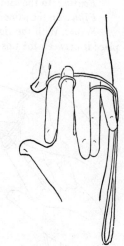

Fig. 779.

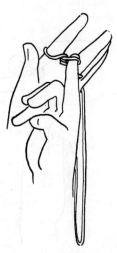

Fig. 780.

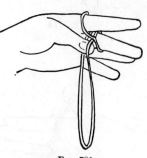

Fig. 781.

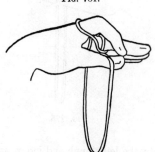

Fig. 782

A DRAVIDIAN TRICK

I obtained this trick from Dr. Haddon, in August, 1904. It was shown him by Dr. S. Levinstein, who learnt it in Leipzig from a travelling troup of Dravidians.

First : Hold the left hand up with the palm to the right, and with the right hand put the loop over the left index and middle finger, so that there is a short palmar string across these fingers and two strings hanging down on the back of the left hand. (Fig. 777.)

Second : Put the right index up under the string on the left palm (Fig. 778), push it between the index and middle finger, and catch the near hanging string (Fig. 779), and draw it all the way out to the right between the left index

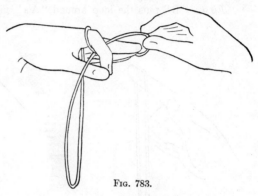

FIG. 783.

and middle finger and under the left palmar string (Fig. 780). Let the two strings of the loop, formed by drawing out the string, hang down on the left palm. One of these strings, the nearer, is an index string and the other a middle finger string. Arrange them in order side by side.

Third : Turn the left hand with the palm down and the fingers directed to the

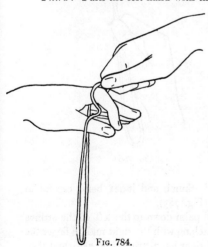

FIG. 784.

right. Bend the left thumb away from you over the hanging index string, and take up on the back of the thumb the hanging middle finger string (Fig. 781). Now put the tips of the left thumb and index together (Fig. 782), and with the right thumb and index remove the loop from the left middle finger (Fig. 783), and let it drop. Without separating the left thumb and index, the loop may be dropped off the left hand by a slight jerk, or pulled off by picking up with the right thumb and index the string which passes over the left index, and pulling it to the right (Fig. 784). This trick is interesting largely because it comes from India, where as yet the field is unexplored.

A FINGER CATCH

A **Chippewa** Chief showed me this catch at the St. Louis Exposition. Dr. Furness saw it done by the Uap boy who taught him "Carrying Money."

Two persons (A and B) and one loop of string are required for this figure.

First: "B" puts the loop around "A's" index finger and holds it, about

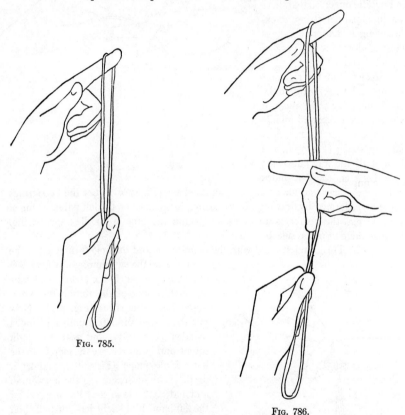

FIG. 785.

FIG. 786.

twelve inches from "A's" finger, with his left thumb and index, being careful to keep the two strings uncrossed and parallel (Fig. 785).

Second: "B" then passes his right hand palm down to the left of the strings (about six inches from "A's" finger) and, catching with the right middle finger the left hand string, draws it to the right past the right hand string (Fig. 786), and then

puts the middle finger down
between the two strings.
Then turning the hand with
the palm up, he puts his
index finger from below between the strings close to
"A's" finger, where they
are uncrossed (Fig. 787).
Now turning the palm down
again, he places the tip of
his middle finger on the tip
of "A's" index (Fig. 788)
and removes his index finger from the loop around it.

Third: If "B" now
pulls the strings he has been
holding with his left hand,
the strings will come off
"A's" index and "B's"
middle finger held tip to tip.

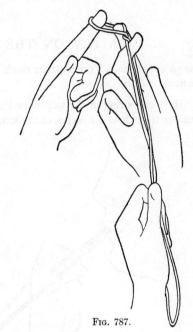

Fig. 787.

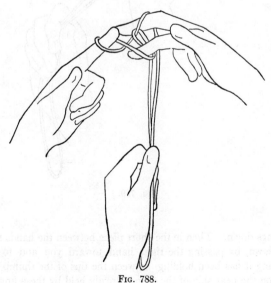

Fig. 788.

A FLY ON THE NOSE

This is an unpublished Torres Straits catch, kindly given me by Dr. Haddon. The native name is *Buli*.

First : Hold one string of the loop between the tips of the thumb and index of each hand so that about six inches of the string passes from hand to hand and

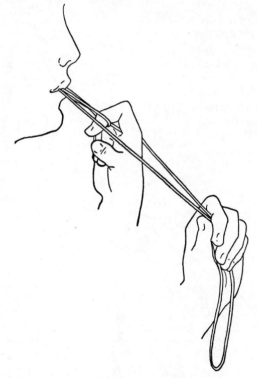

FIG. 789.

a long loop hangs down.   Then in the short piece between the hands make a small ring hanging down, by passing the right hand toward you and to the left and placing the string it has been holding, between the tips of the thumb and index of the left hand, on the near side of the string already held by these fingers.

Second: Hold the ring thus formed between the teeth where the strings cross, the original right hand string crossing below the original left hand string. Hold the long loop straight down with the left hand.

Third: Pass the right index away from you through the long hanging loop, with the palmar surface facing you; then bend the finger toward you and hook it over the lower hanging string of the small ring held in the mouth (Fig. 789). Move

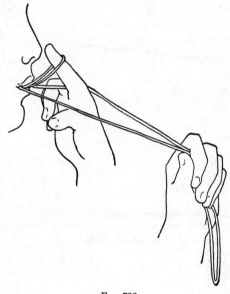

Fig. 790.

the right hand to the right on the near side of the right hanging string of the long loop, and put a twist on the loop held by the right index, by turning the finger to the right and up so that the palmar surface faces you.

Fourth: Move the right hand to the left, and put the right index (with its back from you) away from you through the long hanging loop; then place its tip on the tip of the nose (Fig. 790); release the loop held by the teeth, at the same time pulling down the end of the long hanging loop and protruding the tongue. The string should then come free from the right index.

It is very evident that the twist you put in the right index loop (in the *Fourth* movement) untwists the cross in the ring held by the teeth.

A THUMB CATCH

I learned this catch from the same Osage Indian who taught me the Osage "Diamonds." I am told that it is also known in England.

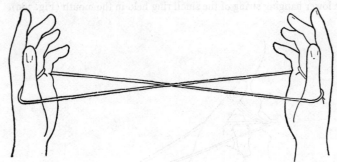

FIG. 791.

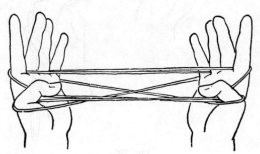

FIG. 792.

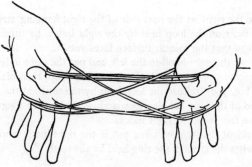

FIG. 793.

First: First Position, with the strings between the hands crossed; the left near string passing over the right near string (Fig. 791).

Second: Opening A, taking up the left palmar string first.

Third: Turn each thumb away from you down into the loop on the index finger, and, holding securely in the bend of the thumb the far thumb string and the

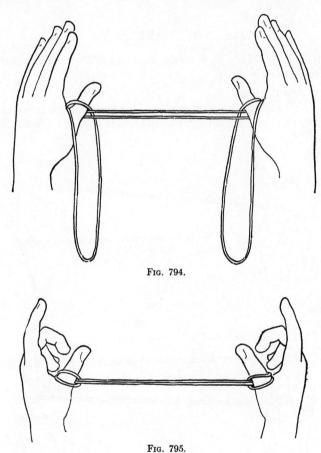

FIG. 794.

FIG. 795.

near index string (Fig. 792), turn the hands with the fingers pointing downward (Fig. 793), and drop from the hands all the strings except those held by the thumbs.

Fourth: Turn the hands with the fingers pointing upward (Fig. 794). Separate the hands (Fig. 795).

By reason of the cross in the string in the First Position when you release the loops in the *Third* movement and draw the hands apart, each little finger loop becomes a slip noose around the opposite thumb. If the cross in the First Position be formed by the right thumb string passing over the left thumb string, you must take up the *right* palmar string first in forming Opening A.

WILL YOU HAVE A YAM?

Dr. Haddon has kindly given me this unpublished Torres Straits catch. The native name is *Lewer* = Food.

First : First Position.

Second : Pass each index away from you over the little finger string and to the far side of it, then draw the string toward you in the bend of the index (Fig. 796,

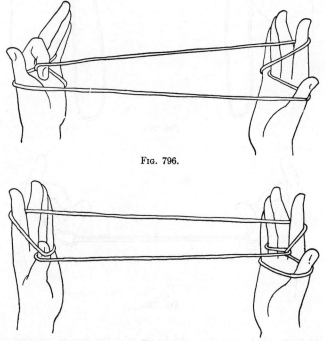

Fig. 796.

Fig. 797.

Left hand); turn the index up toward you in its usual position, thus turning the string around the tip of the finger (Fig. 796, Right hand).

Third : Pass each thumb away from you under the far index string, and pick up from below on the back of the thumb the near index string (Fig. 797, Left hand),

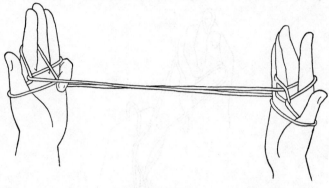

FIG. 798.

which crosses the palm obliquely, and return the thumb under the near thumb string to its position (Fig. 797, Right hand).

Fourth : Pass each little finger toward you over the far index string, and pick up from below on the back of the little finger the near string, which passes directly

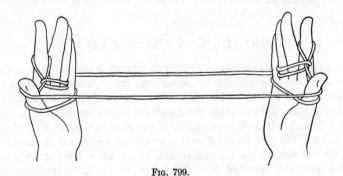

FIG. 799.

from hand to hand (Fig. 798, Left hand), and return the little finger to its position (Fig. 798, Right hand).

Fifth : Pass each thumb away from you, and pick up, from below, the near string of the figure, and return the thumb to its position (Fig. 799).

Sixth : Release the loop from the left index and hold it erect between the left index and thumb (Fig. 800). This loop represents a Yam. Offer this hand to another person: He says, "Have you any food for me?" You say, "I haven't

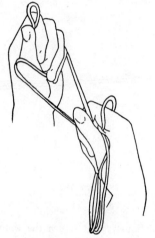

Fig. 800.

any," pulling the right hand strings at the same time; the "Yam" disappears and all the strings come off the left hand. The same can then be repeated with the right hand.

THREADING A CLOSED LOOP

This little trick is probably very widely distributed; it has been observed among the Omahas, the Pawnees and the Kwakiutls; the Japanese, and the Caroline Islanders. Dr. Boas informs Dr. Haddon (see American Anthropologist, v, 1903, p. 218) that there are two shamanistic societies among the Kwakiutls, and that this trick is used to identify the members of one of these societies when they meet in the forest. The members of the other society are recognized by another trick, which, since it requires the use of a stick, does not fall within our subject. The trick has also been described from Argyleshire by Dr. R. C. Maclagan (p. 189) as the "thumb loop."

First : Take a piece of string about eighteen inches long, and, holding it at the middle between the tips of the right thumb and index, wind a portion of one-half of it around the left thumb, toward the body above the thumb, and away from the body under the thumb, the left hand being held with the thumb and index pointing to the right.

Second : In the part of the string which you have been holding between the right thumb and index make a small loop and place it between the tips of the left thumb and index, so that it stands erect; hold it there and remove the right thumb and index.

Third : Pick up between the tips of the right thumb and index the end of the other half of the string, which is hanging down from the far side of the left thumb, then draw it to the right (Fig. 801). Now make several passes with the right hand

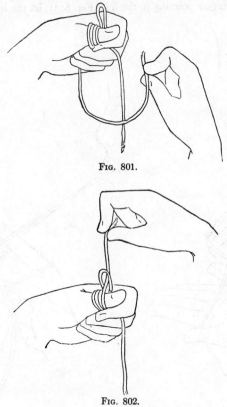

Fig. 801.

Fig. 802.

as if you were trying to thread the end of the right hand string through the erec loop held by the left hand; finally pass the right hand to the left over the left hand, apparently threading the loop, but really drawing the part of the string which hangs from the right hand, between the left thumb and index as far as you can (Fig. 802). The loop, which is still held by the left thumb and index, appears to have been threaded by the right hand string.

A SAW MILL

This little string game was shown to me by a young Irish girl.

First : Take one string of the loop between the teeth and let the rest of the loop hang down in front of you.

Second : Let the right hanging string lie across the palm of the right hand held palm up, the fingers pointing to the left (Fig. 803); let the left hanging string

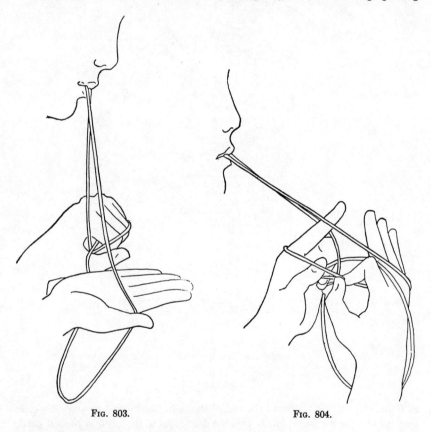

FIG. 803.   FIG. 804.

lie across the left hand held palm up, the fingers pointing to the right. Now holding each string between the thumb and index, close the fingers on the palm, and put a loop in each string, by turning the fist so that the thumb is uppermost and then passing the hand between the hanging string and your body (Fig. 803, Left hand).

Third : Exchange the loops held by the two hands, putting one loop through the other (Fig. 804).

Fourth : A second person now pulls out the hanging loop, and a sawing motion is produced by pulling alternately the loops held by the hands and the loops held by the teeth and the second person (Fig. 805).

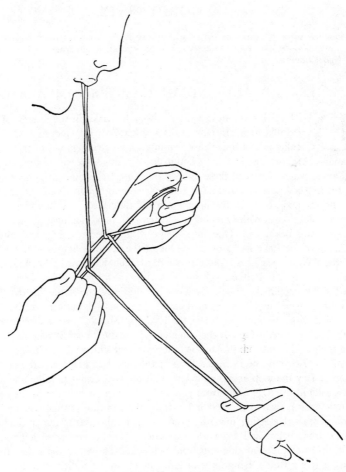

FIG. 805.

CHAPTER IX

ESKIMO AND INDIAN GAMES FROM ALASKA

DURING his recent expedition through Alaska in the interest of the Philadelphia Free Museum of Science and Art, Dr. George B. Gordon kindly collected for me twenty-two interesting string games of the Eskimos and Tanana (Athapascan) Indians. Unfortunately, this book was in type and ready for the press when I learned these figures, therefore I can now give only the drawings of the finished patterns, and a few notes concerning the methods and their relations to the methods used in the figures already described. Of the eighteen Eskimo figures, eight begin with Opening A and ten with new openings; of the four Tanana figures, two begin with Opening A, one with a new opening, and one with the opening of the Eskimo "Mouth." One of the Eskimo figures—the "Wolverine" or the "Wolf"—is in all respects similar to the Klamath "Porcupine," and the "Dog on a Leash," although beginning with a new opening, is otherwise the same as the "Porcupine." The "Cariboo" is precisely the same as the "Cariboo" described by Boas from Baffin-Land. The finished pattern of the "Trap" is identical with the final pattern of the Eskimo "Mouth," but is formed by entirely different methods. One of the Tanana games, the "Bow-String," comes out like the Osage "Thumb Catch," but is otherwise very different. "Crow's Feet" is the familiar "Leashing of Lochiel's Dogs"; the methods, however, are novel and very simple: Lay the loop across your lap, with the two strings parallel and uncrossed; pass each little finger away from you under the near string (the hands being about a foot apart), then pass each index from the far side toward you under the far string; draw this string toward you and pick up the near string on the back of the index, from below and from the near side. Then, sweeping each hand outward, pick up from the near side and from below, on the ball of the index, that part of the far string which, lying on your lap, extends to the right and left of the hands; draw this string toward the centre and bring it up between the two strings passing from hand to hand, letting the loop already on the index slip off, and extend the figure on the index and little fingers.

Many of the methods employed in these figures are new and difficult; among the familiar ones we find Klamath and Navaho movements; one figure begins with the opening of the Loyalty Islands "Well," and another with the opening of the "Leashing of Lochiel's Dogs." We find no instance of the typical Caroline Islands extension of the finished pattern, and no record of the occurrence of the "Real Cat's-Cradle." At Nunivak Island, the Eskimo name for a cat's-cradle string is *ayahaak*, "play string," and for the game itself, *ayahowsit*, "play with a string."

ESKIMO FIGURES

(1) "A Ship," *umiakbuk* (Fig. 806), from King Island, near Cape Prince of Wales. A further development of the figure forms "Two Men" (Fig. 807).

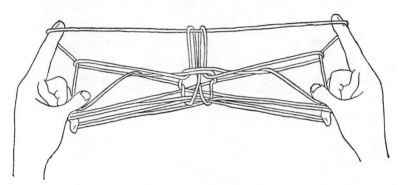

FIG. 806.

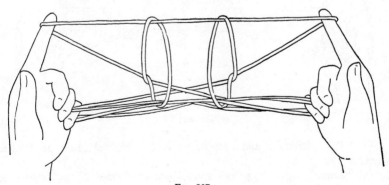

FIG. 807.

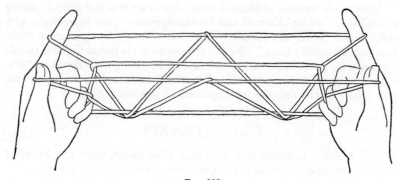

Fig. 808.

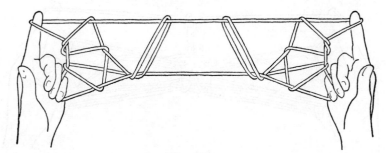

Fig. 809.

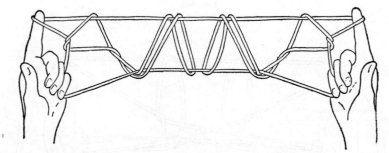

Fig. 810.

(2) "Two Mountains and a Stream," *tituchtak* (Fig. 808), from St. Michael Island.

(3) "Arms," *moguk* (Fig. 809), from which are formed "Legs," *eruk* (Fig. 810), from Nunivak Island.

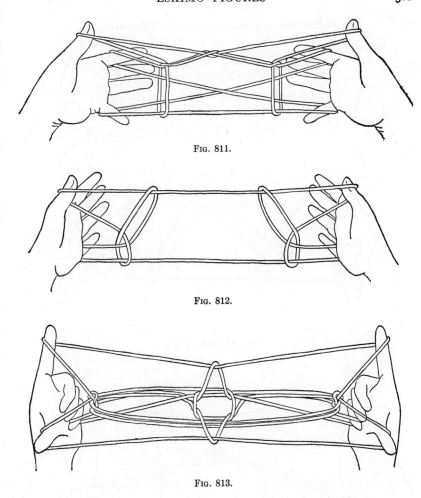

FIG. 811.

FIG. 812.

FIG. 813.

(4) "Siberian House," *kochlinee* (Fig. 811), and afterward "Two Eskimos Running Away," *mugalonik enuck okparuktuk* (Fig. 812), from Big Diomede Island.

(5) "Wolverine," *kojtsick*, from Cape Prince of Wales; also known as the "Wolf," *kulonik*. The same as the "Porcupine" (p. 137).

(6) "Little Boat," *kayak* (Fig. 813), from King Island. The Eskimos say this figure should be called "Two Boats," *malruk-kayak*, because two men are plainly visible; and as a *kayak* will hold only one man there *must* be two boats.

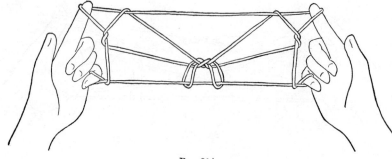

Fig. 814.

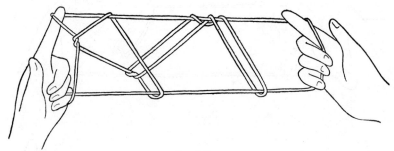

Fig. 815.

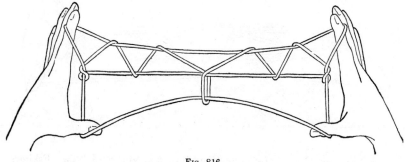

Fig. 816.

(7) "Sea-Gull," *tc-c-kyack* (Fig. 814), from Nunivak Island.

(8) "Lake Fish," *nanvumcheseah* (Fig. 815), from Anvik, on the Yukon River.

(9) "Stairs," *tutumukaligat* (Fig. 816), from Cape Prince of Wales.

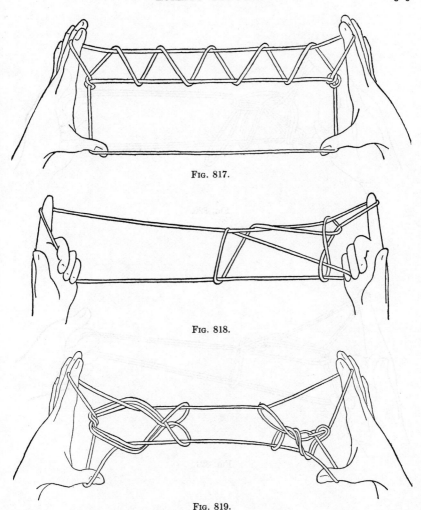

FIG. 817.

FIG. 818.

FIG. 819.

(10) "Clothes Line," *iniarat* (Fig. 817), from Cape Prince of Wales.

(11) "Rabbit," *makadok* (Fig. 818), from Anvik, on the Yukon River. It is known on St. Michael Island as "Bird on Eggs."

(12) "Whale and Fox," *achvuk-tezeuk* (Fig. 819), from Cape Prince of Wales. The whale is stranded on the shore and the fox comes to eat it, but an Eskimo drives it away.

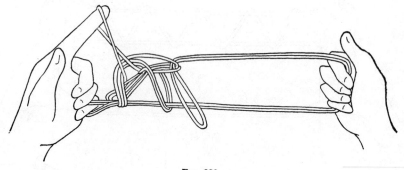

Fig. 820.

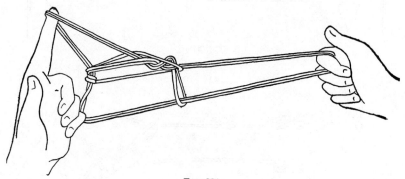

Fig. 821.

(13) "Dog on a Leash," *kaymuchta* (Fig. 820), from Nunivak Island. The leash is pulled off and the dog escapes.

(14) "Nameless" (Fig. 821), from King Island.

(15) "Sealskin Carrying-bag," *aginuk* (Fig. 822), from St. Michael Island; afterward are formed the "Kidneys," *taktuk* (Fig. 823).

(16) "Two Ptarmigans," *mugalonik-okhozgiuk* (Fig. 824), from Cape Prince of Wales.

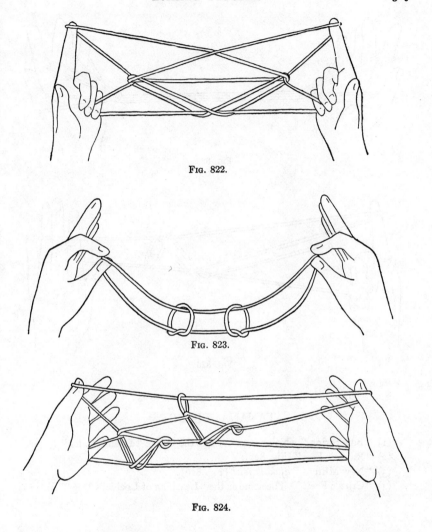

Fig. 822.

Fig. 823.

Fig. 824.

(17) "A Trap," *keezook*, from Cape Prince of Wales. The final pattern is the same as the "Mouth" (p. 282). The finger, caught in the trap, can be worked out between the strings forming the sides of the trap.

(18) "Cariboo," *tuk-tuk*, from St. Michael Island. The same as the Baffin-Land "Cariboo" (p. 124).

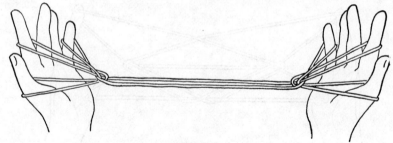

FIG. 825.

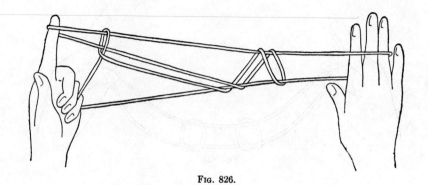

FIG. 826.

TANANA FIGURES

(1) "Bow-String," which comes out like the Osage "Thumb Catch" (p. 350).
(2) "Raven's Feet" (Fig. 825).
(3) "New Mittens," *ajakailaiguk* (Fig. 826).
(4) "Crow's Feet." The same as the "Leashing of Lochiel's Dogs" (p. 116).

FIGURES KNOWN ONLY FROM THE FINISHED PATTERNS

Before it seemed possible to record the method of making string figures a few observers had collected the finished patterns and either made drawings of them or preserved the actual string figures by fastening them on paper. I have brought together such of these as I could obtain, in the hope that other observers will find out the method by which they are made; with our present knowledge it is practically impossible to work back from the finished pattern to the opening movements.

NAURU FIGURES

These patterns are the most elaborate that have ever been collected; yet we are told that in other Pacific islands there are many equally complex. The following fifteen were secured by Mr. E. Stephen, a resident of Nauru, or Pleasant, Island

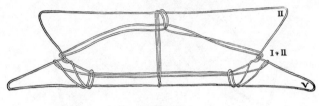

Fig. 827.

of the Marshall group, mounted by him on paper and presented to Dr. W. H. Furness. They are produced with strings made of plaited human hair; in some cases the string is easily sixteen feet long. They are apparently formed on the hands, and Mr. Stephen has indicated on twelve of them the method of extension, which is the same as that used for the Caroline Islands "Coral," where one loop is held on the index (Fig. 827, II), one loop on the little finger (V), and the two middle strings

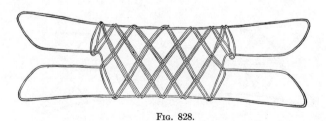

Fig. 828.

between the thumb and index (I and II). I am not sure of the method of extension of the remaining three figures.

(1) Deïmano; the hull of a ship (Fig. 827).
(2) Representation of a mat (Fig. 828).

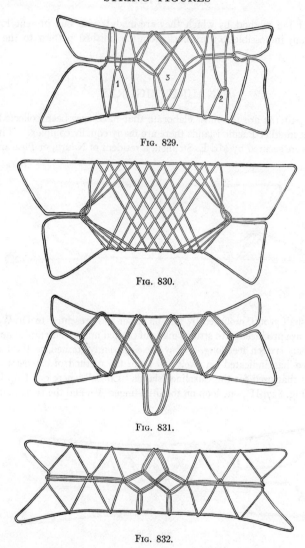

FIG. 829.

FIG. 830.

FIG. 831.

FIG. 832.

(3) Egona (1) and Egameang (2) sitting on a stone (3) (Fig. 829).
(4) Representation of a mat (Fig. 830).
(5) Ijewaioi; a butterfly. The lower loop is held by the teeth (Fig. 831).
(6) Egattamma; a woman (Fig. 832).

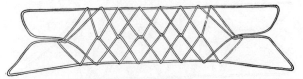

FIG. 833.

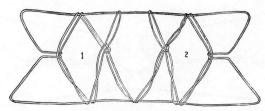

FIG. 834.

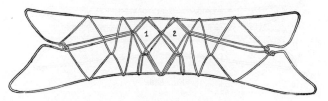

FIG. 835.

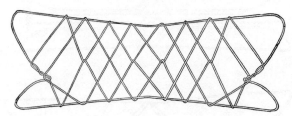

FIG. 836.

(7) Representation of a mat (Fig. 833).
(8) Etima (1) and Etowa (2); Nauru women of rank (Fig. 834).
(9) Echeog (1) and Edawaroi (2); two women (Fig. 835).
(10) Representation of a mat (Fig. 836).

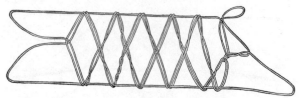

FIG. 837.

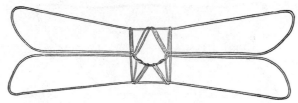

FIG. 838.

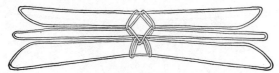

FIG. 839.

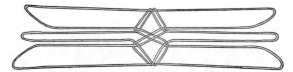

FIG. 840.

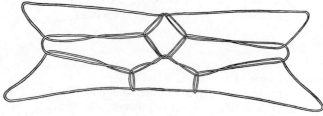

FIG. 841.

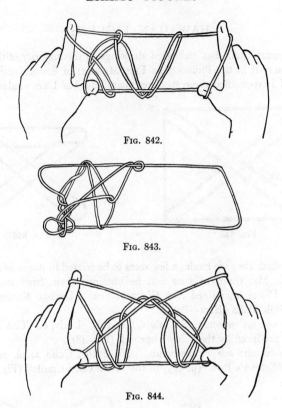

FIG. 842.

FIG. 843.

FIG. 844.

(11) Iiyanibongo; a seasnake (Fig. 837).
(12) Etaroking; a priestess of Nauru in olden times (Fig. 838).
(13) Tinamitto; a Nauru dandy (Fig. 839).
(14) Egarawinago; a lady of quality (Fig. 840).
(15) Ibunemun; a man (Fig. 841).

ESKIMO FIGURES

Dr. Boas in his paper on Cat's-Cradle among the Eskimos of Cumberland Sound (1, p. 229) gives drawings of the three following figures:

(1) Ukaliaqdjung = a Hare (Fig. 842). This figure is very like the Eskimo "Cariboo," turned upside down.

(2) Amaroqdjung = a Wolf (Fig. 843).

(3) Qaqaqdjung Sesinging = a Hill and two Ponds (Fig. 844).

HAWAIIAN FIGURES

Mr. Stewart Culin has published drawings of the majority of the Hawaiian patterns preserved in the Philadelphia Free Museum of Science and Art (1. pp. 222–223). I have studied these specimens carefully, but I am unable to give the

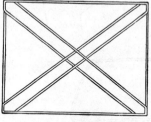

FIG. 845.

FIG. 846.

methods by which they are made; a few seem to be related to stages in our ordinary Cat's-Cradle. Mr. Culin tells us that he obtained them from four Hawaiian sailors from Honolulu, named Aka (Kamehameha), Daviese Kahimoku, Wela-kahao, and Hale Paka (Harry Park).

(1) Hoo-ko-mo; museum No. 21491, Culin 1, pl. xiv, e. This figure is the same as that produced by the "Bow" opening (Fig. 481).

(2) E-ke-ma-nu; ace of diamonds. No. 21492, Culin 1, pl. xiii, e. This figure is the "Soldier's Bed" (p. 325) of the "Real Cat's-Cradle" (Fig. 845).

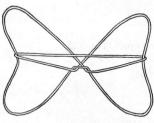

FIG. 847.

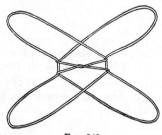

FIG. 848.

(3) Ma-hi-ki; see-saw. No. 21494, Culin, 1, pl. xiii, d (Fig. 846).

(4) Pou; a post. No. 21451, Culin 1, pl. xv, e (Fig. 847). This figure can be made from the "Bow" opening by transferring the index loops to the little fingers, picking up the near little finger strings with the thumbs and finally slipping the lower thumb loops off the thumbs.

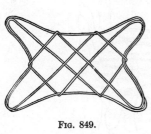

FIG. 849.

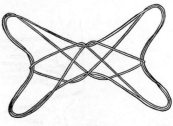

FIG. 850.

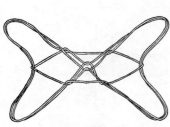

FIG. 851.

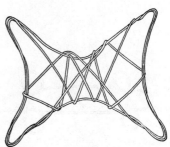

FIG. 852.

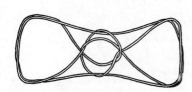

FIG. 853.

FIG. 854.

(5) Pau-ma-wai; a pump. No. 21449, **Culin 1**, pl. xiii, c (Fig. 848).

(6) Po; darkness. No. 21495, **Culin 1**, pl. xiii, b (Fig. 849).

(7) E-ke-pe-ki; ace of spades. No. 21527, **Culin 1**, pl. xiv, c (Fig. 850).

(8) E-ke-ha-ka; ace of hearts. No. 21526, **Culin 1**, pl. xiii, a (Fig. 851).

(9) Ma-ka-pe-na. No. 21493 (Fig. 852).

(10) Ko-he. No. 21452. **Culin 1**, pl. xiv, f (Fig. 853).

(11) Wai-u-la-wa; the breasts. No. 21496, **Culin 1**, pl. xv, c (Fig. 854).

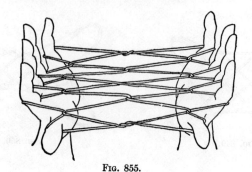

FIG. 855.

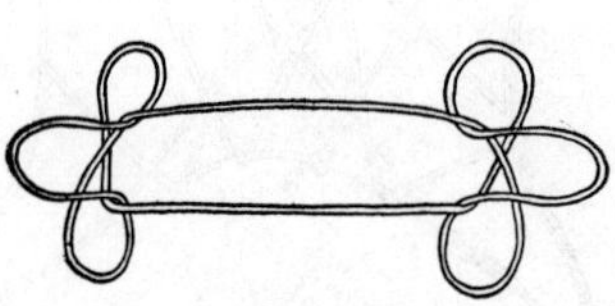

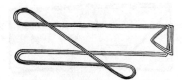

FIG. 856.

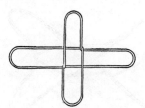

FIG. 857.

FIG. 858.

FIG. 859.

(12) U-pe-na; a net. No. 21498, Culin 1, pl. xiv, b (Fig. 855).

(13) O-ko-le-a-mo. No. 21512, Culin 1, pl. xiv, d (Fig. 856).

(14) Pa-hi-o-lo; a saw. No. 21450, Culin 1, pl. xv, b (Fig. 857).

(15) Pu. No. 21513 (Fig. 858).

(16) Ha-le-ku-mu-ma-ka-a. No. 21515 (Fig. 859).

(17) A-ha-ma-ka. No. 21452. This figure is so distorted that I cannot make it out.

(18) A-na-ma-nu; a bird house. Culin 1, pl. xv, a. This figure is similar to the Zuñi "Top cross beam of a ladder" (Fig. 860), except that the two middle strings are not crossed.

A FIGURE FROM ZUÑI, NEW MEXICO

I have been able to identify most of the figures from Zuñi preserved in the Philadelphia Free Museum. One, however, appears to be new, or is a stage in

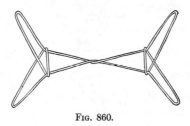

FIG. 860.

the formation of another pattern: Tslem-pis-to-nai, pi-cho-wai-nai = the top cross beam of a ladder. No. 22609 (Fig. 860).

AUSTRALIAN FIGURES

Mr. Walter E. Roth (p. 10) has published drawings of the finished patterns of seventy-four string figures made by the different tribes of Blacks in North Queensland. I have reproduced his ten plates containing these drawings in order that they may be compared with the figures I have described. It will be observed that, as a rule, these patterns are not very elaborate, and that, contrary to what we should expect, they are not similar to the Torres Straits figures Dr. Haddon has collected. Indeed, some of them are closely related to figures obtained by Dr. Furness in the Caroline Islands. For example: "Ten Men" (pl. vi, 7); "One Chief" (pl. v, 5); "Flint and Steel" (pl. vi, 3); "A House" (pl. xii, 4, 5); "Two Chiefs" (pl. iii, 1, pl. v, 4); the second movement of "Carrying Money" (pl. x, 1). One figure appears to be the same as "The Leashing of Lochiel's Dogs" (pl. xii, 1); others resemble the "Storm Clouds" (pl. ix, 2), and the result produced by exchanging index loops after Opening A (pl. v, 6). It does not follow, however, that the figures are formed by the same movements.

The first of Mr. Roth's plates will be found on the next page.

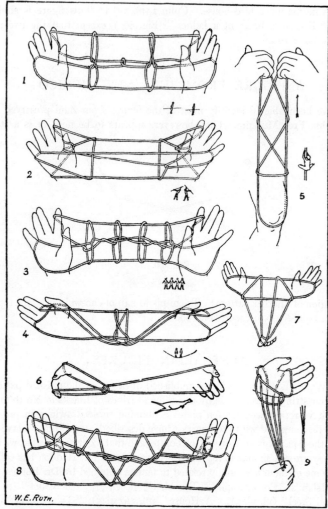

W. E. RUTH.

ROTH'S PLATE III.—MANKIND. ANIMALS

1. Two boys carrying spears. Atherton.
2. Two women fighting with sticks. (Lower) Palmer River. See Pl. VIII, 7, 8.
3. Four boys walking in a row, holding each other's hands. Cape Grafton.
4. Two men walking down a valley. (Three and four people can thus be similarly represented) Cape Grafton, Cape Bedford.
5. Man climbing a tree. (The hands are raised to imitate the progress of the motion.) Cape Bedford. See Pl. VIII, 8.
6. Kangaroo. Princess Charlotte Bay, Pennefather River. See Pl. XII, 1.
7. Pouch: indicative of a kangaroo. Princess Charlotte Bay, Pennefather River.
8. Pouch: and so, a wallaby. (Lower) Tully River.
9. Strictly a spear (see Pl. XII, 1.) but commonly a kangaroo speared. Cape Bedford.

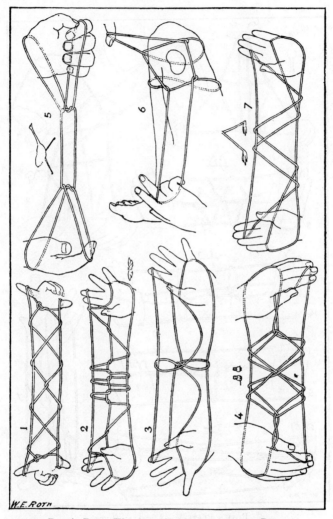

ROTH'S PLATE IV.—ANIMALS: QUADRUPEDS AND BIRDS

1. Bandicoot: indicative of the lobular arrange-~ ment of the internal fat. Cape Bedford. See Pl. VIII, 3.
2. Bat: Flying Fox. Cape Grafton.
3. Flying Fox: the "wings." (Lower) Palmer River.
4. Two rats sitting side by side. (Lower) Tully River.
5. Emu. Princess Charlotte Bay.
6. Emu's nest: with the egg represented by a "match-box" bean.
7. Cassowary: the two legs. (Lower) Tully River.

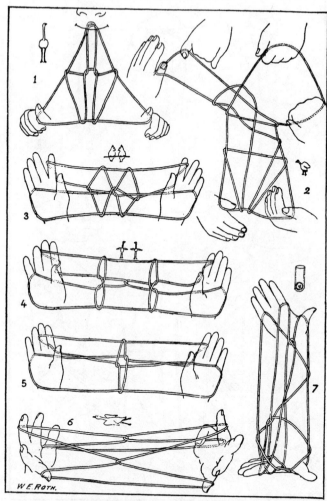

ROTH'S PLATE V.—ANIMALS: BIRDS

1 Cassowary. Atherton.

2 Eagle-hawk. Atherton. For Fish-hawk, see Pl. XI, 4; Hawk's Foot, see Pl. XII, 7.

3 Two cockatoos roosting side by side. (Lower) Tully River.

4. Two white cranes. (Lower) Tully River.

5. Giant crane. (Lower) Tully River.

6. Duck in flight. Princess Charlotte Bay; (Middle) Palmer River.

7. Bird's nest, in the bottom of a hollow stump. Princess Charlotte Bay.

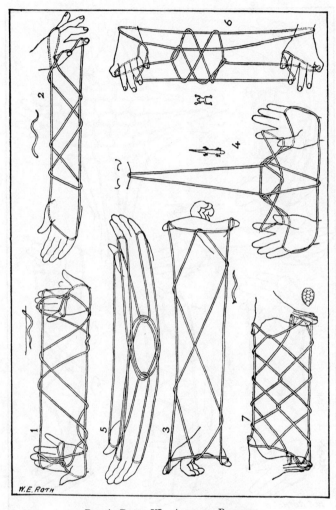

ROTH'S PLATE VI.—ANIMALS: REPTILES

1. Water-snake. Princess Charlotte Bay.
2. Snake, in general. Cape Bedford, Burketown.
3. Deaf-adder. The fingers of the one hand are moved to represent the teeth and mouth. Cape Bedford.
4. Crocodile. Cape Grafton, Cape Bedford, (Middle) Palmer River. See Pl. VIII, 3.
5. Crocodile's nest, with egg. Pennefather River. "Iguana," see Pl. VIII, 3.
6. Frog. Princess Charlotte Bay.
7. Turtle: the scutum. Cape Bedford. Princess Charlotte Bay.

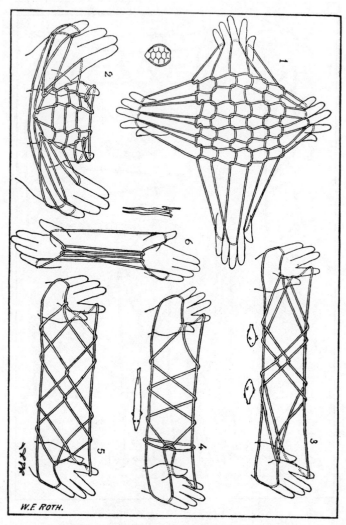

ROTH'S PLATE VII.—ANIMALS: REPTILES AND FISH

1. Tortoise: the scutum. (Middle) Palmer River.
2. Turtle: the scutum. Pennefather River.
3. Two fish. (Lower) Tully River.
4. Fish. Atherton.
5. Mullet skimming along the water. Cape Grafton.
6. Eels carried on a hooked stick (a common method of carrying fish). Cape Bedford.

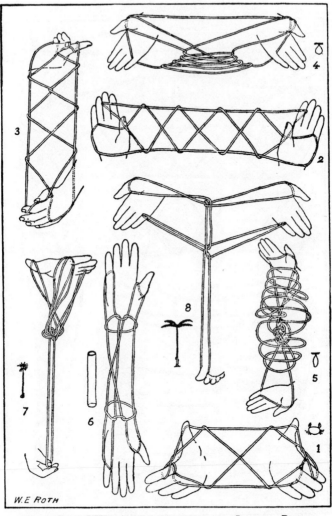

W. E ROTH

ROTH'S PLATE VIII.—ANIMALS: CRUSTACEA AND INSECTS. PLANTS

1. Crab. Cape Bedford.
2. Four shrimps, each square indicative of a crustacean. Princess Charlotte Bay.
3. Honey: the cells of the comb. Cape Bedford. N.B.—This figure has other meanings: e.g., the squares represent the:
   (1) Scales of crocodile. (Middle) Palmer River.
      of iguana, Night Island, Burketown.
   (2) Lobes of fat, bandicoot. (Lower) Palmer River.

4. Wasps' nest. Burketown. See also Pl. XII, 8.
5. Hornets' nest (drawn on the flat). Princess Charlotte Bay.
6. Hollow log: symbolic of the honey inside it. Princess Charlotte Bay.
7. Tree: with woman (thumb) hiding below. Princess Charlotte Bay.
8. Palm-tree: with man (toe) hiding below. Princess Charlotte Bay (at Night Island this figure represents a woman with outstretched arms and legs).

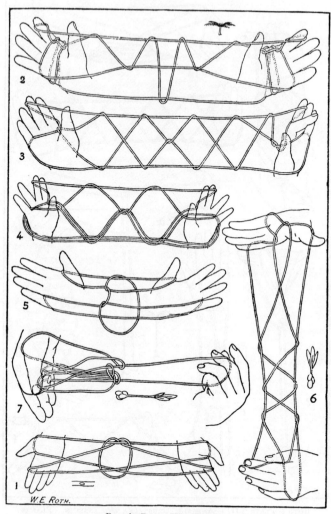

ROTH'S PLATE IX.—PLANTS

1. Hole in limb of tree: opossum, honey, etc.,
   inside it. Princess Charlotte Bay.
2. Zamia (Cycas) tree. Atherton.
3. Zamia: nuts. Atherton.
4. Two coco-nuts. Cape Grafton.

5. Coco-nut. Cape Bedford.
6. Yams. Night Island.
7. Yams. Princess Charlotte Bay. Edible lily
   root: (Lower) Palmer River.

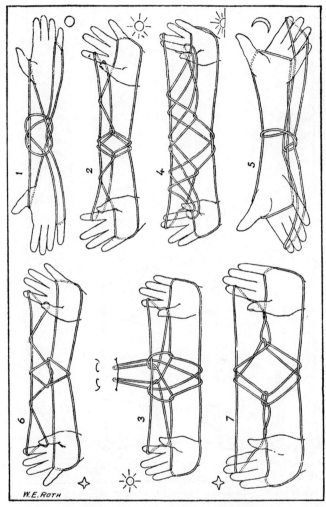

ROTH'S PLATE X.—INORGANIC NATURE

1. Sun: clouded over. Really a stage just previous to—
2. Sun: with full rays. Cape Bedford.
3. Sun: with full rays. Atherton.
4. Sun: setting on the horizon. Cape Grafton, Atherton.
5. Moon. (Lower) Tully River, Atherton, Cape Grafton, Cape Bedford, Princess Charlotte Bay, Burketown.
6. Star. Cape Bedford.
7. Star. (Lower) Tully River.

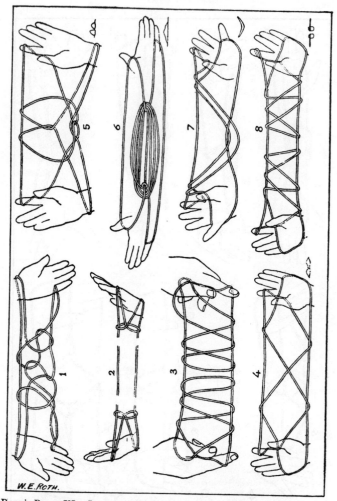

ROTH'S PLATE XI.—INORGANIC NATURE (Continued). MANUFACTURED ARTICLES

1 Clouds. hanging dark and heavy. Really a stage just previous to the following figure, effected by separating the hands as rapidly as possible, so far as the string will allow, and at the same time making a hissing sound to represent the.

2 Lightning. Cape Bedford.

3 Rain Night Island. (Identical with Pl. XI, 8)

4 River: large and broad Princess Charlotte Bay. This figure represents a Fish-hawk on the (Lower) Palmer River, the two squares indicating the outstretched wings.

5 Two rocks sticking out of the water. Cape Grafton. Atherton.

6. Hill, Mountain. Princess Charlotte Bay.

7. Boomerang. (Lower) Palmer River

8. Two Tomahawks. Cape Bedford. (Identical with Pl. XI, 3.)

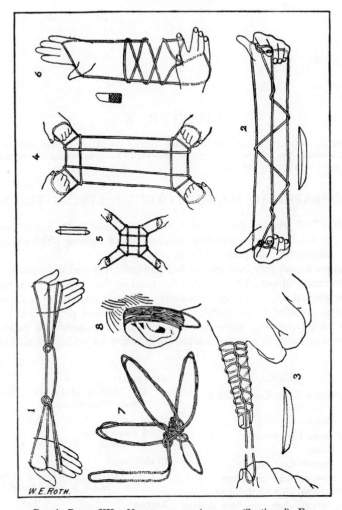

ROTH'S PLATE XII.—MANUFACTURED ARTICLES (Continued), ETC.

1. Four-prong spear. Cape Bedford. It represents a speared kangaroo at Princess Charlotte Bay.
2. Canoe. Cape Grafton, Cape Bedford, Princess Charlotte Bay, Night Island.
3. Bark canoe: the stitches at either extremity. Pennefather River
4. Canoe on water: the four hands rocking it. Cape Bedford

5. Fish-net. (Similar figure to preceding.)
6. Dilly-bag with handle: Princess Charlotte Bay. Shell chest ornament with hanging loop: Atherton.
7. Hawk's Foot. (Lower) Palmer River. (Arranged *on the flat.*)
8. Wasps' nest. Cape Bedford. (Arranged *on the ear.*)

CHAPTER X

GEOGRAPHICAL DISTRIBUTION OF STRING FIGURES

FIGURES whereof the finished patterns are similar to the figures described in this book, but concerning the methods of forming which we have no information, are preceded by an asterisk.

Figures known only from the finished patterns are preceded by two asterisks.

The names adopted for the figures described in this book are given first, the name by which it is known in another country, or tribe, is given below as a synonym. A synonym preceded by an asterisk indicates that a finished pattern is so labelled, but we do not positively know how it is formed. The method of making the few figures preceded by a dagger are known, but have not yet been published.

AFRICA.

BATWA PYGMIES, KASAI VALLEY, CONGO.
Pygmy Diamonds.
The Mouse.

WAJIJI, BRITISH EAST AFRICA.
The Mouse.

ULUNGU, BRITISH EAST AFRICA.
The Leashing of Lochiel's Dogs.
Syn.: *Umuzwa*, a wooden spoon.

KABYLES, ALGERIA (introduced from France).
The Leashing of Lochiel's Dogs.
Syn.: "Cock's Feet."

AMERICA.

APACHES:
An Apache Door.
An Apache Tepee.
The Mouse.

CHEROKEES:
The Leashing of Lochiel's Dogs.
Syn.: "Crow's Feet."

CHIPPEWAS:
A Finger Catch.
The Mouse.

CLAYOQUAHTS:
The Leashing of Lochiel's Dogs.
Syn.: Sea-egg (Echinus) Spear.

ESKIMOS:
ALASKA.
A Cariboo, *tuktuk.*
The Mouth, *rote.*
Breastbone and Ribs, *grut.*
Porcupine.
Syn.: Wolf, *kulonik.*
Wolverine, *kojtsick.*
The Mouse

AMERICA. ESKIMOS—*Continued:*
- †A Ship, *umiakbuk.*
- †Two Mountains and a Stream, *tituchtak.*
- †Arms and Legs, *moguk-eruk.*
- †Siberian House and Two Men, *kochlinee.*
- †Little Boat, *kayak.*
- †Sea-gull, *tc-c-kyack.*
- †Lake Fish, *nanvumcheseah.*
- †Stairs, *tutumukaligat.*
- †Clothes-line, *iniarat.*
- †Eskimo Rabbit, *makadok.*
  - Syn.: Bird Sitting on Eggs.
- †Whale and Fox, *achvuk-tezeuk.*
- †Dog on Leash, *kaymuchta.*
- †Nameless.
- †Sealskin Carrying-bag, *aginuk.*
- †Two Ptarmigans, *mugalonik okhozgiuk.*
- †A Trap, *keezook.*

BAFFIN LAND.
- A Cariboo, *tuktuqdjung.*
- The Circle, *ussuqdjung.*
- **A Hare, *ukaliaqdjung.*
- **A Wolf, *amaroqdjung.*
- **A Hill with Two Ponds, *qaqaqdjung sesinging.*

KLAMATHS:
- (Some Modoc figures may be included among the following:)
  - Owl's Net.
  - Two Elks.
  - A Rabbit.
  - The Sun.
  - A Rattlesnake and a Boy.
  - Two Skunks.
  - Two Foxes.
  - Two Squirrels.
  - A Porcupine.
  - Two Little Boys Running Away.
  - A Little Fish that Hides in the Mud.
  - A Little Boy Carrying Wood.
  - A Brush-house.
  - Six-pointed Star.
  - Two Boys Fighting for an Arrow.

KWAKIUTLS:
- Threading a Closed Loop.

AMERICA—*Continued.* NAVAHOS:
- An Apache Door.
  - Syn.: *Li-sis,* poncho.
- Many Stars, *son tlani.*
- An Owl, *nas-ja.*
- A Second Owl.
- A Third Owl.
- Seven Stars, *dil-ye-he.*
- Two-horned Star, *son-bi-tere.*
  - *Syn.: So-bide-hulonni.*
- Two Coyotes, *ma-i-at-sani-il-watli.*
  - *Syn.: Mai-i-atl-sa-yill-aghueli.*
- Big Star.
- North Star.
  - *Syn.: Big Star, *tsun-tsi.*
- Carrying Wood, *chiz-jo-yet-li.*
- Two Hogans, *naki-hogan* or **atl-sa-hogan**.
- Two Stars.
- An Arrow, *ka.*
- A Man, *hastine denné.*
- A Bow, *atl-ti.*
- Lightning, *atsinil-klish.*
- A Butterfly, *ga-lo-ki* or **ga-hi-ki**.
- A Worm.
- Twin Stars, *sono-tschu.*
- A Lizard.
  - Syn.: *Nashoi-dichizhi.*
- Storm Clouds.
- One Hogan.
- A Second Worm.
- A Bird's Nest, *a-to.*
- The Mouse.
- †Navaho Breastbone and Ribs.

OMAHAS:
- W.
- M.
- The Mouse.
- Threading a Closed Loop.

ONONDAGAS:
- The Leashing of Lochiel's Dogs.
  - Syn.: "Crow's Feet."

OSAGES:
- Osage Diamonds.
- Osage Two Diamonds.
- The Mouse.
- A Thumb Catch.

AMERICA—*Continued.* PAWNEES:
  Threading a Closed Loop.

SALISH, THOMSON RIVER, BRITISH COLUMBIA:
  Dressing a Skin.
  A Fish-spear.
    Syn.: "Pitching a Tent."

TANANAS, ALASKA:
  The Leashing of Lochiel's Dogs.
    Syn.: " Crow's Feet."
  †Bow String.
  †Raven's Feet.
  †New Mittens.

TEWAS, ISLETA, N. M.
  A Brush House, *nathu.*
  Six-pointed Star.
    *Syn.: *Pah-rhu-la,* a star.
  *An Apache Door.
  *Many Stars.
  *Lightning.
    Syn.: *Vo-pi-ri-dai,* lightning.

ZUÑIS:
  *An Apache Door.
    Syn.: *A-tslo-no-no-nai.*
  *A Brush House, *pi-cho-wai, ham-pun-nai.*
  *A Fish-spear.
  *Carrying Wood.
  *Twin Stars.
    Syn.: *Pi-cho-wai; wai-lo-lo,* lightning.
  **Top Cross-beam of a Ladder; *tslem-pis-to-nai; pi-cho-wai-nai.*

AUSTRALIA. NORTH QUEENSLAND.
  *A House.
    Syn.: Canoe on the Water; also a Fish Net.
  *Ten Men.
    Syn.: A Turtle.
  *Flint and Steel.
    Syn.: A Deaf Adder.
  *The Leashing of Lochiel's Dogs.
    Syn.: Four-pronged Spear.
  *One Chief.
    Syn.: Giant Crane.
  **Two Boys Carrying Spears.
  **Two Women Fighting with Sticks.
  **Four Boys Walking in a Row.
  **Two Men Walking Down a Valley.

AUSTRALIA—*Continued:*
  **Man Climbing a Tree.
  **Kangaroo.
  **Pouch; Kangaroo.
  **Pouch; Wallaby.
  **A Spear; A Kangaroo Speared.
  **Bandicoot.
  **Bat.
  **Flying Fox.
  **Two Rats Sitting Side by Side.
  **Emu.
  **Emu's Nest, with Egg.
  **Cassowary.
  **Eagle-hawk.
  **Two Cockatoos Roosting.
  **Two White Cranes.
  **Duck in Flight.
  **Bird's Nest.
  **Water Snake.
  **Snake.
  **Crocodile.
  **Crocodile's Nest, with Egg.
  **Frog.
  **Turtle.
  **Tortoise.
  **Turtle (II).
  **Two Fish.
  **Fish, Mullet.
  **Mullet.
  **Eels Carried on a Hooked Stick.
  **Crab.
  **Four Shrimps.
  **Honey.
  **Wasp's Nest.
  **Hornet's Nest.
  **Hollow Log.
  **Tree.
  **Palm-tree.
  **Hole in Limb of a Tree.
  **Zamia Tree.
  **Zamia Nuts.
  **Two Coconuts.
  **Coconut.
  **Yams (I).
  **Yams (II).
  **Sun, clouded over.
  **Sun, with full rays.

AUSTRALIA—*Continued*:
**Sun, with full rays (II).
**Sun, setting.
**Moon.
**Star.
**Star (II).
**Clouds.
**Lightning.
**Rain.
**River.
**River (II).
     Syn.: A Fish-hawk.
**Two Rocks.
**Hill.
**Boomerang.
**Canoe.
**Bark Canoe.
**Dilly-bag.
**Hawk's Foot.
**Wasp's Nest.

BORNEO.
    The Real Cat's-cradle.

BRITISH NEW GUINEA.
    Kiwai Island at the Mouth of the Fly
        River:
       A Crab, *kokowa*.

CAROLINE ISLANDS.
    Natik:
      Caroline Islands Catch.
      Circles and Triangles, *bur-bur-ani-jau*.
      Ten Men.
      Variation of Ten Men.
      Caroline Islands Triangles.
      House of the Blos-bird, *palangan-im-mun-*
        blos.
      No Name.
      Caroline Islands Diamonds.

    Uap:
      Carrying Money, *runi-ka-fei*.
      Three Stars, *dilipi-tuf*.
      Coral, *melang*.
      Two Chiefs, *logaru-pilun*.
      A House, *naun*.
      One Chief, *pilun*.
      A Turtle.

CAROLINE ISLANDS. Uap—*Continued*:
    Ten Times.
    Flint and Steel, *nifi*.
    Torres Straits Lizard.
    A Finger Catch.
    Hanging.
    Threading a Closed Loop.

CHINA.
    The Real Cat's-cradle.

ENGLAND.
    The Real Cat's-cradle.
    Tallow Dips.
    Threading a Closed Loop.
    Osage Thumb Catch.

EUROPE.
    The Real Cat's-cradle.

HAWAIIAN ISLANDS.
    *Osage Diamonds.
      Syn.: *Ma-ka-lii* and *pu-kau-la*.
    *Osage Two Diamonds.
      Syn.: *Pa-pi-o-ma-ka-nu-i-nu-i*.
    **Hoo-ko-mo*.
    **Ace of Diamonds, *eke-ma-nu*.
    **See-saw, *ma-hi-ki*.
    **A Post, *pou*.
    **A Pump, *pau-ma-wai*.
    **Darkness, *po*.
    **Ace of Spades, *e-ke-pe-ki*.
    **Ace of Hearts, *e-ke-ha-ka*.
    **Ma-ka-u-pe-na*.
    **Ko-he*.
    **The Breasts, *wa-u-la-wa*.
    **O-ko-le-a-mo*.
    **Pu*.
    **Ha-le-ku-mu-ma-ka-a*.
    **A-ha-ma-ka*.
    **A Bird House, *a-na-ma-nu*.

INDIA.
    A Dravidian Trick.

IRELAND.
    Osage Diamonds.
      Syn.: The Ladder; the Fence.
    The Leashing of Lochiel's Dogs.
      Syn.: Duck's Feet.

IRELAND—*Continued*:
Tallow Dips.
The Mouse.
The Real Cat's-cradle.

JAPAN.
The Mouse.
Threading a Closed Loop.
The Real Cat's-cradle.

KOREA.
The Real Cat's-cradle.

LOYALTY ISLANDS. Lifu:
A Well, *tim*.
Fence Around a Well, *sihnag*.

MARSHALL ISLANDS. Nauru:
**Hull of a Ship, *deimano*.
**Egona and Egameang Sitting on a Stone.
**A Butterfly, *ijewaioi*.
**A Woman, *Egattamma*.
**Nauru Woman of Rank, *Etima* and *Etowa*.
**The Woman, *Echeog* and *Edawaroi*.
**A Sea-snake, *iiyanibongo*.
**A Nauru Dandy, *tinamitto*.
**A Lady of Quality, *Egarawingo*.
**A Man, *ibunemun*.
**A Mat (I).
**A Mat (II).
**A Mat (III).
**A Mat (IV).

NEW ZEALAND.
*A House.

PHILIPPINES.
Bagobos:
Bagobo Diamonds.
Bagobo, Two Diamonds.
The Real Cat's-cradle.

PHILIPPINES—*Continued*:
Linao Moros:
Bagobo Diamonds.
Ten Times.
Hanging.
The Mouse.
The Real Cat's-cradle.

Negritos:
Hanging.
The Mouse.

SCOTLAND.
The Leashing of Lochiel's Dogs.
Tallow Dips.

TORRES STRAITS.
Fighting Head-hunters, *ares*.
Sunset, *lem baraigida*, Murray Island.
Syn.: A Star, *dogai*, Mabuiag.
A Fish-spear, *baur*.
A Sea-snake, *pagi*.
Kingfish, *geigi*, Murray Island.
Syn.: The Dugong, *dangal*, Mabuiag.
A Well.
Syn.: Nest of the Ti-bird, *ti-meta;* a
Canoe, *gul.*, Mabuiag.
A Trigger Fish, *nageg*.
Casting the Fish-spear.
A Man and a Bed, *le-sik*.
A Palm Tree, u.
A Canoe with Two Masts, *nar*.
Little Fishes, *tup*.
A Torres Straits Lizard, *monan*, Murray
Island.
Syn.: Intestines of a Turtle, *maita*,
Mabuiag.
The Mouse, *kebe-mokeis*.
Fly on the Nose, *buli*.
Will You Have a Yam, *lewer*, food.

A FEW INVENTED FIGURES—THE SCARAB

The first four movements are the same as the first four movements of the "Well." The strings in the centre of the figure cross so as to form a large X.

Fifth: Bend each thumb away from you into the former thumb loop (now hanging from the top straight string of the figure), and pick up, with the back of the thumb from the palmar side, the lower leg of the X, and pull it toward you through the hanging thumb loop.

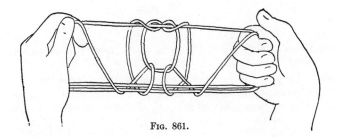

FIG. 861.

Sixth : The same as the *Ninth* movement of the "Crab."

Seventh and *Eighth :* The same as the *Second* and *Third* movements of the "Fence" (Fig. 861).

THE LOZENGE

First : Opening A.

Second : Pass each thumb away from you over the far thumb string and both strings of the index loop, and pick up from below on the back of the thumb the near little finger string, and return the thumb to its position.

Third : Bend each middle finger down into the thumb loops, and pick up from below on the back of the middle finger the lower near thumb string, and return the middle finger to its position.

Fourth: Let the upper thumb loops slip entirely off the thumbs.

Fifth: Pass each thumb away from you, close to the palm (thus taking the twist out of the thumb loop) under all the strings, and pick up from below on the back

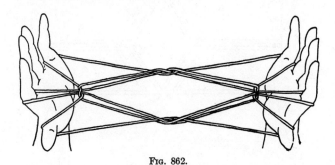

FIG. 862.

of the thumb the far little finger string, and return the thumb to its position, drawing the string toward you between the near index string and the far thumb string, the latter slipping off the thumb during the movement.

Sixth : Release the loops from the little fingers, transfer the middle finger loops to the little fingers, and extend the figure (Fig. 862).

THE SQUARE

First, Second, and *Third:* The same as the first three movements of the "Apache Door."

Fourth: The same as the *Fifth* movement of the "Apache Door."

Fifth: Opening A, taking up the single lower palmar string only.

Sixth: Pick up from below on the back of each thumb the near index string,

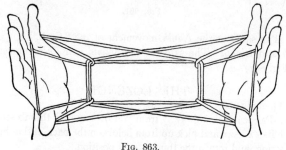

Fig. 863.

return the thumb to its position and slip the two lower thumb loops over the upper loop (the one you have just taken on the thumb) and entirely off the thumb.

Seventh: Pick up from below on the back of each little finger the far index string, return the little finger to its position, and slip the two lower little finger loops

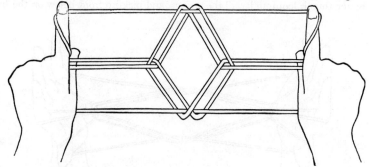

Fig. 864.

over the upper loop (the one you have just taken on the little finger) and entirely off the little finger.

Eighth: Insert each thumb and little finger from below into the index loop of the same hand, withdraw the index, separate widely the thumbs and little fingers, and draw the strings tight (Fig. 863).

VARIATION OF CORAL

First : Opening A.

Second : Exchange the loops on the thumbs, putting the left thumb loop on the right thumb and then the right thumb loop on the left thumb.

Third : Now go through all the movements of the "Coral," beginning with the *Second* movement (Fig. 864. Compare Fig. 359, and pl. x, 1, page 383).

TWO DOLPHINS

First and *Second :* The same as the first two movements of "Many Stars."

Third : Bend each middle finger down toward you over the index strings, and take up from below, on the back of the finger, the far thumb string, and return the middle finger to its position.

Fourth : Separate the thumbs widely from the other fingers, and laying the figure on the knee, withdraw the thumbs gently, and pick up through the thumb

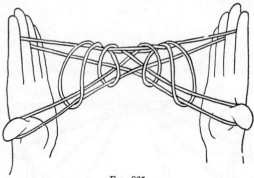

FIG. 865.

loop, on the back of the thumb, the far little finger string.   Take the figure from the knee and draw the strings tight.

Fifth : Wrap the far middle finger string once around the little finger, turning the string away from you and then toward you.   Slip the lower, original, little finger loop over the upper loop and off the little finger.   Repeat on the other hand.

Sixth : Transfer the index loop to the thumb; slip the lower, original thumb loop entirely off the thumb.

Seventh : Release the loops from the little fingers and draw the hands quickly apart (Fig. 865).

VARIATION OF THE CRAB

First, Second, Third, Fourth, and *Fifth:* The same as the first five movements of the "Scarab."

Sixth, Seventh, Eighth, Ninth, and *Tenth:* The same as the *Second, Third, Fourth, Fifth,* and *Sixth* movements of the "Crab." Push the loop which passes

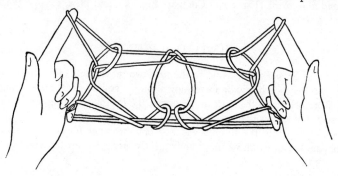

FIG. 866.

around the vertical string running from the index to the little finger, well up, away from the little finger loops.

Eleventh: Keep the index loop well up on the tip of the finger, and pass each

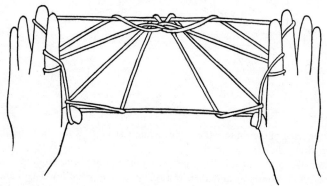

FIG. 867.

thumb away from you, and, picking up on the back of the thumb, draw toward you the lower diagonal string of the loop passing around the vertical string which runs from the index to the little finger.

Twelfth : Now complete the "Crab," beginning with the *Eighth* movement and going through to the very end (Fig. 866).

To put an additional ring around the index loop, repeat this figure, from the *Eleventh* movement to the end.   This may be done any number of times.

SECOND VARIATION OF TEN MEN

The first eight movements are similar to the first eight movements of the "Variation of Ten Men."   Then begin at the *Ninth* movement of "Ten Men," and complete that figure (Fig. 867).

BIBLIOGRAPHY

Andree, R.—1. Correspondenzblatt deutscher anthropologischer Gesellschaft, 1888, p. 54.
2. Mittheilungen der anthropologische Gesellschaft in Wien, 1888, Bd. XVIII, p. 214.
3. Ethnographische Parallen und Vergleiche, Neue Folge, Leipzig, 1889, p. 96.

Boas, Franz.—1. The Game of Cat's-cradle. Internationales Archiv für Ethnographie, I, 1888, p. 229.
2. Das Fadenspiel. Mittheilungen der anthropologische Gesellschaft in Wien, 1888, p. [85].
3. The Central Eskimo. Sixth Annual Report of the Bureau of Ethnology, 1884–85, Washington, 1888, p. 569, three figures.
4. The Eskimo of Baffin Land and Hudson Bay. Bulletin of the American Museum of Natural History, New York, XV., 1901, pp. 151, 161.

Brown, E. E.—University of California Magazine, V, 1899, p. 163.

Buchner, M.—Reise durch den stillen Ozean, Breslau, 1878, p. 269.

Bunce, D.—Australasiatic Reminiscences, Melbourne, 1857, p. 75.

Cock, A. de, en Teirlinck, Is.—Kinderspel en Kinderlust in Zuid-Nederland, Gent, 1903, Derde Deel, pp. 209–211.

Codrington, R. H.—The Melanesians: Studies in their Anthropology and Folk-lore, Oxford, 1891, pp. 30, 31, 341.

Crespigny, C. A. C. de.—Notes on Borneo. Proceedings of the Royal Geographical Society, II, 1858, p. 344.

Culin, Stewart.—1. Hawaiian Games. American Anthropologist, Vol. I, No. 2, n. s., April, 1899, pp. 222, 223, Plates XIII, XIV, XV.
2. Korean Games, with Notes on the Corresponding Games of China and Japan, Philadelphia, 1895, p. 30.
3. Bulletin II, Free Museum of Science and Art, Philadelphia, 1899, p. 106.

Dieffenbach, Ernest.—Travels in New Zealand, London, 1843, II, p. 32.

Ehrenreich, P.—Beiträge zur Völkerkunde Brasiliens. Veröffentl. d. Mus. f. Völkerkunde in Berlin, II, 1891, p. 30.

Ellis, William.—Polynesian Researches, London, 1853.

Eyre, E. J.—Journals of Expeditions of Discovery into Central Australia, London, 1845, II, p. 227.

Fielde, Adele M.—A Corner of Cathay, New York, 1894, p. 87.

Finsch, O.—Ethnologische Erfahrungen und Belegstücke aus der Süd-see. Ann. des k. k. naturhist. Hofmuseums Wien, III, 1888, p. 143; VI, 1891, p. 33.

Gill, W. Wyatt.—Life in the Southern Isles, London, 1876, p. 65.

Gomme, Alice B.—Dictionary of British Folk-lore, Part I, Traditional Games, London, 1894, Vol. I, p. 61.

Gray, Rev. John.—Some Scottish String Figures. Man, August, 1903, 66, p. 117.

Haddon, A. C.—1. The Ethnography of the Western Tribes of Torres Straits. Journal of the Anthropological Institute, XIX, 1890, p. 361.
2. The Study of Man, London and New York, 1898, p. 224.
3. Head-hunters, Black, White, and Brown, London, 1901, pp. 38, 175, 201.
4. (With **W. H. R. Rivers**) A Method of Recording String Figures and Tricks. Man, October, 1902, 109, pp. 146–153.
5. A Few American String Figures and Tricks. American Anthropologist, Vol. V, No. 2, April-June, 1903, p. 213.
6. Reports of the Cambridge Anthropological Expedition to Torres Straits, Vols. I–VI, Cambridge, England.

Hall, Charles Francis.—1. Life with the Esquimaux, p. 316.
2. Arctic Researches, and Life Among the Esquimaux, New York, 1865, p. 129.

Hingston, Margaret A.—"The Candles" String Figure in Somerset. Man, October, 1903, 85, p. 147.

Klutschak, H. W.—Als Eskimos unter den Eskimos, Wien, 1881, pp. 136, 139, three figures.

Maclagan, R. C.—The Games and Diversions of Argylshire, London, 1901, pp. 189, 190.

Mallery, G.—Pictographs of the North American Indians. Fourth Annual Report of the Bureau of Ethnology, 1882–83, Washington, 1886, p. 238.

Matthes, B. F.—Bijdragen tot de ethnologie van Ziud-Celebes, p. 129. Makas en Boeg. Woordenbock, I, V.

Murdoch, John.—Ethnological Results of the Point Barrow Expedition. Ninth Annual Report of the Bureau of Ethnology, 1887–88, Washington, 1892, p. 383.

Nelson, E. W.—The Eskimo about Behring Strait. Eighteenth Annual Report of the Bureau of Ethnology, I, 1896–1897, Washington, 1899, p. 332.

Nister, E.—The Games Book for Boys and Girls, London, 1897, p. 73.

Partington, James Edge, and Heape, Charles.—An Album of the Weapons, Tools, Ornaments, Articles of Dress, etc., of the Natives of the Pacific Islands, drawn and described from examples in public and private collections in England, 1895.

Rivers, W. H. R., and Haddon, Alfred C.—A Method of Recording String Figures and Tricks. Man, October, 1902, 109, pp. 146–153.

Roth, Walter E.—North Queensland Ethnography. Bulletin No. 4, March, 1902. Games, Sports, and Amusements. Home Secretary's Department, Brisbane, p. 10.

Schmeltz, J. D. E.—Internationales Archiv für Ethnographie, I, 1888, p. 230.

Smith, Harlan I.—The Thompson Indians of British Columbia, by James Teit, ed. by Franz Boas. Memoirs of the American Museum of Natural History, New York, Vol. II, Anthropology, Vol. I, 1900, p. 281, Fig. 270.

Smyth, R. Brough.—Aborigines of Victoria, London, 1878, I, p. 178.

Taylor, R.—Te Ika a Maui; or New Zealand and Its Inhabitants, London, 1855, p. 172.

Tenicheff, W.—L'activité de l'homme, Paris, 1898, p. 153.

Thilenius.—Globus, LXXXIII, 1903, p. 20.

Tregear, Edward.—1. The Maoris of New Zealand. Journal of the Anthropological Institute, XIX, 2, November, 1889, p. 115.
    2. The Maori Race, Wanganni, 1904, p. 58.

Turner, W. Y.—The Ethnology of the Motu. Journal of the Anthropological Institute, VII, 1878, p. 483.

Tylor, E. B.—Remarks on the Geographical Distribution of Games. Journal of the Anthropological Institute, IX, 1, August, 1879, p. 26.

Wallace, Alfred R.—The Malay Archipelago, London, 1869, I, p. 183.

INDEX

A CATALOGUE OF
SELECTED DOVER BOOKS
IN ALL FIELDS OF INTEREST

A CATALOGUE OF SELECTED DOVER
BOOKS IN ALL FIELDS OF INTEREST

CONDITIONED REFLEXES, Ivan P. Pavlov. Full translation of most complete statement of Pavlov's work; cerebral damage, conditioned reflex, experiments with dogs, sleep, similar topics of great importance. 430pp. 5⅜ x 8½. 60614-7 Pa. $4.50

NOTES ON NURSING: WHAT IT IS, AND WHAT IT IS NOT, Florence Nightingale. Outspoken writings by founder of modern nursing. When first published (1860) it played an important role in much needed revolution in nursing. Still stimulating. 140pp. 5⅜ x 8½. 22340-X Pa. $2.50

HARTER'S PICTURE ARCHIVE FOR COLLAGE AND ILLUSTRATION, Jim Harter. Over 300 authentic, rare 19th-century engravings selected by noted collagist for artists, designers, decoupeurs, etc. Machines, people, animals, etc., printed one side of page. 25 scene plates for backgrounds. 6 collages by Harter, Satty, Singer, Evans. Introduction. 192pp. 8⅞ x 11¾. 23659-5 Pa. $5.00

MANUAL OF TRADITIONAL WOOD CARVING, edited by Paul N. Hasluck. Possibly the best book in English on the craft of wood carving. Practical instructions, along with 1,146 working drawings and photographic illustrations. Formerly titled Cassell's Wood Carving. 576pp. 6½ x 9¼. 23489-4 Pa. $7.95

THE PRINCIPLES AND PRACTICE OF HAND OR SIMPLE TURNING, John Jacob Holtzapffel. Full coverage of basic lathe techniques—history and development, special apparatus, softwood turning, hardwood turning, metal turning. Many projects—billiard ball, works formed within a sphere, egg cups, ash trays, vases, jardiniers, others—included. 1881 edition. 800 illustrations. 592pp. 6⅛ x 9¼. 23365-0 Clothbd. $15.00

THE JOY OF HANDWEAVING, Osma Tod. Only book you need for hand weaving. Fundamentals, threads, weaves, plus numerous projects for small board-loom, two-harness, tapestry, laid-in, four-harness weaving and more. Over 160 illustrations. 2nd revised edition. 352pp. 6½ x 9¼. 23458-4 Pa. $5.00

THE BOOK OF WOOD CARVING, Charles Marshall Sayers. Still finest book for beginning student in wood sculpture. Noted teacher, craftsman discusses fundamentals, technique; gives 34 designs, over 34 projects for panels, bookends, mirrors, etc. "Absolutely first-rate"—E. J. Tangerman. 33 photos. 118pp. 7¾ x 10⅝. 23654-4 Pa. $3.00

DRAWINGS OF WILLIAM BLAKE, William Blake. 92 plates from Book of Job, *Divine Comedy, Paradise Lost,* visionary heads, mythological figures, Laocoon, etc. Selection, introduction, commentary by Sir Geoffrey Keynes. 178pp. 8⅛ x 11.   22303-5 Pa. $4.00

ENGRAVINGS OF HOGARTH, William Hogarth. 101 of Hogarth's greatest works: *Rake's Progress, Harlot's Progress, Illustrations for Hudibras, Before and After, Beer Street and Gin Lane,* many more. Full commentary. 256pp. 11 x 13¾.   22479-1 Pa. $7.95

DAUMIER: 120 GREAT LITHOGRAPHS, Honore Daumier. Wide-ranging collection of lithographs by the greatest caricaturist of the 19th century. Concentrates on eternally popular series on lawyers, on married life, on liberated women, etc. Selection, introduction, and notes on plates by Charles F. Ramus. Total of 158pp. 9⅜ x 12¼.   23512-2 Pa. $5.50

DRAWINGS OF MUCHA, Alphonse Maria Mucha. Work reveals draftsman of highest caliber: studies for famous posters and paintings, renderings for book illustrations and ads, etc. 70 works, 9 in color; including 6 items not drawings. Introduction. List of illustrations. 72pp. 9⅜ x 12¼. (Available in U.S. only)   23672-2 Pa. $4.00

GIOVANNI BATTISTA PIRANESI: DRAWINGS IN THE PIERPONT MORGAN LIBRARY, Giovanni Battista Piranesi. For first time ever all of Morgan Library's collection, world's largest. 167 illustrations of rare Piranesi drawings—archeological, architectural, decorative and visionary. Essay, detailed list of drawings, chronology, captions. Edited by Felice Stampfle. 144pp. 9⅜ x 12¼.   23714-1 Pa. $7.50

NEW YORK ETCHINGS (1905-1949), John Sloan. All of important American artist's N.Y. life etchings. 67 works include some of his best art; also lively historical record—Greenwich Village, tenement scenes. Edited by Sloan's widow. Introduction and captions. 79pp. 8⅜ x 11¼.
                                                23651-X Pa. $4.00

CHINESE PAINTING AND CALLIGRAPHY: A PICTORIAL SURVEY, Wan-go Weng. 69 fine examples from John M. Crawford's matchless private collection: landscapes, birds, flowers, human figures, etc., plus calligraphy. Every basic form included: hanging scrolls, handscrolls, album leaves, fans, etc. 109 illustrations. Introduction. Captions. 192pp. 8⅞ x 11¾.
                                                23707-9 Pa. $7.95

DRAWINGS OF REMBRANDT, edited by Seymour Slive. Updated Lippmann, Hofstede de Groot edition, with definitive scholarly apparatus. All portraits, biblical sketches, landscapes, nudes, Oriental figures, classical studies, together with selection of work by followers. 550 illustrations. Total of 630pp. 9⅛ x 12¼.   21485-0, 21486-9 Pa., Two-vol. set $15.00

THE DISASTERS OF WAR, Francisco Goya. 83 etchings record horrors of Napoleonic wars in Spain and war in general. Reprint of 1st edition, plus 3 additional plates. Introduction by Philip Hofer. 97pp. 9⅜ x 8¼.
                                                21872-4 Pa. $3.75

THE EARLY WORK OF AUBREY BEARDSLEY, Aubrey Beardsley. 157 plates, 2 in color: *Manon Lescaut, Madame Bovary, Morte Darthur, Salome,* other. Introduction by H. Marillier. 182pp. 8⅛ x 11. 21816-3 Pa. $4.50

THE LATER WORK OF AUBREY BEARDSLEY, Aubrey Beardsley. Exotic masterpieces of full maturity: *Venus and Tannhauser, Lysistrata, Rape of the Lock, Volpone,* Savoy material, etc. 174 plates, 2 in color. 186pp. 8⅛ x 11. 21817-1 Pa. $4.50

THOMAS NAST'S CHRISTMAS DRAWINGS, Thomas Nast. Almost all Christmas drawings by creator of image of Santa Claus as we know it, and one of America's foremost illustrators and political cartoonists. 66 illustrations. 3 illustrations in color on covers. 96pp. 8⅜ x 11¼. 23660-9 Pa. $3.50

THE DORÉ ILLUSTRATIONS FOR DANTE'S DIVINE COMEDY, Gustave Doré. All 135 plates from Inferno, Purgatory, Paradise; fantastic tortures, infernal landscapes, celestial wonders. Each plate with appropriate (translated) verses. 141pp. 9 x 12. 23231-X Pa. $4.50

DORÉ'S ILLUSTRATIONS FOR RABELAIS, Gustave Doré. 252 striking illustrations of *Gargantua and Pantagruel* books by foremost 19th-century illustrator. Including 60 plates, 192 delightful smaller illustrations. 153pp. 9 x 12. 23656-0 Pa. $5.00

LONDON: A PILGRIMAGE, Gustave Doré, Blanchard Jerrold. Squalor, riches, misery, beauty of mid-Victorian metropolis; 55 wonderful plates, 125 other illustrations, full social, cultural text by Jerrold. 191pp. of text. 9⅜ x 12¼. 22306-X Pa. $6.00

THE RIME OF THE ANCIENT MARINER, Gustave Doré, S. T. Coleridge. Dore's finest work, 34 plates capture moods, subtleties of poem. Full text. Introduction by Millicent Rose. 77pp. 9¼ x 12. 22305-1 Pa. $3.50

THE DORE BIBLE ILLUSTRATIONS, Gustave Doré. All wonderful, detailed plates: Adam and Eve, Flood, Babylon, Life of Jesus, etc. Brief King James text with each plate. Introduction by Millicent Rose. 241 plates. 241pp. 9 x 12. 23004-X Pa. $6.00

THE COMPLETE ENGRAVINGS, ETCHINGS AND DRYPOINTS OF ALBRECHT DURER. "Knight, Death and Devil"; "Melencolia," and more—all Dürer's known works in all three media, including 6 works formerly attributed to him. 120 plates. 235pp. 8⅜ x 11¼. 22851-7 Pa. $6.50

MAXIMILIAN'S TRIUMPHAL ARCH, Albrecht Dürer and others. Incredible monument of woodcut art: 8 foot high elaborate arch—heraldic figures, humans, battle scenes, fantastic elements—that you can assemble yourself. Printed on one side, layout for assembly. 143pp. 11 x 16. 21451-6 Pa. $5.00

THE COMPLETE WOODCUTS OF ALBRECHT DURER, edited by Dr. W. Kurth. 346 in all: "Old Testament," "St. Jerome," "Passion," "Life of Virgin," Apocalypse," many others. Introduction by Campbell Dodgson. 285pp. 8½ x 12¼. 21097-9 Pa. $6.95

DRAWINGS OF ALBRECHT DURER, edited by Heinrich Wölfflin. 81 plates show development from youth to full style. Many favorites; many new. Introduction by Alfred Werner. 96pp. 8⅛ x 11. 22352-3 Pa. $5.00

THE HUMAN FIGURE, Albrecht Dürer. Experiments in various techniques—stereometric, progressive proportional, and others. Also life studies that rank among finest ever done. Complete reprinting of *Dresden Sketchbook*. 170 plates. 355pp. 8⅜ x 11¼. 21042-1 Pa. $7.95

OF THE JUST SHAPING OF LETTERS, Albrecht Dürer. Renaissance artist explains design of Roman majuscules by geometry, also Gothic lower and capitals. Grolier Club edition. 43pp. 7⅞ x 10¾ 21306-4 Pa. $3.00

TEN BOOKS ON ARCHITECTURE, Vitruvius. The most important book ever written on architecture. Early Roman aesthetics, technology, classical orders, site selection, all other aspects. Stands behind everything since. Morgan translation. 331pp. 5⅜ x 8½. 20645-9 Pa. $4.00

THE FOUR BOOKS OF ARCHITECTURE, Andrea Palladio. 16th-century classic responsible for Palladian movement and style. Covers classical architectural remains, Renaissance revivals, classical orders, etc. 1738 Ware English edition. Introduction by A. Placzek. 216 plates. 110pp. of text. 9½ x 12¾. 21308-0 Pa. $8.95

HORIZONS, Norman Bel Geddes. Great industrialist stage designer, "father of streamlining," on application of aesthetics to transportation, amusement, architecture, etc. 1932 prophetic account; function, theory, specific projects. 222 illustrations. 312pp. 7⅞ x 10¾. 23514-9 Pa. $6.95

FRANK LLOYD WRIGHT'S FALLINGWATER, Donald Hoffmann. Full, illustrated story of conception and building of Wright's masterwork at Bear Run, Pa. 100 photographs of site, construction, and details of completed structure. 112pp. 9¼ x 10. 23671-4 Pa. $5.00

THE ELEMENTS OF DRAWING, John Ruskin. Timeless classic by great Viltorian; starts with basic ideas, works through more difficult. Many practical exercises. 48 illustrations. Introduction by Lawrence Campbell. 228pp. 5⅜ x 8½. 22730-8 Pa. $2.75

GIST OF ART, John Sloan. Greatest modern American teacher, Art Students League, offers innumerable hints, instructions, guided comments to help you in painting. Not a formal course. 46 illustrations. Introduction by Helen Sloan. 200pp. 5⅜ x 8½. 23435-5 Pa. $3.50

THE ANATOMY OF THE HORSE, George Stubbs. Often considered the great masterpiece of animal anatomy. Full reproduction of 1766 edition, plus prospectus; original text and modernized text. 36 plates. Introduction by Eleanor Garvey. 121pp. 11 x 14¾. 23402-9 Pa. $6.00

BRIDGMAN'S LIFE DRAWING, George B. Bridgman. More than 500 illustrative drawings and text teach you to abstract the body into its major masses, use light and shade, proportion; as well as specific areas of anatomy, of which Bridgman is master. 192pp. 6½ x 9¼. (Available in U.S. only) 22710-3 Pa. $3.00

ART NOUVEAU DESIGNS IN COLOR, Alphonse Mucha, Maurice Verneuil, Georges Auriol. Full-color reproduction of *Combinaisons ornementales* (c. 1900) by Art Nouveau masters. Floral, animal, geometric, interlacings, swashes—borders, frames, spots—all incredibly beautiful. 60 plates, hundreds of designs. 9⅜ x 8-1/16. 22885-1 Pa. $4.00

FULL-COLOR FLORAL DESIGNS IN THE ART NOUVEAU STYLE, E. A. Seguy. 166 motifs, on 40 plates, from *Les fleurs et leurs applications decoratives* (1902): borders, circular designs, repeats, allovers, "spots." All in authentic Art Nouveau colors. 48pp. 9⅜ x 12¼.
23439-8 Pa. $5.00

A DIDEROT PICTORIAL ENCYCLOPEDIA OF TRADES AND IN-DUSTRY, edited by Charles C. Gillispie. 485 most interesting plates from the great French Encyclopedia of the 18th century show hundreds of working figures, artifacts, process, land and cityscapes; glassmaking, paper-making, metal extraction, construction, weaving, making furniture, clothing, wigs, dozens of other activities. Plates fully explained. 920pp. 9 x 12.
22284-5, 22285-3 Clothbd., Two-vol. set $40.00

HANDBOOK OF EARLY ADVERTISING ART, Clarence P. Hornung. Largest collection of copyright-free early and antique advertising art ever compiled. Over 6,000 illustrations, from Franklin's time to the 1890's for special effects, novelty. Valuable source, almost inexhaustible.
Pictorial Volume. Agriculture, the zodiac, animals, autos, birds, Christmas, fire engines, flowers, trees, musical instruments, ships, games and sports, much more. Arranged by subject matter and use. 237 plates. 288pp. 9 x 12.
20122-8 Clothbd. $13.50

Typographical Volume. Roman and Gothic faces ranging from 10 point to 300 point, "Barnum," German and Old English faces, script, logotypes, scrolls and flourishes, 1115 ornamental initials, 67 complete alphabets, more. 310 plates. 320pp. 9 x 12. 20123-6 Clothbd. $15.00

CALLIGRAPHY (CALLIGRAPHIA LATINA), J. G. Schwandner. High point of 18th-century ornamental calligraphy. Very ornate initials, scrolls, borders, cherubs, birds, lettered examples. 172pp. 9 x 13.
20475-8 Pa. $6.00

ART FORMS IN NATURE, Ernst Haeckel. Multitude of strangely beautiful natural forms: Radiolaria, Foraminifera, jellyfishes, fungi, turtles, bats, etc. All 100 plates of the 19th-century evolutionist's *Kunstformen der Natur* (1904). 100pp. 9⅜ x 12¼. 22987-4 Pa. $4.50

CHILDREN: A PICTORIAL ARCHIVE FROM NINETEENTH-CENTURY SOURCES, edited by Carol Belanger Grafton. 242 rare, copyright-free wood engravings for artists and designers. Widest such selection available. All illustrations in line. 119pp. 8⅜ x 11¼. 23694-3 Pa. $3.50

WOMEN: A PICTORIAL ARCHIVE FROM NINETEENTH-CENTURY SOURCES, edited by Jim Harter. 391 copyright-free wood engravings for artists and designers selected from rare periodicals. Most extensive such collection available. All illustrations in line. 128pp. 9 x 12. 23703-6 Pa. $4.50

ARABIC ART IN COLOR, Prisse d'Avennes. From the greatest ornamentalists of all time—50 plates in color, rarely seen outside the Near East, rich in suggestion and stimulus. Includes 4 plates on covers. 46pp. 9⅜ x 12¼. 23658-7 Pa. $6.00

AUTHENTIC ALGERIAN CARPET DESIGNS AND MOTIFS, edited by June Beveridge. Algerian carpets are world famous. Dozens of geometrical motifs are charted on grids, color-coded, for weavers, needleworkers, craftsmen, designers. 53 illustrations plus 4 in color. 48pp. 8¼ x 11. (Available in U.S. only) 23650-1 Pa. $1.75

DICTIONARY OF AMERICAN PORTRAITS, edited by Hayward and Blanche Cirker. 4000 important Americans, earliest times to 1905, mostly in clear line. Politicians, writers, soldiers, scientists, inventors, industrialists, Indians, Blacks, women, outlaws, etc. Identificatory information. 756pp. 9¼ x 12¾. 21823-6 Clothbd. $40.00

HOW THE OTHER HALF LIVES, Jacob A. Riis. Journalistic record of filth, degradation, upward drive in New York immigrant slums, shops, around 1900. New edition includes 100 original Riis photos, monuments of early photography. 233pp. 10 x 7⅞. 22012-5 Pa. $6.00

NEW YORK IN THE THIRTIES, Berenice Abbott. Noted photographer's fascinating study of city shows new buildings that have become famous and old sights that have disappeared forever. Insightful commentary. 97 photographs. 97pp. 11⅜ x 10. 22967-X Pa. $5.00

MEN AT WORK, Lewis W. Hine. Famous photographic studies of construction workers, railroad men, factory workers and coal miners. New supplement of 18 photos on Empire State building construction. New introduction by Jonathan L. Doherty. Total of 69 photos. 63pp. 8 x 10¾. 23475-4 Pa. $3.00

THE DEPRESSION YEARS AS PHOTOGRAPHED BY ARTHUR ROTH-STEIN, Arthur Rothstein. First collection devoted entirely to the work of outstanding 1930s photographer: famous dust storm photo, ragged children, unemployed, etc. 120 photographs. Captions. 119pp. 9¼ x 10¾.
23590-4 Pa. $5.00

CAMERA WORK: A PICTORIAL GUIDE, Alfred Stieglitz. All 559 illustrations and plates from the most important periodical in the history of art photography, Camera Work (1903-17). Presented four to a page, reduced in size but still clear, in strict chronological order, with complete captions. Three indexes. Glossary. Bibliography. 176pp. 8⅜ x 11¼.
23591-2 Pa. $6.95

ALVIN LANGDON COBURN, PHOTOGRAPHER, Alvin L. Coburn. Revealing autobiography by one of greatest photographers of 20th century gives insider's version of Photo-Secession, plus comments on his own work. 77 photographs by Coburn. Edited by Helmut and Alison Gernsheim. 160pp. 8⅛ x 11.
23685-4 Pa. $6.00

NEW YORK IN THE FORTIES, Andreas Feininger. 162 brilliant photographs by the well-known photographer, formerly with Life magazine, show commuters, shoppers, Times Square at night, Harlem nightclub, Lower East Side, etc. Introduction and full captions by John von Hartz. 181pp. 9¼ x 10¾.
23585-8 Pa. $6.00

GREAT NEWS PHOTOS AND THE STORIES BEHIND THEM, John Faber. Dramatic volume of 140 great news photos, 1855 through 1976, and revealing stories behind them, with both historical and technical information. Hindenburg disaster, shooting of Oswald, nomination of Jimmy Carter, etc. 160pp. 8¼ x 11.
23667-6 Pa. $5.00

THE ART OF THE CINEMATOGRAPHER, Leonard Maltin. Survey of American cinematography history and anecdotal interviews with 5 masters—Arthur Miller, Hal Mohr, Hal Rosson, Lucien Ballard, and Conrad Hall. Very large selection of behind-the-scenes production photos. 105 photographs. Filmographies. Index. Originally Behind the Camera. 144pp. 8¼ x 11.
23686-2 Pa. $5.00

DESIGNS FOR THE THREE-CORNERED HAT (LE TRICORNE), Pablo Picasso. 32 fabulously rare drawings—including 31 color illustrations of costumes and accessories—for 1919 production of famous ballet. Edited by Parmenia Migel, who has written new introduction. 48pp. 9⅜ x 12¼. (Available in U.S. only)
23709-5 Pa. $5.00

NOTES OF A FILM DIRECTOR, Sergei Eisenstein. Greatest Russian filmmaker explains montage, making of Alexander Nevsky, aesthetics; comments on self, associates, great rivals (Chaplin), similar material. 78 illustrations. 240pp. 5⅜ x 8½.
22392-2 Pa. $4.50

HOLLYWOOD GLAMOUR PORTRAITS, edited by John Kobal. 145 photos capture the stars from 1926-49, the high point in portrait photography. Gable, Harlow, Bogart, Bacall, Hedy Lamarr, Marlene Dietrich, Robert Montgomery, Marlon Brando, Veronica Lake; 94 stars in all. Full background on photographers, technical aspects, much more. Total of 160pp. 8⅜ x 11¼. 23352-9 Pa. $5.00

THE NEW YORK STAGE: FAMOUS PRODUCTIONS IN PHOTO-GRAPHS, edited by Stanley Appelbaum. 148 photographs from Museum of City of New York show 142 plays, 1883-1939. *Peter Pan*, *The Front Page*, *Dead End*, *Our Town*, O'Neill, hundreds of actors and actresses, etc. Full indexes. 154pp. 9½ x 10. 23241-7 Pa. $6.00

MASTERS OF THE DRAMA, John Gassner. Most comprehensive history of the drama, every tradition from Greeks to modern Europe and America, including Orient. Covers 800 dramatists, 2000 plays; biography, plot summaries, criticism, theatre history, etc. 77 illustrations. 890pp. 5⅜ x 8½. 20100-7 Clothbd. $10.00

THE GREAT OPERA STARS IN HISTORIC PHOTOGRAPHS, edited by James Camner. 343 portraits from the 1850s to the 1940s: Tamburini, Mario, Caliapin, Jeritza, Melchior, Melba, Patti, Pinza, Schipa, Caruso, Farrar, Steber, Gobbi, and many more—270 performers in all. Index. 199pp. 8⅜ x 11¼. 23575-0 Pa. $6.50

J. S. BACH, Albert Schweitzer. Great full-length study of Bach, life, background to music, music, by foremost modern scholar. Ernest Newman translation. 650 musical examples. Total of 928pp. 5⅜ x 8½. (Available in U.S. only) 21631-4, 21632-2 Pa., Two-vol. set $10.00

COMPLETE PIANO SONATAS, Ludwig van Beethoven. All sonatas in the fine Schenker edition, with fingering, analytical material. One of best modern editions. Total of 615pp. 9 x 12. (Available in U.S. only) 23134-8, 23135-6 Pa., Two-vol. set $15.00

KEYBOARD MUSIC, J. S. Bach. Bach-Gesellschaft edition. For harpsichord, piano, other keyboard instruments. English Suites, French Suites, Six Partitas, Goldberg Variations, Two-Part Inventions, Three-Part Sinfonias. 312pp. 8⅛ x 11. (Available in U.S. only) 22360-4 Pa. $6.00

FOUR SYMPHONIES IN FULL SCORE, Franz Schubert. Schubert's four most popular symphonies: No. 4 in C Minor ("Tragic"); No. 5 in B-flat Major; No. 8 in B Minor ("Unfinished"); No. 9 in C Major ("Great"). Breitkopf & Hartel edition. Study score. 261pp. 9⅜ x 12¼. 23681-1 Pa. $6.50

THE AUTHENTIC GILBERT & SULLIVAN SONGBOOK, W. S. Gilbert, A. S. Sullivan. Largest selection available; 92 songs, uncut, original keys, in piano rendering approved by Sullivan. Favorites and lesser-known fine numbers. Edited with plot synopses by James Spero. 3 illustrations. 399pp. 9 x 12. 23482-7 Pa. $7.95

PRINCIPLES OF ORCHESTRATION, Nikolay Rimsky-Korsakov. Great classical orchestrator provides fundamentals of tonal resonance, progression of parts, voice and orchestra, tutti effects, much else in major document. 330pp. of musical excerpts. 489pp. 6½ x 9¼.   21266-1 Pa. $6.00

TRISTAN UND ISOLDE, Richard Wagner. Full orchestral score with complete instrumentation. Do not confuse with piano reduction. Commentary by Felix Mottl, great Wagnerian conductor and scholar. Study score. 655pp. 8⅛ x 11.   22915-7 Pa. $12.50

REQUIEM IN FULL SCORE, Giuseppe Verdi. Immensely popular with choral groups and music lovers. Republication of edition published by C. F. Peters, Leipzig, n. d. German frontmaker in English translation. Glossary. Text in Latin. Study score. 204pp. 9⅜ x 12¼.

23682-X Pa. $6.00

COMPLETE CHAMBER MUSIC FOR STRINGS, Felix Mendelssohn. All of Mendelssohn's chamber music: Octet, 2 Quintets, 6 Quartets, and Four Pieces for String Quartet. (Nothing with piano is included). Complete works edition (1874-7). Study score. 283 pp. 9⅜ x 12¼.

23679-X Pa. $6.95

POPULAR SONGS OF NINETEENTH-CENTURY AMERICA, edited by Richard Jackson. 64 most important songs: "Old Oaken Bucket," "Arkansas Traveler," "Yellow Rose of Texas," etc. Authentic original sheet music, full introduction and commentaries. 290pp. 9 x 12.   23270-0 Pa. $6.00

COLLECTED PIANO WORKS, Scott Joplin. Edited by Vera Brodsky Lawrence. Practically all of Joplin's piano works—rags, two-steps, marches, waltzes, etc., 51 works in all. Extensive introduction by Rudi Blesh. Total of 345pp. 9 x 12.   23106-2 Pa. $14.95

BASIC PRINCIPLES OF CLASSICAL BALLET, Agrippina Vaganova. Great Russian theoretician, teacher explains methods for teaching classical ballet; incorporates best from French, Italian, Russian schools. 118 illustrations. 175pp. 5⅜ x 8½.   22036-2 Pa. $2.50

CHINESE CHARACTERS, L. Wieger. Rich analysis of 2300 characters according to traditional systems into primitives. Historical-semantic analysis to phonetics (Classical Mandarin) and radicals. 820pp. 6⅛ x 9¼.

21321-8 Pa. $10.00

EGYPTIAN LANGUAGE: EASY LESSONS IN EGYPTIAN HIERO-GLYPHICS, E. A. Wallis Budge. Foremost Egyptologist offers Egyptian grammar, explanation of hieroglyphics, many reading texts, dictionary of symbols. 246pp. 5 x 7½. (Available in U.S. only)

21394-3 Clothbd. $7.50

AN ETYMOLOGICAL DICTIONARY OF MODERN ENGLISH, Ernest Weekley. Richest, fullest work, by foremost British lexicographer. Detailed word histories. Inexhaustible. Do not confuse this with Concise Etymological Dictionary, which is abridged. Total of 856pp. 6½ x 9¼.

21873-2, 21874-0 Pa., Two-vol. set $12.00

A MAYA GRAMMAR, Alfred M. Tozzer. Practical, useful English-language grammar by the Harvard anthropologist who was one of the three greatest American scholars in the area of Maya culture. Phonetics, grammatical processes, syntax, more. 301pp. 5⅜ x 8½.   23465-7 Pa. $4.00

THE JOURNAL OF HENRY D. THOREAU, edited by Bradford Torrey, F. H. Allen. Complete reprinting of 14 volumes, 1837-61, over two million words; the sourcebooks for *Walden*, etc. Definitive. All original sketches, plus 75 photographs. Introduction by Walter Harding. Total of 1804pp. 8½ x 12¼.   20312-3, 20313-1 Clothbd., Two-vol. set $50.00

CLASSIC GHOST STORIES, Charles Dickens and others. 18 wonderful stories you've wanted to reread: "The Monkey's Paw," "The House and the Brain," "The Upper Berth," "The Signalman," "Dracula's Guest," "The Tapestried Chamber," etc. Dickens, Scott, Mary Shelley, Stoker, etc. 330pp. 5⅜ x 8½.   20735-8 Pa. $3.50

SEVEN SCIENCE FICTION NOVELS, H. G. Wells. Full novels. *First Men in the Moon, Island of Dr. Moreau, War of the Worlds, Food of the Gods, Invisible Man, Time Machine, In the Days of the Comet*. A basic science-fiction library. 1015pp. 5⅜ x 8½. (Available in U.S. only)
20264-X Clothbd. $8.95

ARMADALE, Wilkie Collins. Third great mystery novel by the author of *The Woman in White* and *The Moonstone*. Ingeniously plotted narrative shows an exceptional command of character, incident and mood. Original magazine version with 40 illustrations. 597pp. 5⅜ x 8½.
23429-0 Pa. $5.00

MASTERS OF MYSTERY, H. Douglas Thomson. The first book in English (1931) devoted to history and aesthetics of detective story. Poe, Doyle, LeFanu, Dickens, many others, up to 1930. New introduction and notes by E. F. Bleiler. 288pp. 5⅜ x 8½. (Available in U.S. only)
23606-4 Pa. $4.00

FLATLAND, E. A. Abbott. Science-fiction classic explores life of 2-D being in 3-D world. Read also as introduction to thought about hyperspace. Introduction by Banesh Hoffmann. 16 illustrations. 103pp. 5⅜ x 8½.
20001-9 Pa. $1.75

THREE SUPERNATURAL NOVELS OF THE VICTORIAN PERIOD, edited, with an introduction, by E. F. Bleiler. Reprinted complete and unabridged, three great classics of the supernatural: *The Haunted Hotel* by Wilkie Collins, *The Haunted House at Latchford* by Mrs. J. H. Riddell, and *The Lost Stradivarious* by J. Meade Falkner. 325pp. 5⅜ x 8½.
22571-2 Pa. $4.00

AYESHA: THE RETURN OF "SHE," H. Rider Haggard. Virtuoso sequel featuring the great mythic creation, Ayesha, in an adventure that is fully as good as the first book, *She*. Original magazine version, with 47 original illustrations by Maurice Greiffenhagen. 189pp. 6½ x 9¼.
23649-8 Pa. $3.50

UNCLE SILAS, J. Sheridan LeFanu. Victorian Gothic mystery novel, considered by many best of period, even better than Collins or Dickens. Wonderful psychological terror. Introduction by Frederick Shroyer. 436pp. 5⅜ x 8½.   21715-9 Pa. $6.00

JURGEN, James Branch Cabell. The great erotic fantasy of the 1920's that delighted thousands, shocked thousands more. Full final text, Lane edition with 13 plates by Frank Pape. 346pp. 5⅜ x 8½.
23507-6 Pa. $4.50

THE CLAVERINGS, Anthony Trollope. Major novel, chronicling aspects of British Victorian society, personalities. Reprint of Cornhill serialization, 16 plates by M. Edwards; first reprint of full text. Introduction by Norman Donaldson. 412pp. 5⅜ x 8½.   23464-9 Pa. $5.00

KEPT IN THE DARK, Anthony Trollope. Unusual short novel about Victorian morality and abnormal psychology by the great English author. Probably the first American publication. Frontispiece by Sir John Millais. 92pp. 6½ x 9¼.   23609-9 Pa. $2.50

RALPH THE HEIR, Anthony Trollope. Forgotten tale of illegitimacy, inheritance. Master novel of Trollope's later years. Victorian country estates, clubs, Parliament, fox hunting, world of fully realized characters. Reprint of 1871 edition. 12 illustrations by F. A. Faser. 434pp. of text. 5⅜ x 8½.   23642-0 Pa. $5.00

YEKL and THE IMPORTED BRIDEGROOM AND OTHER STORIES OF THE NEW YORK GHETTO, Abraham Cahan. Film *Hester Street* based on *Yekl* (1896). Novel, other stories among first about Jewish immigrants of N.Y.'s East Side. Highly praised by W. D. Howells—Cahan "a new star of realism." New introduction by Bernard G. Richards. 240pp. 5⅜ x 8½.   22427-9 Pa. $3.50

THE HIGH PLACE, James Branch Cabell. Great fantasy writer's enchanting comedy of disenchantment set in 18th-century France. Considered by some critics to be even better than his famous *Jurgen*. 10 illustrations and numerous vignettes by noted fantasy artist Frank C. Pape. 320pp. 5⅜ x 8½.   23670-6 Pa. $4.00

ALICE'S ADVENTURES UNDER GROUND, Lewis Carroll. Facsimile of ms. Carroll gave Alice Liddell in 1864. Different in many ways from final Alice. Handlettered, illustrated by Carroll. Introduction by Martin Gardner. 128pp. 5⅜ x 8½.   21482-6 Pa. $2.00

FAVORITE ANDREW LANG FAIRY TALE BOOKS IN MANY COLORS, Andrew Lang. The four Lang favorites in a boxed set—the complete *Red, Green, Yellow* and *Blue* Fairy Books. 164 stories; 439 illustrations by Lancelot Speed, Henry Ford and G. P. Jacomb Hood. Total of about 1500pp. 5⅜ x 8½.   23407-X Boxed set, Pa. $14.95

HOUSEHOLD STORIES BY THE BROTHERS GRIMM. All the great Grimm stories: "Rumpelstiltskin," "Snow White," "Hansel and Gretel," etc., with 114 illustrations by Walter Crane. 269pp. 5⅜ x 8½.
21080-4 Pa. $3.00

SLEEPING BEAUTY, illustrated by Arthur Rackham. Perhaps the fullest, most delightful version ever, told by C. S. Evans. Rackham's best work. 49 illustrations. 110pp. 7⅞ x 10¾.
22756-1 Pa. $2.50

AMERICAN FAIRY TALES, L. Frank Baum. Young cowboy lassoes Father Time; dummy in Mr. Floman's department store window comes to life; and 10 other fairy tales. 41 illustrations by N. P. Hall, Harry Kennedy, Ike Morgan, and Ralph Gardner. 209pp. 5⅜ x 8½.
23643-9 Pa. $3.00

THE WONDERFUL WIZARD OF OZ, L. Frank Baum. Facsimile in full color of America's finest children's classic. Introduction by Martin Gardner. 143 illustrations by W. W. Denslow. 267pp. 5⅜ x 8½.
20691-2 Pa. $3.50

THE TALE OF PETER RABBIT, Beatrix Potter. The inimitable Peter's terrifying adventure in Mr. McGregor's garden, with all 27 wonderful, full-color Potter illustrations. 55pp. 4¼ x 5½. (Available in U.S. only)
22827-4 Pa. $1.25

THE STORY OF KING ARTHUR AND HIS KNIGHTS, Howard Pyle. Finest children's version of life of King Arthur. 48 illustrations by Pyle. 131pp. 6⅛ x 9¼.
21445-1 Pa. $4.95

CARUSO'S CARICATURES, Enrico Caruso. Great tenor's remarkable caricatures of self, fellow musicians, composers, others. Toscanini, Puccini, Farrar, etc. Impish, cutting, insightful. 473 illustrations. Preface by M. Sisca. 217pp. 8⅜ x 11¼.
23528-9 Pa. $6.95

PERSONAL NARRATIVE OF A PILGRIMAGE TO ALMADINAH AND MECCAH, Richard Burton. Great travel classic by remarkably colorful personality. Burton, disguised as a Moroccan, visited sacred shrines of Islam, narrowly escaping death. Wonderful observations of Islamic life, customs, personalities. 47 illustrations. Total of 959pp. 5⅜ x 8½.
21217-3, 21218-1 Pa., Two-vol. set $12.00

INCIDENTS OF TRAVEL IN YUCATAN, John L. Stephens. Classic (1843) exploration of jungles of Yucatan, looking for evidences of Maya civilization. Travel adventures, Mexican and Indian culture, etc. Total of 669pp. 5⅜ x 8½.
20926-1, 20927-X Pa., Two-vol. set $7.90

AMERICAN LITERARY AUTOGRAPHS FROM WASHINGTON IRVING TO HENRY JAMES, Herbert Cahoon, et al. Letters, poems, manuscripts of Hawthorne, Thoreau, Twain, Alcott, Whitman, 67 other prominent American authors. Reproductions, full transcripts and commentary. Plus checklist of all American Literary Autographs in The Pierpont Morgan Library. Printed on exceptionally high-quality paper. 136 illustrations. 212pp. 9⅛ x 12¼.
23548-3 Pa. $7.95

YUCATAN BEFORE AND AFTER THE CONQUEST, Diego de Landa. First English translation of basic book in Maya studies, the only significant account of Yucatan written in the early post-Conquest era. Translated by distinguished Maya scholar William Gates. Appendices, introduction, 4 maps and over 120 illustrations added by translator. 162pp. 5⅜ x 8½.
23622-6 Pa. $3.00

THE MALAY ARCHIPELAGO, Alfred R. Wallace. Spirited travel account by one of founders of modern biology. Touches on zoology, botany, ethnography, geography, and geology. 62 illustrations, maps. 515pp. 5⅜ x 8½.
20187-2 Pa. $6.95

THE DISCOVERY OF THE TOMB OF TUTANKHAMEN, Howard Carter, A. C. Mace. Accompany Carter in the thrill of discovery, as ruined passage suddenly reveals unique, untouched, fabulously rich tomb. Fascinating account, with 106 illustrations. New introduction by J. M. White. Total of 382pp. 5⅜ x 8½. (Available in U.S. only) 23500-9 Pa. $4.00

THE WORLD'S GREATEST SPEECHES, edited by Lewis Copeland and Lawrence W. Lamm. Vast collection of 278 speeches from Greeks up to present. Powerful and effective models; unique look at history. Revised to 1970. Indices. 842pp. 5⅜ x 8½.
20468-5 Pa. $8.95

THE 100 GREATEST ADVERTISEMENTS, Julian Watkins. The priceless ingredient; His master's voice; 99 44/100% pure; over 100 others. How they were written, their impact, etc. Remarkable record. 130 illustrations. 233pp. 7⅞ x 10 3/5.
20540-1 Pa. $5.00

CRUICKSHANK PRINTS FOR HAND COLORING, George Cruickshank. 18 illustrations, one side of a page, on fine-quality paper suitable for watercolors. Caricatures of people in society (c. 1820) full of trenchant wit. Very large format. 32pp. 11 x 16.
23684-6 Pa. $5.00

THIRTY-TWO COLOR POSTCARDS OF TWENTIETH-CENTURY AMERICAN ART, Whitney Museum of American Art. Reproduced in full color in postcard form are 31 art works and one shot of the museum. Calder, Hopper, Rauschenberg, others. Detachable. 16pp. 8¼ x 11.
23629-3 Pa. $2.50

MUSIC OF THE SPHERES: THE MATERIAL UNIVERSE FROM ATOM TO QUASAR SIMPLY EXPLAINED, Guy Murchie. Planets, stars, geology, atoms, radiation, relativity, quantum theory, light, antimatter, similar topics. 319 figures. 664pp. 5⅜ x 8½.
21809-0, 21810-4 Pa., Two-vol. set $10.00

EINSTEIN'S THEORY OF RELATIVITY, Max Born. Finest semi-technical account; covers Einstein, Lorentz, Minkowski, and others, with much detail, much explanation of ideas and math not readily available elsewhere on this level. For student, non-specialist. 376pp. 5⅜ x 8½.
60769-0 Pa. $4.50

AMERICAN ANTIQUE FURNITURE, Edgar G. Miller, Jr. The basic coverage of all American furniture before 1840: chapters per item chronologically cover all types of furniture, with more than 2100 photos. Total of 1106pp. 7⅞ x 10¾.   21599-7, 21600-4 Pa., Two-vol. set $17.90

ILLUSTRATED GUIDE TO SHAKER FURNITURE, Robert Meader. Director, Shaker Museum, Old Chatham, presents up-to-date coverage of all furniture and appurtenances, with much on local styles not available elsewhere. 235 photos. 146pp. 9 x 12.   22819-3 Pa. $5.00

ORIENTAL RUGS, ANTIQUE AND MODERN, Walter A. Hawley. Persia, Turkey, Caucasus, Central Asia, China, other traditions. Best general survey of all aspects: styles and periods, manufacture, uses, symbols and their interpretation, and identification. 96 illustrations, 11 in color. 320pp. 6⅛ x 9¼.   22366-3 Pa. $6.95

CHINESE POTTERY AND PORCELAIN, R. L. Hobson. Detailed descriptions and analyses by former Keeper of the Department of Oriental Antiquities and Ethnography at the British Museum. Covers hundreds of pieces from primitive times to 1915. Still the standard text for most periods. 136 plates, 40 in full color. Total of 750pp. 5⅜ x 8½.
23253-0 Pa. $10.00

THE WARES OF THE MING DYNASTY, R. L. Hobson. Foremost scholar examines and illustrates many varieties of Ming (1368-1644). Famous blue and white, polychrome, lesser-known styles and shapes. 117 illustrations, 9 full color, of outstanding pieces. Total of 263pp. 6⅛ x 9¼. (Available in U.S. only)   23652-8 Pa. $6.00